North America in Colonial Times

in

Colonial Times

**An Encyclopedia
for Students**

North America in Colonial Times

An Encyclopedia for Students

Jacob Ernest Cooke and Milton M. Klein, *Editors*

Volume 1

CHARLES SCRIBNER'S SONS
Macmillan Library Reference USA
Simon & Schuster Macmillan
New York

SIMON & SCHUSTER AND PRENTICE HALL INTERNATIONAL
London Mexico City New Delhi Singapore Sydney Toronto

Developed for Scribners by Visual Education Corporation, Princeton, N.J.

For Scribners
PUBLISHER: Karen Day
MANAGING EDITOR, *Encyclopedia of the North American Colonies:* David L. Bain (d. 1992)
COVER DESIGN: Irina Lubenskaya

For Visual Education
PROJECT DIRECTOR: Darryl Kestler
WRITERS: Dale Anderson, Cindy S. George, John Haley, Charles Roebuck, Rebecca Stefoff
EDITORS: Amy Livingston, Sara Mullen, Charles Roebuck
ASSOCIATE EDITOR: Jacqueline Morais
MAP AND ART EDITOR: Liz Ryan-Sax
COPYEDITING SUPERVISOR: Maureen Pancza
COPY EDITOR: Marie Enders
INDEXER: Stephen Ingle
PHOTO RESEARCH: Sara Matthews
PRODUCTION SUPERVISORS: Anita Crandall, Ellen Foos
DESIGN: Maxson Crandall
ELECTRONIC PREPARATION: Cynthia C. Feldner, Fiona Torphy
ELECTRONIC PRODUCTION: Elise Dodeles, Lisa Evans-Skopas, Deirdre Sheean, Isabelle Verret

Library of Congress Cataloging-in-Publication Data

North America in colonial times : an encyclopedia for students / Jacob Ernest Cooke and Milton M. Klein, editors.
    p.   cm.
    Adaptation and revision of Encyclopedia of the North American colonies for young readers.
    Includes bibliographical references and index.
    Summary: An encyclopedia of the history of the American colonies and Canada, including Native Americans, Spanish missions, English and Dutch exploration, the slave trade, and the French and Indian War.
    ISBN 0-684-80538-3 (set : alk. paper).— ISBN 0-684-80534-0 (v.1 : alk. paper).— ISBN 0-684-80535-9 (v.2 : alk. paper).— ISBN 0-684-80536-7 (v.3 : alk. paper).— ISBN 0-684-80537-5 (v.4: alk. paper)
    1. Europe—Colonies—America—History—Encyclopedias, Juvenile. 2. North America—History—Encyclopedias, Juvenile. [1. North America—History—Colonial period, ca. 1600–1775—Encyclopedias.] I. Cooke, Jacob Ernest, 1924– . II. Klein, Milton M. (Milton Martin), 1917– . III. Encyclopedia of the North American colonies.
E45.N65   1998
970.02—dc21
    98-29862
    CIP
    AC

Table of Contents

Maps

Color Plates

Volume 1
Color plates for Daily Life are between pages 110 and 111.

Volume 2
Color plates for Art and Architecture are between pages 118 and 119.

Volume 3
Color plates for People are between pages 118 and 119.

Volume 4
Color plates for Conflict are between pages 118 and 119.

Table of Contents

Volume 2

Table of Contents

Volume 3

Volume 4

Table of Contents

Preface

*T*he early history of those regions of North America that became the United States has long been a subject of study for scholars. Indeed, some of the latest advances in the writing of American history—in such areas as demography, law, and studies on women, African Americans, Native Americans, childhood, the poor, and the disadvantaged—have stemmed from work done by these students of the British colonial past. On the other hand, the history of other parts of North America has not attracted as much attention.

In 1993, Charles Scribner's Sons set out to remedy this deficiency with a new *Encyclopedia of the North American Colonies.* Its three volumes dealt not only with the former British colonies on the mainland of North America but also with all the cultures that developed on the continent from the time of the first European settlement until these political units ceased to be colonies of European powers and became independent states. The *Encyclopedia* therefore included the events that occurred in the first Norse settlements; in New Netherland, the short-lived Dutch outpost in North America; in the small Russian settlements of the Pacific Northwest; in New France and Louisiana; and in the Spanish Borderlands that stretched from Florida to California.

The warm reception accorded this *Encyclopedia* has suggested the desirability of a version more suited to younger readers, and the present *North America in Colonial Times* is the result of that consideration. Without sacrificing any of the scholarly quality of the original *Encyclopedia,* the present version has been modified in several ways. The text is now arranged alphabetically, making the work more accessible to students; the language has been adjusted to a level appropriate for middle and high school students; and the long, complex entries of the parent work have been broken down into shorter entries on more specific subjects.

The page format is also designed to aid students. Rather than the two full text columns in the parent work, *North America in Colonial Times* uses a major column for the entries and a minor column for items that explain and enrich the text: definitions of difficult or unfamiliar terms, time lines that place long articles in perspective chronologically, and sidebars that highlight interesting aspects of the material. To further increase the work's accessibility, cross-references to related articles appear both within the text and at the end of most entries.

More than 200 black-and-white illustrations enhance the pages of *North America in Colonial Times.* Depicting leading figures of the day, daily life, colonial art, and architecture, they help bring history to life for the student. Of particular use are the 16 maps of North America in different time periods, showing the routes of European explorers, colonies established by European powers, and the homelands of various Native American tribes. Finally, 16 pages of full-color plates illustrate important topics.

The editors of *North America in Colonial Times* were intimately associated with the production of the *Encyclopedia.* Jacob Ernest Cooke was the editor in chief of that publication, and Milton M. Klein was one of the associate editors. Both are widely published scholars in the field of early American history. Neal Salisbury of Smith College, a specialist in Native American history, acted as consultant on this important area of colonial history. Eleanor Brown, librarian at Mount Vernon High School in New York, and Beverley Ackert, a retired teacher of economics and government, have reviewed the entries to evaluate their suitability for middle and high school students.

Transforming the *Encyclopedia of the North American Colonies* into the present version has been a team effort. Visual Education Corporation of Princeton, New Jersey, assumed the responsibility of reshaping the material for younger readers and ensuring that it was accessible and accurate. The editors and consultants provided guidance in this undertaking, and Karen Day of Scribners offered encouragement.

The editors and all those involved in the publication of these volumes trust that the contents will arouse students' interest in and enhance their knowledge of this important period in our history. Covering almost three centuries, the

Preface

colonial period saw the emergence of some of the most important issues in later American history—race relations, the status of women, the role of religion, the political process, the treatment of the disadvantaged, and education—and the creation of the folkways that have shaped our culture. It is only remembrance of things past that can sharpen our understanding of contemporary events; and it is the task of the historian to bring that past to life. As Pulitzer-Prize-winning historian Michael Kammen has so aptly observed:

The historian is the memory of civilization. A civilization without memory ceases to be civilized. A civilization without history ceases to have identity. Without identity there is no purpose; without purpose, civilization will wither.

Jacob Ernest Cooke
Milton M. Klein

Time Line of North America in Colonial Times

ca. 20,000 B.C.	*The first human inhabitants of the Americas cross from Siberia into Alaska.*
A.D. 985	*Erik the Red establishes a Norse colony in Greenland.*
ca. 1000	*Leif Eriksson lands on the coast of North America.*
ca. 1420	*Prince Henry of Portugal establishes a school of navigation at Sagres, from which seamen set out and discover the Canary, Madeira, and Azores islands.*
1492	*Christopher Columbus, attempting to sail west to Asia, finds the "New World."*
1494	*The Treaty of Tordesillas divides the world between the Spanish and Portuguese empires.*
ca. 1500	*The French begin fishing off the coast of Newfoundland.*
	The Mohawk, Oneida, Onondaga, Cayuga, and Seneca peoples unite to form the Iroquois Confederacy.
1507	*Martin Waldseemüller calls the land explored by Columbus "America" in honor of Amerigo Vespucci, an Italian navigator who was the first to use the term "New World."*
1513	*Juan Ponce de León claims Florida for Spain.*
1518	*African slaves are brought to Hispaniola (Haiti and Dominican Republic) to work in gold mines.*
1518–1521	*Hernando Cortés conquers the Aztecs in Mexico.*
1519–1522	*Ships under the command of Ferdinand Magellan sail around the world.*
1524	*Giovanni da Verrazano explores the North American coast.*
1534–1536	*Jacques Cartier explores the Gulf of St. Lawrence and the St. Lawrence River as far as Montreal.*
1539–1543	*Hernando de Soto explores North America from Florida to the Mississippi River.*
1540–1542	*Francisco Vásquez de Coronado explores the Southwest as far as the Grand Canyon.*
1562–1568	*John Hawkins makes slave-trading voyages from Africa to the West Indies.*
1564	*France establishes Fort Caroline in Florida but quickly loses it to the Spanish.*
1565	*Pedro Menéndez de Avilés founds St. Augustine in Florida.*
1565–1574	*Spain sets up missions and forts between Florida and Virginia.*
1572	*Chief Powhatan unites Algonquian-speaking tribes in the Chesapeake region to form the Powhatan Confederacy.*
1578	*Francis Drake sails around South America and lands in present-day California.*
1583	*Sir Humphrey Gilbert leads an expedition to Newfoundland.*
1585–1590	*The English attempt twice to establish a colony at Roanoke Island. The second settlement mysteriously disappears.*
1598	*Juan de Oñate founds the colony of New Mexico.*
1602	*Bartholomew Gosnold explores the Atlantic coast from southern Maine to Narragansett Bay and transmits smallpox to his Indian trading partners.*

1604 Samuel de Champlain and Pierre du Gua de Monts establish a French settlement at Port Royal in Acadia (present-day Nova Scotia).

1606 James I of England grants charters to the Virginia Company and the Plymouth Company to colonize the Atlantic coast of North America.

1606–1608 The Plymouth Company establishes Saghadoc, an unsuccessful colony in present-day Maine.

1607 Colonists found Jamestown, the first permanent English settlement, in Virginia.
Massasoit becomes chief of the powerful Wampanoag of New England.

1608 Samuel de Champlain establishes a French settlement at Quebec.

1609 Henry Hudson explores the Hudson River as far north as present-day Albany.
Santa Fe is founded in New Mexico.

1612 New varieties of tobacco are planted in Virginia, launching a tobacco boom in the Chesapeake region.

1613 English forces destroy the Acadian town of Port Royal.

1614 Captain John Smith explores the New England coast.
New Netherland Company gains a monopoly on trade in the Dutch colony.

1616 Africans arrive in Bermuda, the first slaves in the English colonies.

1619 The Dutch bring the first blacks to Virginia.

1620 The Pilgrims establish Plymouth colony.

1622 Powhatan Indians fight the English in Virginia.

1624 Thirty families arrive in the Dutch colony of New Netherland.

1625 Jesuits arrive in Quebec.

1626 Peter Minuit becomes director general of New Netherland and buys Manhattan Island from the Indians.

1628 The English take over Acadia and Quebec, which are returned to France in 1632.

1630 The Massachusetts Bay Company establishes a new colony at Boston.

1630–1642 The Great Migration brings 16,000 settlers from England to the Massachusetts Bay colony.

1632 George Calvert, Lord Baltimore, receives a grant to found the colony of Maryland.

1633 French Jesuits establish Quebec College.

1633–1638 English colonists begin settling along the Connecticut River.

1636 Roger Williams founds the colony of Rhode Island.
Harvard College is established at Cambridge, Massachusetts.

1636–1637 In the Pequot War, English colonists in Connecticut destroy most of the Pequot tribe.

1636–1638 Anne Hutchinson challenges the authority of religious leaders in Massachusetts, is exiled, and settles in Rhode Island.

1638 Peter Minuit founds New Sweden on the Delaware River.

1639 North America's first hospital, the Hôtel-Dieu, is established in Quebec.

1641 The Bay Psalm Book, *the first book printed in the English colonies, appears in Boston.*

1642   *French fur traders establish a base at Montreal.*

1642–1649   *The English Civil War pits supporters of the monarch against Parliamentarians (mostly Puritans). King Charles I is executed in 1649, and England becomes a commonwealth.*

1643   *Massachusetts Bay, Plymouth, Connecticut, and New Haven colonies form the New England Confederation.*

1646–1665   *Iroquois Indians raid the Algonquin, Huron, and other neighboring tribes, driving refugees into Quebec and the Great Lakes region.*

1647   *Peter Stuyvesant becomes director general of New Netherland.*

1649   *Maryland passes the Act of Toleration establishing religious freedom for Christians; the act is repealed in 1654.*

1650   *Poems by Anne Bradstreet, the first published American poet, are printed in London.*

1652–1654   *First war between English and Dutch colonists.*

1653–1660   *England is ruled by Oliver Cromwell, Lord Protector of the Commonwealth.*

1654   *The first Jews arrive in New Amsterdam.*

1655   *Peter Stuyvesant conquers New Sweden, ending Swedish colonization in North America.*

1660   *The first Navigation Act requires all goods going into or out of the English colonies to be carried on English ships. The English monarchy is restored under Charles II.*

1663   *Louis XIV of France declares New France a royal province. Charles II of England gives eight proprietors a grant for the colony of Carolina.*

1664   *English naval forces capture New Netherland, which is renamed New York.*

1665–1667   *Second war between the English and the Dutch.*

1666–1667   *French colonial forces attack the Iroquois Confederacy and force it to accept French terms for peace.*

1668   *The English establish Charles Fort at the mouth of the Rupert River in present-day Canada.*

1669   *John Locke draws up the Fundamental Constitutions, a proposed plan of government for the Carolinas.*

1670   *The Hudson's Bay Company gains control of the fur trade in the Hudson Bay region.*

1672   *Royal African Company gains a monopoly on the English slave trade to America and the West Indies.*

1672–1674   *In the third war between the English and the Dutch, the Dutch temporarily regain control of New York.*

1673   *Louis Jolliet and Father Jacques Marquette explore the Mississippi River.*

1675–1676   *King Philip's War: Wampanoag leader Metacom, called King Philip, leads Indians of southern New England in an unsuccessful uprising against the English.*

1676   *Bacon's Rebellion: Virginia settlers, led by Nathaniel Bacon, seize control of the colony.*

1680   *Pueblo Revolt: Pueblo Indians drive Spanish from New Mexico.*

1681   *William Penn receives a charter to establish Pennsylvania from King Charles II of England.*

1682   *English colonists attack Quebec.*
       René-Robert Cavelier, Sieur de La Salle, claims Mississippi River valley for France, calling it Louisiana.

1686–1689   *King James II of England creates the Dominion of New England, which includes the colonies of New Hampshire, Massachusetts, Rhode Island, Connecticut, New York, and New Jersey. Sir Edmund Andros is renamed governor of the new province.*

1687   *Father Eusebio Francisco Kino establishes mission settlements in Pimeria Alta (modern Arizona).*

1688   *Protestant monarchs William II and Mary ascend the throne in England in what is called the Glorious Revolution.*

1689–1691   *Glorious Revolution in America: Colonists revolt against the Dominion of New England and receive new charters from William and Mary.*

Leisler's Rebellion: Jacob Leisler seizes control in New York and is executed in 1691.

1689–1697   *King William's War brings French and English colonies and their Indian allies into conflict.*

1692–1693   *Salem witchcraft trials: Nineteen people are hanged as witches in Massachusetts.*

1693   *The College of William and Mary is founded in Virginia.*

1696   *Carolina adopts the first slave laws in the British mainland colonies.*

Spain reconquers New Mexico from the Pueblo Indians.

1699   *Pierre Le Moyne d'Iberville founds the first French settlement in Louisiana.*

1701   *Anglicans create the Society for the Propagation of the Gospel (SPG) to convert Indians and Africans.*

Yale College is established in New Haven.

Antoine de la Mothe Cadillac founds Detroit.

1702–1713   *Queen Anne's War brings new conflict between French and English colonists and their Indian allies.*

1707   *The Act of Union unites England and Scotland into the United Kingdom of Great Britain.*

1709   *African and Indian slavery is legalized in New France.*

1710   *British forces conquer Port Royal in Acadia and rename it Annapolis Royal.*

1711–1713   *Tuscarora War: Carolina colonists join the Yamassee to defeat the Tuscarora Indians.*

1713   *Treaty of Utrecht: France gives up Acadia, Newfoundland, and Hudson Bay to Great Britain.*

1715–1728   *Yamassee War: Yamassee attack South Carolina towns and plantations and are defeated by British and Cherokee forces.*

1718   *Jean Baptiste Le Moyne de Bienville founds New Orleans.*

1729   *North and South Carolina become separate royal colonies.*

1729–1731   *Natchez Revolt in Louisiana.*

1730   *The Great Wagon Road is begun. It eventually stretches from Philadelphia to Georgia.*

1731   *Benjamin Franklin establishes a circulating library in Philadelphia.*

1732   *Franklin publishes* Poor Richard's Almanack.

1733   *James Oglethorpe founds Georgia as a refuge for British debtors.*

British Parliament passes the Molasses Act, taxing sugar and molasses from the French West Indies.

1734–1735 Clergyman Jonathan Edwards leads a religious revival in Massachusetts.

1735 The trial of publisher John Peter Zenger in New York promotes the principle of freedom of the press.

1737 "Walking Purchase": Delaware Indians sell the colony of Pennsylvania the entire Lehigh Valley.

1738–1745 Great Awakening: English preacher George Whitefield sparks religious revivals throughout the British colonies.

1739 Stono Rebellion: Slaves in South Carolina revolt and are stopped by the militia.

1740s Eliza Pinckney begins indigo cultivation in South Carolina.

1741 Rumors of plots by slaves to revolt lead to arrests and executions in New York.
Russian explorer Vitus Bering lands in Alaska.

1743 Benjamin Franklin establishes the American Philosophical Society in Philadelphia.

1744–1748 King George's War: European war between Britain, France, and Spain spreads to North America.

1746 College of New Jersey (later Princeton University) is founded.

1754 French and Indian War begins when Virginia sends its militia, led by George Washington, to challenge the French in the Ohio Valley. France and Britain officially declare war in 1756.

1755 Britain expels French colonists from Acadia. Many Acadians migrate to Louisiana.

1759–1760 British forces under General James Wolfe capture Quebec. A year later, the French surrender at Montreal.

1762 Spain declares war on Great Britain.

1763 Treaty of Paris: Great Britain wins Florida from Spain and Canada and Cape Breton from France. Spain gains Louisiana. Britain issues proclamation forbidding colonists to settle west of the Appalachian Mountains.
Touro Synagogue opens in Newport, Rhode Island.

1763–1766 Chief Pontiac of the Ottawa leads an alliance of Indians against the British in the Great Lakes region.

1764 The Sugar Act imposes high import taxes on non-British sugar, leading to colonial protests.

1765 The Stamp Act provokes outrage and widespread protest in the colonies and is repealed.

1766 British Parliament passes the Declaratory Act to emphasize its "full power and authority" over the colonies.

1767 Jesuits are expelled from Spanish territories. Franciscans take over the western missions.
In the British colonies, the Townshend Acts impose new taxes on certain imported items.

1769 Junípero Serra founds the first Spanish mission in California at San Diego.

1770 Boston Massacre: British troops fire into a crowd, killing five colonists.

1773 Boston Tea Party: Colonists protest the tea tax by dumping a shipload of tea into Boston harbor.
Publication of Poems on Various Subjects, Religious and Moral by Phillis Wheatley, a slave in Boston.

1774   *Parliament passes the Intolerable Acts to strengthen British authority in Massachusetts.*

In the Quebec Act, Parliament extends the borders of Quebec province southward and grants religious freedom to Catholics, angering American colonists.

The First Continental Congress meets in Philadelphia.

1775   *Battles are fought at Lexington and Concord.*

The Second Continental Congress assembles in Philadelphia.

George Washington takes command of the Continental Army.

1776   *Thomas Paine's* Common Sense *is published in Philadelphia.*

American colonists issue the Declaration of Independence to explain their separation from Great Britain.

1777   *Under military pressure, Cherokee Indians yield their lands to North and South Carolina.*

Vermont declares its independence from New York and New Hampshire.

1778   *Captain James Cook explores the northern Pacific coast.*

1779   *Spain declares war on Britain and enters the American War of Independence.*

1781   *American troops under George Washington and French forces under General Rochambeau defeat British troops led by General Charles Cornwallis at Yorktown, Virginia, winning independence for the United States.*

1783   *Treaty of Versailles: Great Britain recognizes the independence of the United States of America. Florida is returned to Spain.*

1784   *New Brunswick province is established in Canada as a refuge for American Loyalists.*

1789~1793   *Alexander Mackenzie reaches the Pacific coast by traveling overland across Canada.*

1791   *Constitution Act: Britain divides the province of Quebec into Lower Canada (Quebec) and Upper Canada (Ontario).*

1792   *Captain George Vancouver explores the west coast of Canada.*

1794   *Slavery is abolished in French colonies.*

1799   *The Russian-American Company is chartered and given a monopoly to conduct trade in Alaska.*

1800   *Spain returns Louisiana to France.*

1803   *Louisiana Purchase: France sells Louisiana to the United States for $15 million.*

1812~1841   *The Russian-American Company maintains a base at Fort Ross, in northern California.*

1819   *The United States acquires Florida from Spain.*

1821   *Mexico declares independence from Spain.*

1825~1832   *Stephen F. Austin brings American colonists to Texas.*

1833   *Great Britain declares an end to slavery in all its possessions, beginning in 1834.*

1840   *The Act of Union reunites Upper and Lower Canada and grants them self-rule.*

1867   *The British North America Act establishes the Dominion of Canada.*

Russia sells Alaska to the United States.

Abenaki Indians

See second map in Native Americans (vol. 3).

* palisade fence of stakes forming a defense

Abenaki was the name given to two clusters of loosely related Native American tribes in New England. The territory of the Western Abenaki covered most of present-day New Hampshire and Vermont and extended into Canada as far as the headwaters of the St. Lawrence River. The Eastern Abenaki, which included the Penobscot and Kennebec tribes, occupied what is now Maine and southeastern Quebec. During colonial times, the Abenaki sometimes included other groups, such as the MIC-MAC INDIANS of Nova Scotia.

Way of Life.   The Abenaki lived by hunting and fishing, raising corn, and gathering wild plant foods from forests and meadows. Because their homelands had rocky soil and a short growing season, agriculture played a smaller role in their economy than in those of other northeastern tribes. Many of the Abenaki settled in river valleys, where the land was more fertile. They often built palisades* around their villages as a protection against attack by enemies such as the IROQUOIS.

The lifestyle of the Abenaki changed with the seasons. In the spring, during the fish runs, they lived in villages near rivers. In the fall, the settlements broke up as families scattered to hunt. In the winter, the families gathered in their villages again.

The family was the focus of Abenaki society. Related families lived together in large households, and several households formed a village. Each village had two chiefs—a war chief and a civil chief—but these chiefs had little authority. They served mainly as advisers. Most important decisions were made jointly by all the adult men and women of the village.

Relations with Europeans.   Although the Abenaki tribes shared both language and ethnic background, they did not always act in unison when dealing with Europeans. Each tribe pursued what it saw as its own interests. Abenaki relations with Europeans were influenced largely by the different goals of the French and English colonists.

The French, who were interested primarily in the fur trade, did not appear to pose much of a threat. The English, on the other hand, sought to expand their settlements into Abenaki territory—and they had formed an alliance with the rival Iroquois. These factors pushed most Abenaki tribes into a close association with the French.

Beginning in the 1670s, the threat of English expansion touched off a series of wars between the Abenaki and the English. These wars took place while France and England were struggling for control of North America. Sometimes the fighting was limited to conflicts between the Abenaki and England's allies, the Iroquois. At other times, the Abenaki fought English settlers and troops directly. Throughout the wars, the Abenaki used arms supplied by the French and often fought alongside French troops. With a strategy that combined raiding and retreating, the Abenaki successfully limited the advance of English colonists into their territory. However, the prolonged hostilities had a damaging effect on the Indians' society and economy.

By the 1720s, the French position was weakening, and the Abenaki were becoming divided. Some tribes wanted to continue their alliance with France. Others hoped to remain neutral or to form relations with the British—in part because they had become dependent on British trade goods. With the defeat of France in the FRENCH AND INDIAN WAR in 1763, the Abenaki were forced to give up much of their best land.

Similar divisions split the Abenaki during the AMERICAN REVOLUTION, when both the British and Americans sought their support. In the end, Abenaki communities fought on each side. After winning independence, Americans took over more of the Indians' land. Some Abenaki withdrew to Canada. Others retreated to the most remote areas of New England and resumed their traditional way of life. Abenaki Indians still live in Canada and New England today.

Acadians

See map in New France (vol. 3).

Cajuns of Louisiana

The Acadians who came to Louisiana in the mid-1700s settled primarily in areas west of New Orleans. Their descendants, known as Cajuns from a local pronunciation of the word *Acadian*, continue to live in close-knit communities there.

The Cajuns developed a unique culture. Their language is a mixture of French, Spanish, Native American, and African American dialects. Their cuisine includes spicy specialties such as gumbo and jambalaya. Cajun music—played by an accordion, a fiddle, and a triangle—has its own special sound.

*T*he people of Acadia, a French colony in eastern Canada, developed a distinctive society and culture. The British won control of this region in the 1700s, and they eventually forced the Acadians to leave their homeland and migrate to other parts of North America.

The Colony of Acadia. In 1605 Samuel de CHAMPLAIN established a small French settlement at Port Royal (present-day Annapolis Royal in NOVA SCOTIA). This was the beginning of the colony of Acadia—a name that may have come from the Native American word *aquoddiake.* In the 1620s French trading companies began bringing settlers to the new colony, and by 1700 the number of people living in scattered areas around Port Royal had reached 1,400. The settlement continued to expand until Acadia included all of Nova Scotia, Ile-Saint-Jean (now Prince Edward Island), Ile Royale (now Cape Breton Island), and parts of the Gaspé Peninsula in Quebec and present-day New Brunswick.

The Acadians formed a distinct group. Most of the early settlers had come from southern France and spoke a dialect of French. Some belonged to large extended families who had moved together from France. As a result of their language and strong family ties, these people formed a very close-knit society.

The Acadians made their living by farming and fishing. Most lived on small farms in fertile river valleys, where they grew grains and vegetables and raised a variety of livestock. A special feature of Acadian agriculture was the use of dikes, made of earth and reinforced by logs and branches. The dikes allowed the farmers to use the marshland along the coast for cultivation. Dike building required a great deal of community cooperation, and this contributed to the sense of solidarity in Acadian society. Most Acadians also engaged in a small trade with the MICMAC INDIANS of Nova Scotia and provided agricultural goods to both French and British colonies.

The Troubles of the Acadians. Much of Acadia's history reflected the struggle between France and Great Britain for control of North America. The boundaries of the colony were never clearly defined, and disputed territory was traded back and forth between the two countries a number of times in the 1600s and early 1700s. Caught in the middle of this power struggle, the Acadians suffered greatly from raids on their settlements and from political upheaval.

Port Royal, the main town in the French colony of Acadia, fell to the British in 1710. The town became Annapolis Royal in Nova Scotia. John Hamilton painted this scene of it in the 1750s.

* cede to yield or surrender

In 1713 France ceded* Acadia to Britain under the TREATY OF UTRECHT. Yet British control of the territory and its French-speaking people remained weak for another 50 years. During this period, the British repeatedly tried to get the Acadians to swear an oath of allegiance to Britain. The Acadians resisted, hoping to remain neutral and have friendly relations with both the British and the French. They believed that neutrality would help guarantee their safety and spare them the consequences of war. The Acadians simply wanted to be left alone with their lands, their culture, and their Catholic religion, and to continue trading with everyone.

Peace in Acadia ended in 1744 with the beginning of the War of the Austrian Succession, also known as KING GEORGE'S WAR. French officials encouraged the Acadians to remain loyal to France. Most Acadians decided to remain neutral, but a few did take up arms for the French. Questioning the Acadians' loyalty and neutrality, the British once again insisted that they swear an oath of allegiance to Britain. When the Acadians resisted, the British decided to remove all Acadians from the region and place them in other British colonies along the Atlantic coast.

Deportation. In 1755 British troops began raiding Acadian settlements and rounding up the people. Some Acadians fled to safety in territory that was still under French control. Others hid in the forests of Acadia. Those captured by the British were put on boats and deported to Protestant colonies, where they often faced harsh treatment because of their Catholic faith. In the British effort to scatter the refugees throughout the colonies, many Acadians became separated from their families. American poet Henry Wadsworth Longfellow wrote of the heartbreak of their forced migration and separations in his long poem *Evangeline.*

The Great Upheaval, as the Acadians called this period, lasted officially from 1755 to 1763. Many Acadians, however, continued wandering for years in search of a safe haven. As early as 1756, they began leaving the British colonies to seek refuge elsewhere. Some went to France or to French colonies in the West Indies. Many went to the Spanish colony of LOUISIANA, where they established a distinctive French-speaking culture and became known as Cajuns. Still other Acadians made their way back to Canada and began reestablishing their lives there. Today, reminders of Acadian culture can be found in Nova Scotia and among the Cajuns of Louisiana. (*See also* **Canada; Migration Within the Colonies; New France.**)

Acts of Toleration

* *toleration* acceptance of the right of individuals to follow their own religious beliefs

* *proprietor* person granted land and the right to establish a colony

* *repeal* to undo a law

* *Glorious Revolution* bloodless revolution in England in 1688 in which James II, a Catholic, was replaced as monarch by Protestants William and Mary

Religious freedom was rare in colonial America. Colonial governments tended to permit the practice of only one religion. In the 1600s, however, two laws—one passed in MARYLAND and one in England—called for toleration* of religious differences. These Acts of Toleration provided the first steps toward greater religious freedom in the English colonies of North America.

Maryland passed the first of Act of Toleration in 1649. The colony, founded as a haven for Roman Catholics fleeing persecution in England, also welcomed large numbers of Protestants. This soon resulted in tensions between people of the two faiths. In an effort to ease these tensions, the proprietor* of the colony, Cecil CALVERT (the second Lord Baltimore), arranged in 1649 for the Maryland assembly to pass an "Act Concerning Religion." The law did not allow complete freedom of religion, as it applied only to Christians who believed in the idea of the trinity—God the Father, Jesus Christ, and the Holy Ghost. Nevertheless, the law marked an important first step toward religious freedom. In addition to guaranteeing freedom of worship, it also prohibited individuals from using harsh names against people of other Christian faiths. Unfortunately, the law did not promote great toleration, and in any case the Maryland assembly repealed* the act in 1654.

A second Act of Toleration affected all the English colonies. The Glorious Revolution* of 1688 brought decades of religious conflict in England to an end. The next year the English Parliament passed the Act of Toleration of 1689. This act, which granted religious freedom to all Protestants, applied to England and its colonies. Although the act fell short of ensuring complete religious freedom—it included neither Catholics nor Jews—it did call for toleration for people of various Protestant faiths.

The AMERICAN REVOLUTION reinforced the idea of personal liberty, and most states included religious freedom in their new constitutions. But it was not until the ratification of the Bill of Rights in 1791 that all citizens of the United States gained full religious freedom. (*See also* **Freedom of Religion.**)

Acts of Trade

See *Navigation Acts.*

Adams, Abigail

1744–1818
First Lady and noted letter writer

Abigail Adams was the wife of patriot and future President John Adams. She supported her husband's political goals but advised him to include American women in his call for rights. She is best known for the lively, descriptive letters she wrote.

*A*bigail Adams was the wife of patriot John ADAMS, who became the second President of the United States. Throughout her husband's political career, she provided him with support and encouragement. She is known primarily through the hundreds of lively letters she wrote.

Raised by her grandmother in Weymouth, Massachusetts, Abigail Adams lived at some distance from her friends and relatives. At an early age, she formed the habit of letter writing to keep in touch. In 1764 she married John Adams, and the couple had five children.

In 1776 John Adams was attending the SECOND CONTINENTAL CONGRESS, which was then debating the issue of American independence. Abigail Adams wrote to her husband on March 31, urging him to "remember the ladies" in drawing up a new code of laws:

> Do not put such unlimited power into the hands of the husbands. . . . If particular care and attention is not paid to the ladies, we are determined to foment [mount] a rebellion and will not hold ourselves bound by any laws in which we have no voice, or representation.

She hoped for an end to the legal principle of coverture, which prevented married women from acting on their own and possessing property. John Adams and his fellow lawmakers, however, did not abolish coverture. They believed that men should continue to own family property and represent families in government.

In the years following the DECLARATION OF INDEPENDENCE, John Adams's leading role in the new nation often kept him away from his home in Massachusetts. During this period, Abigail Adams cared for their children, managed her husband's business affairs, took care of the family farm, and continued to write letters that painted a vivid picture of the times. After the signing of the peace treaty between the Americans and the British, she joined her husband in Paris and accompanied him to London where he served as American ambassador.

Abigail Adams was in the midst of American public life during the years her husband served as Vice President (1789–1797) and President (1797–1801) of the United States. In 1801 she and John returned to Massachusetts, where she spent her remaining years.

Adams, John

1735–1826
American patriot, revolutionary, and President

A leader of the independence movement in the American colonies, John Adams played an important role in the creation of the United States. After the AMERICAN REVOLUTION, he became the first Vice President and the second President of the new nation. Though not always popular, Adams served his country with distinction for more than a quarter of a century.

Early Years. John Adams grew up on a farm in Braintree, Massachusetts, a town south of Boston. His parents wanted him to attend college, but the young Adams disliked school. At age 13, Adams told his parents that he wanted to become a farmer. His father responded by giving him some of the dirtiest, most miserable farm chores. The work convinced young John that going to college was not such a bad idea. He studied hard and entered Harvard College at age 15—a typical age for college at the time.

Adams thrived in Harvard, adding to his course work by reading as many as two books a day. Through his reading, Adams absorbed the main ideas of the ENLIGHTENMENT—faith in the power of human reason, an emphasis on science, and the belief that people and their rulers were bound together by a social contract*. After graduating from college, Adams taught school for a year in Worcester, Massachusetts. He then decided to pursue a career in law and, after two years of study, he moved back to Braintree and opened a law practice.

In the 1760s, Adams's life began to take shape. At age 29, he married Abigail Smith, an intelligent woman of strong convictions and a deep commitment to duty—a person very much like himself. John and Abigail eventually had five children. Also during this period—a time of increasing tensions between Great Britain and the colonies—Adams began to play a role in public life.

social contract idea popular in the 1700s that governments came into existence as a result of an agreement among people to give up some of their rights in order to have an orderly society

Leader for Independence.

Adams first made a name for himself in 1765 by writing statements of protest against the STAMP ACT, a British law requiring the colonists to buy special stamps for various types of documents and printed materials. Adams argued that the law was invalid because the colonists had never agreed to it. At the same time, he disapproved of the mass protests and mob violence that erupted in response to the Stamp Act.

Throughout his life, Adams showed both a fear of popular uprisings and a respect for the rule of law. Those feelings lay behind Adams's conduct in 1770. Resentment of the British continued to mount in Boston. In March 1770, a mob of Bostonians taunted a group of British soldiers stationed in the town. The soldiers opened fire on the crowd, killing five colonists. The incident became known as the BOSTON MASSACRE. Determined that the accused soldiers should receive a fair trial, Adams agreed—at some risk to his own reputation—to defend them. He and the other defense attorneys won acquittals for seven of the nine defendants. The jury found the two others guilty but on the lesser charge of manslaughter instead of murder.

During the conflicts with Britain of the 1770s, Adams played an increasingly larger role in Massachusetts—and beyond. In 1773 he applauded the BOSTON TEA PARTY organized by his cousin Samuel ADAMS, calling it "the grandest event which has yet happened since the controversy with Britain opened." Soon afterward, Adams was chosen to represent Massachusetts at the FIRST CONTINENTAL CONGRESS in Philadelphia. At the congress Adams did not yet urge independence, shrewdly recognizing that many representatives from other colonies considered the delegates from Massachusetts too radical. Instead, he helped draft documents asserting the colonists' rights and declaring that the British Parliament did not have the power to tax the colonies. He also voted to approve the Suffolk Resolves, which urged colonists to end imports of all British goods, begin organizing militias*, and disobey the Intolerable Acts—legislation meant to strengthen British authority in the colonies.

militia army of citizens who may be called into action in a time of emergency

By the time of the SECOND CONTINENTAL CONGRESS in 1775, colonists had already fought British troops at the Battles of LEXINGTON AND CONCORD. Adams was now firmly committed to independence, but he realized that many other delegates to the congress did not share his view. Nevertheless, he convinced the congress to raise an army for defense and proposed that George WASHINGTON be made its commander. He also urged the congress to begin taking steps to increase production of food, ships, and other wartime supplies. Meanwhile, colony after colony began asking the congress for advice on establishing new governments. Adams used this opportunity to advance his own ideas, arguing in favor of creating systems resembling colonial governments, with a governor, a council, and an assembly.

In June 1776, the congress finally passed a resolution calling for independence from Great Britain. Adams joined Thomas JEFFERSON, Benjamin FRANKLIN, and two others on the committee that drafted the DECLARATION OF INDEPENDENCE. Adams later recalled that he declined to write the document himself because he was "obnoxious, suspected, and unpopular" and because Jefferson wrote "ten times better" than he did. Though he contributed little to writing the document, Adams argued powerfully and persuasively during the debate in the congress over independence. Jefferson later called him "the pillar of support [for the Declaration] . . . [and] its ablest advocate and defender."

Later Career. During the American Revolution, Adams remained in congress and also served on diplomatic missions to America's ally, France, and to the Netherlands. When the war ended, he joined Benjamin Franklin and John Jay on the commission that negotiated a peace treaty with Great Britain. Afterward, he served as the new nation's first ambassador to Britain.

Adams later served two terms under George Washington as the first Vice President of the United States. He succeeded Washington as President in 1797 and held the office for one term. During his presidency, Adams tried to maintain American neutrality at a time when France and Great Britain were at war. In doing so, he lost the support both of groups that were strongly anti-French and of those favoring war against Britain. He also lost popularity because of his military preparedness program. Even more unpopular were the Alien* and Sedition* Acts of 1798, which authorized the President to deport aliens considered dangerous to the peace and security of the United States. Passed during a time when the country seemed headed for war with France, the laws allowed officials to punish anyone who criticized the government. Many Americans considered these acts a serious attack on basic freedoms and liberties, and they blamed Adams for their passage.

Defeated by Thomas Jefferson in the presidential election of 1800, Adams retired from public life. He spent the next 25 years reading, thinking, and writing about various public issues. He also began a lively exchange of letters with Jefferson in which they discussed their views on recent history and current events. At the same time, Adams watched the political rise of his son, John Quincy Adams, who became President of the United States in 1825. Adams died on the same day as Thomas Jefferson—July 4, 1826—the fiftieth anniversary of the Declaration of Independence. (*See also* **Adams, Abigail.**)

Wrong Date for Independence

The Fourth of July is actually not the date the United States became a nation. The Second Continental Congress voted for independence on July 2. However, July 4 was the day the congress approved the text of the Declaration of Independence. After the vote on July 2, John Adams predicted that the day would forever be celebrated with fireworks and jubilation. He was wrong about the date—but right about the celebration.

---

* *alien* noncitizen
* *sedition* conduct or language that leads people to disobey the laws of the state

Adams, Samuel

1722–1803
Revolutionary statesman

* *propaganda* information presented in a way to influence people

* *effigy* dummy of a person

Samuel Adams played a key role in leading the British colonies to independence. As a young Massachusetts politician, he fought against British attempts to limit the rights of the colonists. He served in both the First and the Second Continental Congress and signed the Declaration of Independence.

Samuel Adams helped lead Massachusetts—and the British colonies in North America—along the road to independence. In his writings Adams used techniques of propaganda* to convince colonists that the British government was determined to take away their rights. With great political skill, he helped organize opposition to the British.

Early Years. Born to a well-to-do Boston family, Sam Adams attended Harvard College. He later earned a master of arts degree at Harvard by arguing in his thesis that citizens had a responsibility to the interest of their community, even if that meant resisting their ruler. Adams had more success in his studies than he did in finding a career. He started a business with money from his father, but the enterprise soon failed. Next he served as Boston's tax collector. Because he fell behind in collecting the taxes, however, he ended up owing the city a considerable sum of money.

For the rest of his life Adams was in constant financial trouble, often relying on the help of friends for himself and his family to survive. His cousin John ADAMS, another Revolutionary leader, criticized him for not looking "enough to himself and his family."

Revolutionary Leader. Although impractical in personal affairs, Samuel Adams was a brilliant politician dedicated to the cause of the rights of Britain's American colonists. His early efforts were not aimed at winning independence. Rather, he led an attempt to take power from a group of wealthy men of property who controlled Massachusetts politics. The leader of that group was Thomas HUTCHINSON, the colony's lieutenant governor and chief justice.

When the British PARLIAMENT passed the SUGAR ACT in 1764 and the STAMP ACT in 1765, Adams saw an opportunity for rousing opposition to Hutchinson and his supporters. The Sugar and Stamp acts were designed to raise money by taxing the colonists. Adams and other colonists claimed that such taxes violated their rights. Under the British constitution, they argued, no person could be taxed without having representation in Parliament. The colonists enjoyed no such representation.

Colonists' resentment of the Stamp Act focused on Hutchinson's brother-in-law, Andrew Oliver, the official distributor of stamps for Massachusetts. A mob of angry colonists burned an effigy* of Oliver and then looted his house. Two weeks later, in another riot, a mob looted Hutchinson's house.

In 1766 Adams and his followers won control of the Massachusetts legislature. They used this power to keep Hutchinson and two of his relatives from being elected to the governor's council. Deeply involved in growing conflict between the rebellious colonists and British authorities, Adams forced the British to recall their appointed governor. He also made life difficult for Hutchinson, who remained in Boston as the representative of the British crown. Adams considered Hutchinson an "enemy of liberty." Hutchinson wrote that he doubted that the colonies contained a "greater incendiary" (troublemaker) than Adams.

A Powerful Pen. In addition to his organizing ability, Adams was relied on for his writing skill. He wrote most of the official papers of the Massachusetts legislature. Through newspaper articles and letters to leaders in Massachusetts and the other colonies, he helped spread the idea that the colonists needed to stand up for their rights.

At the same time, Adams was working to establish a network of opposition leaders throughout the colonies. He joined the SONS OF LIBERTY, an organization formed to protect colonial liberties. In 1768 he sent a "Circular Letter" to the assemblies of the other colonies urging a boycott* of British imports. He also worked to fuel Bostonians' resentment of the British soldiers stationed in their city. When a group of the soldiers fired on a crowd of colonists on March 5, 1770, killing five colonists, Adams called the incident the BOSTON MASSACRE.

In the next few years, while tensions in the colonies eased, Adams continued to work to assert colonists' rights. He organized COMMITTEES OF CORRESPONDENCE throughout Massachusetts to state the rights of the colonists and communicate them to the world. In one of its first actions, the Boston committee adopted a declaration of rights written by Adams. In it, he proclaimed that colonists enjoyed the natural rights to life, to liberty, and to property—ideas that later became part of the American DECLARATION OF INDEPENDENCE. In his declaration, Adams also claimed that colonial assemblies were independent of the British Parliament.

By 1773 tensions were rising again. Adams made public some letters written by Hutchinson in which Hutchinson—now governor—stated his opposition to the claims of colonial rights. That same year, Parliament passed the TEA ACT. Adams seized the opportunity for demonstrating the colonists' anger at British actions. When ships loaded with tea arrived in Boston, Adams and others tried to have the ships returned to Britain with their cargo untouched. Hutchinson would not agree. At a mass meeting on December 16, Adams gave the signal, and a group of Bostonians disguised as Mohawk Indians carried out his plan for solving the tea problem. They dumped the cargo into Boston harbor. Their rebellious act came to be known as the BOSTON TEA PARTY.

Determined to punish Massachusetts, the British responded with the INTOLERABLE ACTS. One measure closed Boston harbor. Another strengthened the hand of the British rulers in Massachusetts and limited self-government. Adams led the opposition to these measures. He convinced the Boston town meeting* to approve a strict boycott of British goods and then sent the news of the boycott to the other colonies, asking them to take similar steps.

Adams became convinced that a meeting of representatives from all the colonies was needed to organize effective measures against the British. In 1774 he went to Philadelphia to represent Massachusetts at the FIRST CONTINENTAL CONGRESS. Before leaving Boston, he called a meeting of like-minded colonists that passed the Suffolk Resolves, a document that put Massachusetts in a virtual state of rebellion.

Later Career. Adams also served in the SECOND CONTINENTAL CONGRESS, where he promoted the cause of independence and signed the Declaration of Independence. After this, however, he played a smaller role in national affairs. He sat in the congress until 1781, helping to write the

* *boycott* refusal to buy goods as a means of protest

Master Politician at Work

The day after the Boston Massacre, Adams organized a mass meeting. He warned Thomas Hutchinson, then acting governor, that further violence would occur if the British troops were not withdrawn from the city. The British commander said that one of the two regiments could be removed. Adams seized the opening, saying that if one regiment could be moved both could be moved. When Hutchinson asked for time to decide, Adams left—and staged another mass rally. The angry crowd made the threat of disorder very real. Adams declared that if Hutchinson refused to act, the resulting violence would be his fault. Hutchinson gave in and allowed the troops to withdraw.

* *town meeting* assembly of male citizens to discuss and vote on community issues

* **Articles of Confederation** plan approved in 1781 to establish a national legislature with limited powers

Articles of Confederation* that created the first government of the United States of America. After returning to Massachusetts, Adams helped write that state's new constitution. From 1789 to 1793 he served as lieutenant governor and, from 1794 to 1797, as governor of his state. He lived his remaining years in "honorable poverty." (*See also* **American Revolution.**)

Africa

See map in Slave Trade (vol. 4).

*A*frica played an important role in the colonial period as a source of slave labor for the Americas. During the 1600s and 1700s, millions of Africans were sent across the Atlantic Ocean to work on plantations in the Caribbean islands and in North and South America.

SLAVERY had a long history in Africa. Europeans became involved in the SLAVE TRADE in the 1400s when the Portuguese were looking for a sea route to India. The Portuguese explored the west and then the east coast of Africa and established coastal settlements from which to carry on a trade in gold, spices, ivory, and slaves.

The Portuguese sent most of the Africans they enslaved back to Portugal, but some were taken to the Cape Verde Islands, off the western coast of Africa. The Spaniards sent African slaves to work on the sugar plantations in the Canary Islands. Both Portugal and Spain used profits from the slave trade to finance further exploration and business ventures. In time other European countries, also seeking to profit from the African trade, established forts and trading posts along the African coast.

In North America, the Portuguese and Spanish at first used Native American slaves to work in gold mines and on plantations. But as Indian populations declined as a result of harsh treatment by Europeans and European diseases,

Throughout the colonial period, Africa was important to the American colonies as a source of slave labor and a market for New England rum. This engraving shows traders acquiring slaves at Fort des Maures, a trading post in western Africa, in the late 1700s.

colonists came to rely increasingly on African slaves. The Spanish introduced Africans in their Caribbean colonies as early as 1502, and the Portuguese soon became a major supplier of slaves for the Americas.

The Dutch, French, and English began shipping African slaves to the Americas, and the slave trade grew rapidly. The first Africans arrived in Virginia in 1619. In the 1700s, Africa became a key link in a pattern of trade that involved the shipment of manufactured goods from Europe, slaves from Africa, and agricultural products from the Americas.

Throughout the colonial period, most slaves brought to the Americas came from an area along the west coast of Africa that extended from present-day Senegal to Angola. A small number also arrived from the island of Madagascar and the coastal regions of East Africa. The slaves came from a wide variety of cultural, political, and economic backgrounds and spoke hundreds of different languages.

The Africans brought important skills to the Americas, such as a knowledge of rice cultivation, which proved useful in colonial agriculture. They also brought cultural traditions that helped shape new and distinct African American cultures throughout colonial North and South America. (*See also* **African American Culture; Exploration, Age of; Trade and Commerce.**)

African American Culture

*I*n the 1600s and 1700s, the SLAVE TRADE brought millions of Africans to the Americas. African American culture was shaped by the fact that these people had come to the New World against their will. Adapting to life in the American colonies, black slaves and their children and grandchildren developed a distinctive culture that blended African and American traditions.

Adapting to a New Life. Most blacks in the American colonies had come from the west coast of Africa, a region with many different tribal groups, languages, and customs. As these people adapted to their new environment, they began to develop a sense of common identity based, in part, on their experiences as slaves.

African Americans who lived in the northern colonies, where slaves were widely scattered, tended to adopt many aspects of white culture. In contrast, blacks in the southern colonies, where large numbers of slaves lived in close quarters, preserved African traditions for a long time. A special situation arose in northern cities, where African Americans developed an urban black culture that drew from both African and white societies.

By the late 1700s, a distinct African American culture had developed in the colonies, and most blacks saw themselves as African Americans. Their identity was evident in their religion, music, and dance. At the same time, organizations such as the African Society and the African Baptist Church reflected the pride that many blacks felt in their heritage.

Religion. Many Africans believed in multiple gods, and African American slaves were open to new religions. Over time slaves accepted the Christianity of their owners, but their version of Christianity had many African overtones. African American church services included joyous songs. Their funerals combined grief with exuberant music and dancing, expressing both a sense of loss at the death of a loved one and happiness that the deceased would soon be in a better place and would be reunited with his or her ancestors.

The Bible played a central role in colonial times in the faith of all Christians, but African Americans interpreted the Bible in their own fashion. For them, the Scriptures told a story of oppression*, liberation, and hope. Although many blacks could not read, they came to know the Bible through their preachers, who read it aloud during religious services and interpreted it. African American worship included an open display of feelings, shouting, and body movement. This emotionalism was incorporated by southern white preachers during the GREAT AWAKENING, a period of religious revival that began in the mid-1700s. After the Great Awakening, white Christian groups expressed their faith with more open feeling as well.

Music, Dance, Folktales.   African American music grew out of African musical tradition, with its complex rhythms, improvisation*, and emotional outpouring. Black field-workers sang songs that often used satire* to describe the harsh work of slavery. In their free time, they liked to sing and play instruments, including instruments that originated in Africa such as banjos, tambourines, rattles, and drums. Drumming was less important in the colonies than in Africa because whites discouraged it, fearing that the drums might inspire rebellion among the slaves.

African American dance and body movement were closely linked to music in African culture. The dances usually featured improvisation, strong rhythms, smooth movements, and almost no body contact among dancers. In the absence of drums, African Americans used hand clapping, thigh slapping, and foot stomping to set the rhythm. Even when blacks learned European-style dances, they adapted them to traditional African styles of dance.

Folktales entertained and helped educate blacks in the North American colonies. Storytelling was an important means of passing along ideas to slaves who could not read. Many stories highlighted the injustice of slavery, often through satire, and exposed the emptiness of white claims to superiority. Stories also relied on the use of comparisons and symbols, such as animals, to camouflage ideas that whites might consider dangerous. Through folktales, African Americans could both learn about their past and safely ridicule white society.

Food and Clothing.   Blacks brought a familiarity with certain foods from their African homelands. Okra, black-eyed peas, yams, and peanuts all became part of African American cooking, as did the use of frying rather than roasting. Black cooks were eventually acknowledged as among the best chefs in the colonies.

African American clothing also showed the influence of African traditions. Although blacks tended to wear European-style clothing, they adapted such clothing to their own tastes. During hot summer months, slaves often wore little clothing and frequently went barefoot. On festive

* *oppression* unjust or cruel exercise of authority

* *improvisation* art created on the spot rather than planned in advance
* *satire* humor that makes fun of something bad or foolish

See color plate 4, vol. 2.

Election Day

In the 1700s, African Americans celebrated a festival rooted in African traditions of authority and changing roles. Called Negro Election Day, the festival was marked by the selection of African American kings and governors who were honored in a grand parade. The celebration included dancing, music, games, and other rowdy activities that lasted well into the night. Election Day festivals were more common in northern areas than in the South. Many southern colonists viewed the selection of black royalty as a dangerous idea that might threaten their own authority.

occasions, African Americans enjoyed brightly colored clothing similar to the bold fabrics favored in Africa. Both men and women also wore kerchiefs on their heads and large hoop earrings, in traditional African style. African Americans continued to dress in this way after the colonial period.

Patterns of Family and Work. Some slaveholders tried to encourage the development of stable family relationships among their slaves. This not only helped create a dependable and growing work force, but it also reduced the threat of rebellion by unhappy slaves. In many respects, though, family relationships among African Americans remained fragile. Slave marriages had no legal status, and families could be separated without their consent. High death rates among blacks and the much greater number of men than of women also made it more difficult for blacks to establish stable family lives.

In both personal relationships and work, blacks maintained the African tradition of communal ties. African Americans preferred to work together in groups, sharing the labor. They also tended to develop, whenever possible, elaborate systems of kinship relationships and friendships that extended beyond their immediate families. Such communal relationships were a distinctive feature of colonial African American culture. (*See also* **Family; Food and Drink; Languages; Literature; Medical Practice; Music and Dance; Recreation and Sports.**)

Aged, the

See *Old Age.*

Agriculture

Agriculture played a central role in the economy of colonial North America. The colonists raised crops and livestock for their own use and sold any extra goods to earn money. As a result, farming activities dominated the lives of most colonial families.

The first colonists in North America lived largely on wild plants, fish, and game animals—a diet that did not supply their basic food needs. Their attempts to grow European crops and follow European farming methods were disastrous. The situation improved when they adopted some Native American crops and farming techniques that suited the land and climate.

During the early colonial period, people living in different regions of North America developed distinct forms of agriculture. Each region had its own particular blend of crops, farming methods, division of labor, and property ownership. These agricultural patterns lasted well beyond the colonial period.

British Agriculture

The British colonies followed a wide range of agriculture patterns—from the small family farms of New England to the large PLANTATIONS of the South. The crops and farming methods varied according to the climate, patterns of settlement and land distribution, and economic needs of the region.

Agriculture

Agriculture was the most important economic activity in all the British colonies. Crops ranged from tobacco and rice in the South to corn and wheat in New England and the middle colonies. This 1794 woodcut shows a farm in New Jersey.

A View at Pahaquarrie, Sussex County, New-Jersey.

Principal Crops and Animals. In the northern colonies, farmers focused primarily on meeting the food needs of their families and local communities. The main crop in the New England colonies was corn, also known as MAIZE. Adopted from the Native Americans, corn grew in abundance and ripened early, helping to replace food supplies exhausted after the long, cold winters. Other Native Americans crops—beans, pumpkins, and squash—became part of the colonial farmers' produce. In New England, settlers also grew wheat, rye, barley, and oats. Raising livestock was important, too. Almost every colonial farm had several cattle, a few pigs, and perhaps a small flock of sheep. Farmers often allowed livestock to graze freely in meadows and forests, and built fencing around fields to keep them away from crops.

The colonists of New York, New Jersey, and Pennsylvania—middle colonies—raised wheat as a local food crop and an export product. Many farmers grew other grains, grasses to feed livestock, and flax for making linen cloth. Larger farms and estates often had orchards and vegetable gardens. The main livestock of the region were cattle, pigs, and sheep. Some farmers also raised horses for riding and pulling wagons and plows. Although cattle were kept primarily for meat, milk production became increasingly important during the 1700s. Many large farms produced milk, butter, and cheese for both home and market.

* cash crop crop grown primarily for profit

Cash crops* dominated the agriculture of the Chesapeake region—Maryland and Virginia. The main cash crop was TOBACCO, another product adopted from Native Americans. Many farmers relied on tobacco to earn money for most of their food, clothing, and other supplies. Some also grew corn and wheat, but these crops generally provided a much smaller income. Chesapeake farmers also raised cattle, pigs, and sheep, primarily as food for their families. As in the north, most livestock roamed free.

The lower southern colonies, which included the Carolinas and Georgia, had two principal cash crops—tobacco and RICE. These crops flourished in the hot, humid coastal lowlands of the eastern part of the region. Indigo, a

Homespun Linens

Many farm families planted flax along with food crops. They raised the flax to make linen for clothing and household use. Flax production involved very hard work, usually divided up among family members. Men sowed the flax seeds in spring, and women uprooted the plants in midsummer. Then the plants had to be dried, de-seeded, and soaked in creeks to rot away vegetable matter. Next the flax was "broken" between special crushing blades. Finally the fibers were cleaned and separated, ready to be spun into yarn and eventually woven into linen.

* *indentured servant* person who agreed to work a certain length of time in return for passage on a ship to the colonies

plant used to make blue dyes and inks, was another important crop. In the hilly interior to the west, farmers grew corn and wheat, mostly as food crops rather than cash crops. Lumber also brought in money in some forested areas. Southern farmers kept large herds of free-roaming livestock and often produced a surplus of meat for export. In some parts of the region, cattle raising became a very profitable business.

Land Ownership and Farm Labor. When the New England colonies were founded in the 1600s, the English monarch granted land to groups of wealthy individuals known as proprietors. The proprietors distributed home lots, fields, and meadows to settlers, leaving pasture land to be shared. For the most part, New England farms remained small and could provide enough food only for the family.

In New England, the community—rather than individual farmers—made many agricultural decisions. As a group, citizens determined the shapes of fields, crops to be planted, and times of planting and harvesting. Farmers and their wives and children worked on their own farms and also helped with community projects such as clearing forests and fencing fields. Some villages cooperated on livestock raising, hiring shepherds to drive all the local animals to and from pastures. As towns grew larger, New England life became less centered on the community, and farmers made more individual decisions about their land.

A variety of ethnic groups settled in the middle colonies, creating a number of distinctive farming communities set apart by the form of farm labor they used and the styles of barns and fences they built. Properties ranged in size from small farms in rural Pennsylvania to large estates in the Hudson River valley of New York. On small farms, families generally did all the work themselves. Larger farms, however, relied greatly on other farm workers, including indentured servants*, seasonal laborers, and slaves. By the mid-1700s, many farms in the region were run by tenant farmers, who received a home, garden, and pasture from a large landowner in exchange for rent and for some labor on the landowner's farm.

In the 1600s, individual farmers dominated farming in the Chesapeake region and southern colonies. Most of the early Chesapeake farmers had gained land through the headright system, a system in which British trade companies gave small parcels of land to people who paid their own passage to America. Many of the Chesapeake region colonists eventually moved to the southern colonies, seeking cheap land.

Beginning in the early 1700s, the Chesapeake region and southern colonies both saw the development of plantations. These large farms, located primarily in lowland areas, required many workers. To supply the labor, planters began relying increasingly on slaves from the West Indies and Africa. The typical plantation of the colonial period had about 200 acres and three or four slaves, but large estates could have thousands of acres and hundreds of slaves. The plantation system, based on tobacco and rice crops, developed into an agricultural economy unlike any other in North America. By the mid-1700s, black slaves outnumbered whites in several areas of the South, and their backbreaking labor brought great wealth to many white southerners.

15

* *scythe* farm cutting tool with a long, curving blade

* *thresh* to crush grain plants so that the seeds or grains are separated from the stalks and the husks

* *crop rotation* changing crops each season to allow the soil to recover its nutrients

Technology.   The English colonists learned some farming techniques from Native Americans. The Indians showed the early settlers how to plant corn in rows among tree stumps. They taught them to build up small mounds of dirt around the base of each plant to secure its roots, support its stalk, and retain moisture. Following the example of the Indians, the colonists planted beans, pumpkins, and squash among the corn rows.

The early settlers had brought few farm implements with them, so they adopted various Indian farming tools such as digging sticks and hoes made of wood and animal bone. Over time the colonists acquired and began to use more traditional European farm implements, such as plows, scythes*, shovels, and axes.

The English colonists developed special techniques for raising certain crops. To grow tobacco, for example, slaves or other workers planted seeds in midwinter, hoed fields in early spring, transplanted seedlings to the fields in May, weeded and pruned plants in summer, and harvested the crop in late summer. Tobacco leaves then had to be dried and cured, first on the ground and then by hanging the plants in airy barns called tobacco houses. Planters involved in rice cultivation also followed special procedures. They found that they could improve yields and control weeds more effectively by flooding the rice fields with water. Slaves built dams to regulate the flow of water from nearby swamps so that fields could be flooded and drained. After harvest, the rice stalks were dried, threshed* by hand, and thrown in the air to separate the grain from its chaff, or outer covering.

By the mid-1700s, cattle grazing, lumbering, and overuse of the soil had begun to wear out farmland in many British colonial areas. The problem was most severe in New England with its poor soil. Farmers tried to reverse this process by fertilizing extensively with fish remains and animal manure. They used simple crop rotation* methods, such as leaving fields unplanted in some years. Farmers also planted various grasses imported from Europe to enrich the soil. However, such attempts were only partially successful. Many small-scale farmers found it increasingly difficult to raise enough crops to meet their needs. As a result, some settlers migrated westward in the 1700s, in search of better land and opportunities.

Dutch Agriculture

The DUTCH WEST INDIA COMPANY established the colony of NEW NETHER-LAND in the early 1600s as a center for the fur trade, but the company soon began to encourage the development of agricultural settlements as well. From the beginning, the Dutch focused on raising crops for market rather than for family use.

Types of Settlement.   The Dutch developed three types of agricultural settlements in New Netherland. The first consisted of small, isolated farms—called *bouweries*—and plantations. A *bouwery* had both livestock and crops, while a plantation had only crops. The West India Company gave free land to individuals to establish these farms and told farmers which crops to plant. The company also hired farmers to work for a set number of years on company-owned farms.

A second type of agricultural settlement was made up of patroonships, or manors. Individuals who brought 50 settlers to New Netherland received about 18 miles of land along the Hudson or some other river. The patroon, the owner of the land, hired farmers and supplied them with livestock and farm equipment in return for half the harvest and half the milk, butter, cheese, and livestock produced for sale.

The last type of agricultural settlement consisted of agricultural towns established by the West India Company. In these towns, the company gave colonists house lots, garden plots, a few acres of farmland, and a small amount of marshland to provide hay for cattle. Among the agricultural towns founded in the mid-1600s was Breukelen, which eventually became the city of Brooklyn (now a part of New York City).

Principal Crops and Animals. The colonists of New Netherland planted a variety of Native American crops, including corn, tobacco, beans, squash, and pumpkins. They also grew European grains, such as wheat, rye, and barley. These settlers had carried from Europe various kinds of apple and pear trees to plant in their orchards, as well as seeds for vegetables and herbs.

Livestock played an important role in agriculture in New Netherland. The early colonists had brought along Dutch breeds of cattle, pigs, and sheep, but they also purchased livestock from English colonists. Although the English cattle did not grow as large or produce as much milk as the Dutch cattle, they were cheaper and could survive unsheltered in the winter. The colonists let their pigs roam free in woods and marshes to hunt for food and also fed them corn. Sheep, raised primarily for wool, were not as plentiful as in the English colonies. Dutch farmers tended to raise goats, which were cheaper than sheep and gave good milk. They also kept horses and oxen for pulling plows and wagons.

Technology. Many of the tools found on farms in New Netherland were similar to those used in other North American colonies. The plow and wagon, however, had distinctly Dutch designs. Dutch wagons had two pairs of narrow wheels, with the rear wheels usually larger than the ones in front. The body of the wagon had a deep board in front, a shorter board in back, and a curved rail on top. American pioneers heading west after the 1720s used covered wagons, known as Conestoga wagons, that were based on the design of these early Dutch wagons.

French Agriculture

Like the Dutch, the French originally established settlements in North America as centers for the fur trade. In the early years of French settlement in the St. Lawrence River valley, men often farmed or gardened to supplement their earnings. However, as settlements expanded, farming became the main occupation of most French colonists. This process occurred at different times in the various French colonial areas. Farming became the principal economic activity in Acadia (Nova Scotia and New Brunswick) in the mid-1600s, in Canada (the St. Lawrence region) in the late 1600s, and in the colony of Louisiana in the 1720s. While the agriculture of these regions shared common elements, each region developed certain distinct features.

Remember: *Words in small capital letters have separate entries, and the index at the end of Volume 4 will guide you to more information on many topics.*

Agriculture

* **lentil** kind of bean

Principal Crops and Animals.   In both Acadia and Canada, the main crop was wheat because bread was a staple food in the French diet. Farmers supplemented their wheat crop with lentils* and vegetables. Most French colonial farmers grew only enough of these products to meet their own needs. In coastal areas of Acadia, farmers often caught fish for their own use and sold the surplus to local markets. In Acadia's mild climate, farmers also planted orchards to supply apples, pears, plums, cherries, and other fruits.

The crops grown in Louisiana were quite different. With its warm climate and access to the port of NEW ORLEANS, farmers there were able to grow and export profitable crops such as tobacco, indigo, COTTON, rice, sugar, and wood products. Farmers also produced abundant supplies of corn, lentils, vegetables, and fruits for their own use and for sale.

Basic livestock in the French colonies included cows and pigs, with some oxen to pull plows and wagons. Canadian farmers sometimes raised horses for transportation, using them to pull sleds over ice and snow in winter. In the St. Lawrence region and Acadia, livestock could not graze outdoors during the long winter months. Farmers had to use some of their land to grow grasses and grains to be stored for the animals to eat in winter. For this reason, they generally raised only enough cows and pigs to provide meat and milk for themselves. The slaughtering of these animals became a yearly autumn ritual. In Louisiana, livestock could graze year round, so farmers did not need to grow crops for animal food. As a result, they often kept larger herds.

Settlement and Farms.   In the St. Lawrence region, rivers provided the principal means of access to settlements, and people usually traveled from one settlement to another by boat. Farmhouses were generally built near the river bank, with the property forming a long rectangle with the narrow end by the river. In Acadia, on the other hand, settlements could be reached by land or sea. As a result, farms tended to develop in a variety of shapes, with the fields usually clustered around the farm buildings.

In Louisiana early farm settlements often grew up near Native American villages, where produce could be traded for animal pelts*. Many of these settlements were also located on or near rivers and bayous*, providing easy access to New Orleans and other ports on the Mississippi River. Because of the emphasis on cash crops, farms in Louisiana tended to be much larger than those in the St. Lawrence Valley and Acadia. During the 1700s, Louisiana developed a plantation system similar to that in the southern British colonies.

* **pelt** skin and fur of an animal
* **bayou** marshy creek off a larger body of water

Technology.   In Canada and Acadia, agriculture depended almost entirely on manual labor and simple hand tools, such as hoes, shovels, and scythes. Some farmers also used heavy wheeled plows, which required oxen or horses to pull them. All family members helped on small family farms. Men had the primary responsibility for heavy field work. Women worked in the home, in the barnyard, and sometimes in the fields. Young children had various small chores and were expected to contribute to the heavier labor as they grew older. When a son neared adulthood, he would begin clearing fields and preparing land for his own farm. He was, however, expected to continue helping with the family farm until he had a family of his own. Some colonists with large farms could afford to hire workers, particularly at planting and harvest time.

To supplement their farm incomes, farmers sometimes learned other skills and took other jobs. In Canada, for example, many men took seasonal work in the fur trade, often paddling canoes for professional fur traders.

Large plantation owners of Louisiana required many workers to produce their cash crops. They relied on slaves for this labor. Slave labor reduced the need for costly equipment and allowed the farmers to make a larger profit. Even small farms often had one or two slaves to help hoe, plant, prune, weed, pick, and process crops such as tobacco and cotton.

A distinctive feature of farming in Acadia was the cultivation of salt-water marshes that had been reclaimed from the sea. The Acadians built earthen dikes to hold back the sea and keep the marshes from flooding the land. Many of the men who built the dikes came from coastal regions of France, where they had learned the special skills needed to build dikes. The process required many workers and community cooperation.

Native American Agriculture

Long before the first European colonists arrived in North America, many Native American societies on the continent had developed complex agricultural economies. Although based primarily on farming, these economies also incorporated hunting and gathering of wild plants, nuts, and berries.

Native American agriculture was as diverse as the tribes, climate, and landscape of the continent. Differences in environment and economic need affected the crops and farming methods Indians used. The importance of agriculture also varied. In general, farming dominated in the eastern part of the continent, fishing was essential in FLORIDA, CALIFORNIA, and the Pacific Northwest, and gathering played a major role in the Southwest. Hunting dominated the activities of all other areas. Despite the great diversity of Native American agriculture, it had several common features—the same basic food crops, the absence of livestock, and seasonal shifts from farming to hunting.

Principal Crops. Three crops—corn, beans, and squash—formed the basis of Native American agriculture throughout North America. The Indians grew hundreds of varieties of these vegetables, suited for particular climates and uses. They grew sweet corn for eating fresh, flour corn for grinding into cornmeal, and popcorn. Common types of beans included lima beans, kidney beans, and string beans. Pumpkins were a popular variety of squash.

Indians supplemented their diet by gathering, hunting, and fishing. They gathered nuts, berries, fruits, and seeds. Hunting and fishing provided meat and fish, as well as fur and skins for clothing and bones for tools. One of the most important nonfood crops was tobacco, which the Native Americans used in rituals and ceremonies.

Technology. The Native Americans' basic tools were the digging stick—a pointed stick from four to six feet long—and a hoe with a blade of wood or animal bone. Both tools were used in planting and weeding. With no plows or work animals, Indian agriculture depended entirely on human labor. In the 1700s, however, some eastern tribes began following European practices, including the use of plows and the raising of livestock.

Remember: Consult the index at the end of Volume 4 to find more information on many topics.

Agriculture

Native American agriculture revolved around three basic crops: corn, beans, and squash. Colonists adopted these crops and learned many useful techniques from the Indians. This 1585 painting by John White shows the fields of the Secotan Indians of Pamlico Sound in what is now North Carolina.

In forested regions, Native Americans cleared land by cutting and burning trees and brush. They grew crops among the stumps that remained, using hoes to loosen the soil and form small mounds of dirt in which to plant seeds. When the soil's nutrients were exhausted, they left the fields fallow—abandoned them for several years—and cleared new ones. The rich soils in lowland areas of the Southeast allowed almost continuous farming. In some regions of the Southwest, Indians irrigated their fields to increase productivity.

While hunting and fishing took place during much of the year, gathering was generally seasonal, depending upon the availability of various wild plants. Drying and freezing meat also took place in specific seasons.

Native Americans practiced a rather rigid division of labor. Hunting was men's work, while women and children did most of the gathering. Both men and women cleared fields, but women and children had responsibility for cultivating, weeding, and harvesting crops. Women also prepared food and made pottery and baskets for gathering and storing food. Such divisions of labor helped Indians survive with little agricultural technology.

Spanish Cowboys

The techniques, clothing, and language of the American cowboy originated in the ranches of the Spaniards. The custom of using horses to herd cattle already existed in Spain. The *vaqueros*—herders of cattle—simply brought the practice to North America. The *vaqueros* developed the techniques of the roundup and branding. They wore boots with tall heels to hold their feet in the stirrups. They also wore leather chaps to cover pant legs and protect them from low bushes. Common cowboy terms—chaps, lariat, lasso, and corral—have Spanish origins.

Spanish Agriculture

Agriculture in the Spanish areas of North America developed from a blend of European and Indian farming methods and crops. These practices were followed in the lands of present-day Florida, Louisiana, TEXAS, ARIZONA, NEW MEXICO, and California. Throughout these areas, Spanish settlers adapted familiar foods and techniques to their new environment. In the process, they also transformed Native American ways of life.

Principal Crops. The Spanish settlers preferred to eat foods they were familiar with, such as white bread. For this reason, they brought wheat to the Americas. In Florida, they also planted oranges, lemons, and limes and created Florida's citrus industry.

In New Mexico, first settled by Spaniards in 1598, farming was difficult. The region was extremely dry and not well suited to growing wheat. Tools were crude—or nonexistent—and Spanish farmers struggled with wooden plows that often broke in the rocky soil. They threshed grain by driving herds of goats over the harvest until the wheat kernels were separated. These difficulties caused chronic food shortages. In the early years, settlers supplemented their scanty harvests with crops provided by Native Americans. Over time the Spaniards began to eat corn, the Indians' staple grain. When Texas was settled in the 1700s, corn became a staple food there as well.

When the Spanish took over Louisiana in the 1760s, they attracted additional settlers and the economy expanded. Rice, the chief grain in the region, became an export crop, as did tobacco. Sugar production also became widespread. By 1802, Louisiana had 75 plantations growing sugarcane.

In California, Native Americans provided the farm labor for the MISSIONS built by Franciscan priests. The Franciscans taught the Indians to work on the mission farms and attempted to convert them to Christianity. By the 1780s, the missions had become highly productive and dominated California's agricultural economy.

Wheat and corn were the chief grains in California. After 1800 California also became a major producer of hemp, which was used to make rope. Between 1803 and 1810, hemp production soared from 500 pounds to 120,000 pounds a year. The market collapsed, however, after Father Miguel HIDALGO, a Mexican priest, led an uprising against Spanish rule.

Livestock. The Spaniards brought cattle to North America and tried to establish large ranches. In Florida the cattle industry struggled at first, but eventually some large ranches were established near Gainesville and on the St. Johns and St. Marks rivers. Ranchers drove their herds to the city of ST. AUGUSTINE for sale. Hides and dried beef were shipped to Havana, Cuba, a major Spanish port in the Caribbean. The cattle industry died in the early 1700s, when British forces invaded Florida and destroyed the ranches.

Both cattle and sheep were important livestock in the arid lands of New Mexico. The cattle—originally 1,000 head—were used as beasts of burden as well as for meat. Sometimes this meat was in great demand from other areas. To protect the local food supply, New Mexico's governor ruled in 1659 that cattle could not be removed from the colony. After the PUEBLO REVOLT of 1680, the Spaniards left

New Mexico for 12 years. When they regained control of the area, they revived the livestock herds with stock from Mexico. In the 1700s, sheep became increasingly important. By 1800 New Mexico had far more sheep than it needed and shipped 20,000 head a year to other areas, making sheep its most valuable export.

Cattle were the principal livestock in Texas. The ranches that developed there created the cowboy culture that became legendary in the American West. Although the herds grew dramatically, ranchers were not able to profit from their success. Spanish policy made it difficult for them to sell their livestock, though they did carry on an illegal trade with French Louisiana. That trade ended in the late 1700s, when Louisiana came under Spanish control and developed a cattle industry of its own.

Native Americans also affected the livestock industry in the Spanish colonies. Their frequent raids prevented the expansion of ranching for many years in Texas and Arizona. Ranching did not flourish in Arizona until the late 1700s, when the Spanish viceroy* was able to achieve peace with the APACHE INDIANS. As part of the settlement, about half the cattle slaughtered in Arizona each year were given to the Apache.

California had large herds of cattle and sheep—more than 160,000 head in total in 1800. Thousands of horses roamed California as well. By 1805 authorities had to kill large numbers of horses to prevent them from eating or trampling crops.

Water and Land Rights. In New Mexico, settlers without land could appeal to the governor for a lot. If no other person claimed it, the land was theirs. In that dry environment, they began by building irrigation ditches. Communities often worked together to construct the main channel first and then build side ditches to carry water to the fields. They elected an overseer, who controlled the flow of water to each farm and led the annual effort to clean out the ditches.

Irrigation was also important in Arizona and Texas. In Arizona, government and mission authorities devised a clever scheme for sharing water: the mission and the nearby fort used the water on alternate weeks. In Texas, arrangements were less friendly—some disputes over water rights lasted for many generations. (*See also* **Labor; Land Ownership; Ranching; Slavery.**)

* *viceroy* person appointed as a monarch's representative to govern a province or colony

Albany

Albany, the present-day capital of New York State, was one of the oldest settlements in the American colonies. Originally a fur trading post named Fort Orange, it developed into an important commercial center during the colonial period.

In 1624 the DUTCH WEST INDIA COMPANY, a trading company, established Fort Orange at a place where the Hudson and Mohawk rivers met. It replaced an earlier Dutch fort that had been abandoned because of flooding. Fort Orange attracted fur traders and merchants, as well as a number of Dutch families that settled in the area and began farming.

Fort Orange's location at the junction of two rivers was a natural crossroads between the interior and the Atlantic coast. The settlement became a principal trading center for furs, and it grew rapidly. By the mid-1650s, over

1,000 people lived in the area. The settlement around Fort Orange gained self-rule in 1652 and became known as Beverwyck.

When the English gained control of NEW NETHERLAND in 1664, they captured Fort Orange and Beverwyck and renamed the settlement Albany in honor of the Duke of York and Albany, the brother of the English king. Under British rule, Albany's role as a busy river port and commercial center led to continued growth. It received a charter* incorporating it as a city in 1686.

In the 1750s, Albany played an important role in the FRENCH AND INDIAN WAR, and many British troops were stationed there. In 1754 the city was the site of the ALBANY CONGRESS, at which some British colonists proposed the formation of a colonial union. During the American Revolution, the British tried to capture Albany because of its military importance, but they failed. Albany became the capital of New York in 1797.

* **charter** written grant from a government conferring certain rights and privileges

Albany Congress (1754)

*T*he Albany Congress was a meeting of British colonial officials and chiefs of the IROQUOIS CONFEDERACY in the summer of 1754 in Albany, New York. The British called the meeting to strengthen their bonds with the Iroquois. Although the congress did not fully achieve that goal, it did produce a plan for uniting the colonies under a single central government.

About 150 Iroquois attended the Albany Congress, along with colonial representatives from New York, Massachusetts, Rhode Island, Connecticut, New Hampshire, Pennsylvania, and Maryland. Uneasy about France's growing power in Canada and fighting on the western frontier, British officials hoped to negotiate a treaty of alliance with the Iroquois. The Iroquois came to the meeting to complain about their treatment by the British and to protest the growing movement of colonists onto Indian lands. After receiving gifts and promises of protection, the Iroquois renewed their alliance with the British. The continued loyalty of the Iroquois remained doubtful, however, because the colonial officials did not really deal with the Indians' concerns.

After the Iroquois left the meeting, the delegates to the congress began to consider a topic often discussed throughout the colonies—the possibility of forming a colonial federation* as a means of defense against Native Americans and European powers. Benjamin FRANKLIN of Pennsylvania, one of the colonial leaders, called for a voluntary union of the colonies under "one general government" headed by an appointed president. Under this plan, known as the Albany Plan, the new unified government would manage Indian affairs, oversee public lands, raise and control a colonial army, build forts and ships, and levy taxes.

The Albany delegates adopted the plan, but the British government rejected it because it gave too much power to the colonies. The colonial legislatures rejected the Albany Plan as well because individual colonies did not have enough power. When the colonists rebelled against British policies in the 1760s and 1770s, the Albany Plan emerged again as a starting point for discussions of national unity. (*See also* **French and Indian War.**)

* **federation** organization of separate states with a central government

Alcohol

See *Food and Drink; Taverns.*

See *Standish, Miles.*

maritime related to the sea or shipping

The Aleuts are a group of native people who live in Alaska. They inhabit a long string of islands, known as the Aleutians, and the western peninsula of Alaska. Relative latecomers to North America, the Aleuts arrived only about 5,000 to 7,000 years ago. Although related to the ESKIMO, they have their own language and culture. The name *Aleut* came from Russian explorers, but these people call themselves *Unangan,* which means "the people."

The Aleuts were maritime* hunters who survived on fish and sea mammals such as seals, sea otter, walrus, and occasionally whales. Skilled sailors, they could travel long distances in their open skin-covered boats, called kayaks. They lived in small villages in dwellings made of pits about three or four feet deep, covered with a frame of driftwood or whalebones. They used dried grass or animal skins to insulate their homes and covered everything with sod.

In 1741 Russian explorers discovered the Aleutian Islands. Russian fur traders searching for seals, foxes, and sea otters soon followed. The Russians treated the Aleuts like slaves and used them for their superior hunting skills. Many Aleuts were killed by the Russians, and many more died of diseases brought by the newcomers. By the mid-1800s only about 2,000 Aleuts remained.

When the United States purchased rights to Alaska in 1867, the Aleutian Islands came under American rule, and the Aleut population slowly began to recover. The influence of the Russians can still be seen, as every Aleut community has a Russian Orthodox Church. (*See also* **Russian Settlements.**)

Alexander, Mary Spratt Provoost

1693–1760
New York businesswoman

Mary Spratt Provoost Alexander was one of the most successful businesswomen in the American colonies. Her life and career linked the British colony of NEW YORK with its Dutch heritage.

Mary Spratt was born in New York City. Her father was a Scottish merchant and her mother, Maria DePeyster, came from a prominent Dutch family of merchants and politicians. Her mother, who married three times and was widowed twice, managed her husbands' businesses after their deaths. This was a fairly common practice among the Dutch, and Mary Spratt would later follow the custom herself.

Known as a high-spirited young woman, Mary Spratt was probably about 18 when she married Samuel Provoost, a merchant. The couple had three children. Mary Spratt Provoost became her husband's business partner, investing the money she inherited from her parents in his shipping and trading ventures. When her husband died about eight years later, she assumed full responsibility for the business.

In 1721 Mary Spratt Provoost married James Alexander, a Scottish lawyer who became a leading figure in New York and New Jersey politics. During their 35-year marriage, she had seven more children. She spent the rest of her life caring for her children, encouraging and sometimes participating in Alexander's political activities, and successfully managing the merchant business inherited from her first husband.

As time passed, Mary Spratt Provoost Alexander continued to expand her trading business. She imported goods from abroad and sold them in her store in New York, along with items manufactured in the colonies. It was said that at the peak of her business, nearly every ship that docked in New York harbor carried a shipment for Mary Spratt Provoost Alexander in its cargo. At her death she left behind a substantial fortune. Her shrewdness and business skills had brought her both prosperity and prominence in the world of colonial trade.

Algonquian

See *Languages: Native American.*

Allen, Ethan

ca. 1737–1789
Soldier and patriot

* *militia* army of citizens who may be called into action in a time of emergency

*E*than Allen, a frontiersman in the British colonies, struggled to gain political independence for VERMONT. He also helped the colonists win an important military victory in the early years of the AMERICAN REVOLUTION. Perhaps Allen is best known as the leader of the GREEN MOUNTAIN BOYS, an independent militia*.

Little is known of Ethan Allen's early life. Born in Litchfield, Connecticut, he served briefly in the FRENCH AND INDIAN WAR. By 1769 Allen had settled in a mountainous region in New England called the New Hampshire Grants. Both New York and New Hampshire claimed this area, which is now the state of Vermont.

Allen and his brothers became involved in the dispute over this territory. They were fiercely opposed to "Yorkers," those who favored union with New York. In 1770 Allen became commander of the Green Mountain Boys, formed to defy the government of New York. Allen and his followers were so effective at harassing their opponents that New York's governor offered a reward of 100 pounds for Allen's capture.

The outbreak of the American Revolution brought a temporary halt to this territorial dispute. Allen quickly joined the Revolutionary fight. In May 1775, he and the Green Mountain Boys, along with colonial troops led by Benedict ARNOLD, captured the British outposts at FORT TICONDEROGA and Crown Point. Four months later Allen took part in an American expedition against Canada.

The British captured Allen in Canada and held him prisoner until 1778. Upon his release, he decided not to rejoin the Revolutionary cause and returned instead to Vermont. Vermont had declared its independence in 1777, but the Continental Congress did not recognize its status as a separate state. Allen devoted himself to winning Vermont's independence and statehood.

In 1780 Allen began talks with the British about the possibility of making Vermont a part of Canada. The American victory in the Revolution ended these talks before any agreement could be reached. When Allen died on February 12, 1789, Vermont was still negotiating over statehood. It finally became a separate state in 1791.

American Indians

See *Native Americans; individual Indian groups.*

American Philosophical Society

* **philosophical** pertaining to philosophy, or "the love of knowledge"

*T*he American Philosophical* Society, founded by Benjamin FRANKLIN in 1743 in Philadelphia, is the oldest learned society in the United States. In the years before the American Revolution, the society provided Americans with an opportunity to demonstrate their intellectual independence with scientific projects and publications equal to those of European societies.

Although the idea for such an organization came from naturalist John BARTRAM, Franklin was the society's founder. The original members included Franklin, Bartram, a physician named Thomas Bond, and a number of other prominent Philadelphians. The members held meetings, read papers they had written, and elected members from other colonies. Franklin hoped the organization would spark scientific and technological progress in the American colonies. It failed to meet his expectations, and he complained that its members were "very idle."

During the 1760s, as feelings of American patriotism swept the colonies, a group of young Philadelphia QUAKERS formed the American Society to promote progress in agriculture, manufacturing, and other areas of "useful knowledge." The two societies soon became rivals, but merged in 1769 as the American Philosophical Society. Benjamin Franklin became president and Thomas Bond, vice president. Because Franklin was in Britain at the time, Bond took the leadership and organized the new society's first major scientific project—astronomical observations of the planet Venus.

The American Philosophical Society's reports on Venus, published in 1771 and distributed among scholarly organizations in Europe, helped establish the society's reputation in America and overseas. European societies began sending copies of their own publications to the American Philosophical Society. This exchange of ideas and documents with European scholars improved the society's standing and enriched its library.

After the American Revolution, the American Philosophical Society became the leading scientific organization in the United States. Although it never fulfilled Franklin's vision as a source of technological and mechanical inventions, it did play a significant role in the intellectual and scientific life of the new nation. Scholars looked to the society for knowledge and inspiration, and its activities encouraged the formation of similar organizations. Today the American Philosophical Society of Philadelphia continues to publish scholarly materials and maintains a large collection of books and articles about the history of science in America. (*See also* **Astronomy; Science.**)

American Revolution

*I*n the spring of 1775, fighting broke out in Massachusetts between British troops and colonial volunteer forces. News of the battles swept through the American colonies and launched a much larger struggle—the war for American independence. Lasting more than six years, the war led to the creation of a new nation, the United States of America. For the first time in modern history, a colonial people had fought a war for independence and won. In the process, Great Britain lost a significant part of its American empire.

Prelude to Revolution.

Serious tension between Britain and its American colonies began to emerge in the mid-1700s. The FRENCH AND INDIAN WAR ended in 1763. It had cost the British a great deal of money to wage war against the French, and they thought the colonies should share some of the expense. After all, Britain had helped defend the colonists from the French and their Indian allies, and they would continue to defend them in the future.

The British imposed a number of taxes on the colonists to raise money to help pay its war debts. The colonists protested vehemently, arguing that the taxes were unlawful because they were citizens of Britain but had no representatives in Parliament to defend their interests and their rights. The British government took two other steps that aroused great opposition in the colonies. In the PROCLAMATION OF 1763 it declared that colonists could no longer settle the lands west of the Appalachian Mountains. This was an attempt to prevent further conflicts between Native Americans and settlers along the FRONTIER. Moreover, Britain began to station large numbers of troops in the colonies to defend the colonists from possible French attacks and to keep peace between the settlers and the Indians. The American colonists considered the Proclamation of 1763 an unfair restriction of their right to move west to new lands, and they saw the increase in British troops in the colonies as a threat to their freedom. Colonial leaders protested these policies with pamphlets, boycotts* of British goods, and sometimes mob action. Each time the British tried to impose a new tax, the colonists organized measures to resist it. The situation in the colonies worsened dramatically when Britain passed the TEA ACT OF 1773. Protests against the act led to the BOSTON TEA PARTY, a bold act of defiance against British authority. To punish the Bostonians for their rebellious behavior, the British Parliament passed a series of harsh laws that became known as the INTOLERABLE ACTS.

In September 1774, colonial delegates met in Philadelphia to discuss the Intolerable Acts and the larger issue of colonial rights. The members of this FIRST CONTINENTAL CONGRESS issued a formal protest and threatened to stop all colonial trade with Britain unless Parliament repealed* the Intolerable Acts. They also urged the colonies to form militias* in case the dispute with Britain turned into open conflict. When the delegates ended the congress, they agreed to meet again the following spring.

War and Independence.

Before the congress could meet again, the colonists clashed with British troops. In April 1775, British soldiers stationed in BOSTON marched into the countryside to seize arms and other supplies held by colonial militia. Shooting broke out and 49 colonists died in the Battles of LEXINGTON AND CONCORD. The American Revolution had begun.

When the SECOND CONTINENTAL CONGRESS assembled in May, the delegates voted to organize a national military force. For commander in chief of the CONTINENTAL ARMY, they chose George WASHINGTON. Meanwhile, thousands of American troops gathered around Boston where British soldiers were still camped. Fighting erupted again in June in the Battle of BUNKER HILL. The British won the battle but suffered heavy casualties*. The American forces proved that they could stand up to the British army. As news of this bloody battle spread, colonists everywhere began preparing for war.

See map in British Colonies (vol. 1).

* **boycott** refusal to buy goods as a means of protest

* **repeal** to undo a law
* **militia** army of citizens who may be called into action in a time of emergency

See color plate 7, vol. 4.

* **casualty** person who is killed or injured

Foreign Aid

A number of Europeans came to North America to help the colonists fight the British. Most played important roles in the Revolutionary War. Thaddeus Kosciusko of Poland built fortifications at West Point, New York, that helped maintain American control of the Hudson River. Casimir Pulaski, also from Poland, organized a cavalry and helped train soldiers on horseback. During the difficult winter at Valley Forge, Baron Friedrich von Steuben of Germany trained the Continental Army and turned it into an effective fighting force. The Marquis de Lafayette, a French nobleman, led American troops and became one of Washington's most trusted officers.

* **patriot** American colonist who supported independence from Britain

Most delegates to the Second Continental Congress believed that peace could still be restored. In July 1775 they sent King GEORGE the OLIVE BRANCH PETITION, a document asking him to cancel the new taxes and remove other obstacles to peace. The king refused the peace petition and declared the colonists rebels. His rejection ended any hope of peace.

In the meantime, delegates to the congress had begun debating the issue of independence from Great Britain. Many colonists still did not want to break away from British rule. Support for independence grew after the appearance of *Common Sense,* a pamphlet by Thomas PAINE. Published in January 1776, the pamphlet presented forceful arguments in favor of independence, convincing many colonists that separation from Britain was necessary and desirable.

In June 1776, delegate Richard Henry LEE of Virginia asked the Continental Congress to declare independence from Britain. The congress formed a committee to draft a document stating the reasons for such an action. Thomas JEFFERSON wrote the declaration. On July 2, 1776, delegates of 12 of the 13 colonies voted in favor of independence. The delegates from New York had been instructed by their legislature to take no action on the issue. Two days later, the Continental Congress approved the DECLARATION OF INDEPENDENCE. New York added its vote for independence on July 9.

The War in the North. The early phases of the Revolutionary War took place in the northern colonies. In late 1775, an American invasion of the British colony of Canada collapsed with a defeat at the city of Quebec. Americans had hoped to persuade Canadians to join the fight for independence, but Canada remained under British rule. The summer and fall of 1776 brought more bad news for the American patriots*. In several battles near NEW YORK CITY, Washington's troops met the huge armies of British commander in chief William Howe. Howe's forces quickly defeated the Americans and forced them to retreat to PHILADELPHIA. Stung by these losses, Washington planned a bold move. On Christmas night, he crossed the Delaware River and staged a surprise attack on a British camp in Trenton, New Jersey. This unexpected victory for Washington's forces was followed by another in January 1777 at nearby Princeton. These small successes helped revive the confidence of the Americans.

A more important victory occurred in the fall of 1777. The British had planned to isolate New England by gaining control of the Hudson River valley. Their strategy collapsed when American forces led by General Horatio Gates won two battles at Saratoga, New York, forcing British general John Burgoyne to surrender on October 17. Saratoga marked a turning point in the war. It ended the British threat to New England and convinced France to help the Americans in their struggle against the British. French aid proved to be a vital factor in winning the war.

The winter of 1777–1778 was bitterly cold, an extremely difficult time for Washington and his army. Camped at Valley Forge, outside Philadelphia, the American soldiers faced shortages of food, clothing, and blankets. They suffered terribly from the cold and from disease. Many abandoned the army and returned to their homes. Those who remained, however, received a thorough military training from the German baron Friedrich Wilhelm von

Steuben and other European officers, who had come to help the Americans. The Continental Army that emerged in the spring was a stronger, more effective force.

The war in the north came to a standstill in 1778. Minor battles were fought, but little ground was gained or lost. British general Sir Henry Clinton moved his army from Philadelphia to New York City, and Washington's army spent the next three years camped outside of the city, waiting. In the west, militia commander George Rogers Clark captured the settlements of Kaskaskia, Cahokia, and Vincennes from the British, but he was unable to take the important fort of Detroit.

The War Moves South. The British shifted their focus to the South, where they hoped to gain the support of many LOYALISTS. They seized Savannah, Georgia, in December 1778, and Charleston, South Carolina, in May 1780. After a victory at Camden, South Carolina, Britain seemed assured of winning in the South. In the fall of 1780, however, the tide began to turn. American soldiers and militiamen under the command of General Nathanael Greene launched a campaign of quick strikes against the British. The Americans won important victories in South Carolina at Kings Mountain and Cowpens. In March 1781 Greene's troops narrowly lost a battle at Guilford Courthouse in North Carolina, but British general Charles Cornwallis withdrew to Wilmington, North Carolina, after suffering heavy losses.

Faced with increasing resistance in the southern colonies, British general Charles Cornwallis decided to move north. He marched his troops to Yorktown,

Led by George Washington, patriot forces defeated the British at the Battle of Princeton on January 3, 1777. The victory lifted American spirits, but the War for Independence was to continue another four and one-half years.

Virginia, a site on a peninsula in Chesapeake Bay. While Cornwallis waited for much needed supplies and reinforcements, American troops led by Washington and French troops under General Comte de Rochambeau surrounded the British and blocked all land routes to their camp. Meanwhile, a French fleet patrolled Chesapeake Bay, preventing the British from sending assistance to the Yorktown forces by sea. Caught in a trap, Lord Cornwallis surrendered to American commander in chief George Washington on October 19, 1781. The Yorktown surrender brought an end to the Revolutionary War.

Peace and Independence. News of the surrender at Yorktown stunned the British and convinced them it was time to accept the independence of the American colonies. Peace talks began in Paris in the spring of 1782, with negotiations lasting for many months. Finally, in September 1783, the British and the Americans signed the Treaty of Paris. The treaty acknowledged the independence of the United States and set the western boundary of the new nation at the Mississippi River. After a long, difficult struggle, the American colonists had created a new nation and adopted a republican* form of government.

* *republican* form of government in which the people elect government officials

Ingredients of Victory. How did the colonies defeat Great Britain, one of the most powerful nations of Europe? Despite its wealth and great army and navy, Britain had several disadvantages in the war. Its troops had to fight in unfamiliar lands, and most military supplies and reinforcements had to travel across the Atlantic Ocean. Furthermore, British commanders made some serious mistakes in the war and failed to adapt their strategies and tactics to the conditions they found in North America.

The Americans also faced some handicaps at the start of the war. They lacked an organized and well-trained army. The Continental Congress had difficulty raising money for the war and convincing individual states to support its policies. In addition, American patriots had to deal with thousands of Loyalists who lived among them and remained faithful to Britain. Yet, Americans enjoyed crucial advantages. One was the assistance they received from France and other rivals of Britain. Perhaps the most decisive factor, though, was the determination of the American patriots. With the majority of Americans deeply committed to independence, Britain would have had to conquer and occupy a vast territory filled with hostile people in order to win the war.

Effects of the Revolution. The Revolution upset the lives of countless Americans. Fearing harsh treatment from American patriots, about 60,000 to 80,000 Loyalists fled to Canada and Britain during and after the war. Much of their land and property was seized and sold by state governments. The Revolution also had a devastating effect on Native Americans. Indians were divided during the war—some supported the British and others aided the colonists. The Treaty of Paris gave all land east of the Mississippi River to the United States. This opened the way to further white settlement of western lands and increased conflict with Native Americans, who in the following years were pushed farther and farther west.

Many African Americans fought in the Revolutionary War—on both sides. To attract black recruits, both the British and Americans promised

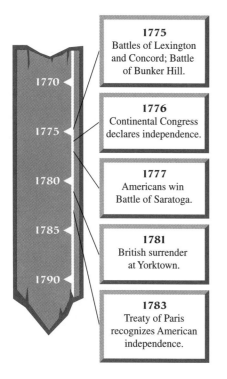

1775
Battles of Lexington and Concord; Battle of Bunker Hill.

1776
Continental Congress declares independence.

1777
Americans win Battle of Saratoga.

1781
British surrender at Yorktown.

1783
Treaty of Paris recognizes American independence.

1770
1775
1780
1785
1790

freedom from slavery. After the war, slavery continued in the United States, although the British did free those who had served in their army and several states liberated slaves who had fought for independence. Women contributed to the war effort as well. Many provided food and clothing for colonial troops. Some women, such as Mary Hayes ("Molly Pitcher") and Deborah Sampson, even served on the battlefront. Numerous women ran businesses and farms while their husbands, brothers, and fathers served in the army. Despite such efforts, women had no greater rights after the Revolution than before the war.

One of the most lasting effects of the American Revolution was the impact of its ideas. The war and the Declaration of Independence served as an inspiration to colonial peoples throughout the world. In the early 1800s, Mexico and colonies in South America began to break away from Spain. Other colonial peoples followed, and the desire for independence has remained a motivating force for people everywhere. (*See also* **Independence Movements; Revolutionary Thought; Taxation.**)

| Amish |
See *Protestant Churches: German Sects.*

| Anasazi Indians |
See *Native Americans: Early Peoples of North America.*

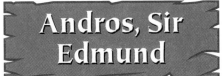

1637–1714
British colonial governor

Sir Edmund Andros was best known as the governor of the DOMINION OF NEW ENGLAND, an organization of English colonies formed in the late 1600s. Although an able administrator, Andros was impatient and rigid. His policies made him extremely unpopular among the colonists.

Born on the island of Guernsey in the English Channel, Andros began his career in the English colonies in 1666, when he went to the West Indies to help defend the islands against the Dutch. He obtained a large piece of land in Carolina in 1672. Two years later, he became governor of New York, where he helped resolve boundary disputes with Connecticut.

In 1686 King James II decided to consolidate the New England colonies into one royal province in an effort to improve the defenses of the colonial frontier. New York and New Jersey were later added to the province. The king abolished the existing colonial governments and appointed Andros to supervise the whole region, which became known as the Dominion of New England.

The colonists vehemently protested the loss of their governments and interference with their rights. Ignoring their protests, Andros enforced the laws with firmness and severity and created widespread opposition. His attempts to change the system of landholding angered landowners. His interference in religion caused resistance among the PURITANS in Massachusetts. Finally, Andros's rigid enforcement of the NAVIGATION ACTS regulating trade led to the hostility of the merchants throughout the region.

When the colonists learned in 1689 that James II had been replaced on the English throne by William and Mary, they seized Andros, sent him back to England, and jailed his prominent supporters. Andros later returned to North America to serve as governor of Virginia. (*See also* **Colonial Administration.**)

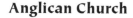
Anglican Church

See *Protestant Churches.*

Animals

* domesticated raised by humans as farm animals or pets

Settlers in the North American colonies lived in close contact with the animal world. Wild animals, many of them unfamiliar to Europeans, formed the basis of the FUR TRADE and became a source of food. Domesticated* animals, primarily ones brought from Europe, played a major role in colonial agriculture. The abundant animal life in North America provided an important resource for the colonists, one they used both wisely and foolishly.

Wild Animals. For thousands of years before European colonists came to North America, the Native Americans hunted deer, turkey, and other game birds, as well as small game such as rabbits and squirrels. They caught various kinds of fish, including salmon and trout, in the oceans, rivers, and lakes and gathered shellfish along the seacoasts. In some areas their way of life was built upon the native WILDLIFE. In the far north, the Indians relied on whales and seals for food and other important items. On the Great Plains, they depended heavily on the BUFFALO. Using weapons that required great skill, including bows and arrows, Native Americans generally killed only what they needed.

When the European colonists came to North America, they also hunted wildlife, both for food and to eliminate animals they feared such as wolves and bears. Using firearms, colonial hunters killed animals in great numbers. The result was a dramatic reduction in animal populations that had remained stable for generations. By the late 1600s, wild turkeys became scarce in New England, and wolves were eliminated from most of that region by the late 1700s. A similar fate awaited the buffalo after the colonial period.

* pelt skin and fur of an animal

The fur trade also took an enormous toll on North American wildlife. Beginning in the 1500s, European explorers and trappers seeking pelts* hunted and traded with Native Americans. The pelts of beavers, bears, otters, wildcats, foxes, raccoons, and deer had great value in Europe, and the fur trade played a central role in the early colonial economy. The fur trade did not stop until hunters had almost exterminated many types of furbearing wild animals.

Domesticated Animals. The European colonists brought HORSES, cattle, sheep, pigs, goats, and other livestock when they came to North America. Livestock raising became an essential part of the agriculture of British, Dutch, and French colonies, while cattle RANCHING was important in the economy of the Spanish Borderlands.

European livestock flourished in North America, and their numbers grew dramatically. In some areas the increase in livestock eventually contributed to soil erosion and other environmental changes. In addition, some livestock escaped into the forests and became wild. Within a generation of settlement, herds of wild cattle and pigs roamed forests throughout the eastern colonies. By the late 1600s, wild horses had begun spreading from the Spanish Borderlands onto the Great Plains.

Livestock provided colonists with meat, milk, and products such as wool and leather hides. Domesticated animals were also important for work and transportation. Settlers used horses and oxen to pull plows, and they often traveled on horseback or in carriages or wagons drawn by horses.

Some animals provided entertainment and sport for the colonists. Horse racing became a popular recreation, especially in the South. In Virginia the passion for horse racing led to the development of the quarter horse, a new breed that was capable of great bursts of speed. Other colonial sports involving animals seem cruel by modern standards. Colonists enjoyed gambling on cockfights—bloody battles between two roosters wearing sharp blades on their legs. Baitings—letting a pack of dogs loose upon a trapped bear or bull—were popular in frontier communities. Although city-dwelling Americans tried to make the colonies more "civilized" by passing laws against such blood sports, illegal baitings and cockfights continued to attract spectators and gamblers throughout the colonial period. (*See also* **Agriculture; Environmental Impact of Colonization; Hunting.**)

Anishnabe Indians

See *Ojibwa Indians.*

Annapolis, Maryland

Annapolis, the capital of MARYLAND, was founded in the mid-1600s. One of the first "planned" cities in America, Annapolis became an important commercial and cultural center during the colonial period. Present-day Annapolis preserves much of its colonial character.

In 1649 several families of PURITANS left Virginia and fled to Maryland because of religious persecution. They settled on the Severn River close to CHESAPEAKE BAY. The Puritans called their settlement Providence, but the name was later changed to Anne Arundel Town after the wife of Cecil Calvert, the colony's proprietor*.

In 1694 Sir Francis Nicholson, the governor of Maryland, transferred the colonial capital from St. Mary's to Anne Arundel Town, a more centrally located site. The new capital was given a new name—Annapolis, in honor of Princess (later Queen) Anne of England. Governor Nicholson designed a new layout for the town that featured circles with streets radiating outward like the spokes of a wheel. These circles, which included the capital building and the main church, became central points of Annapolis. The governor's plan also involved zoning, with certain areas of the town restricted to either commercial or residential use. The residential sections contained house lots of different sizes for wealthy, middle class, and poorer families.

* ***proprietor*** person granted land and the right to establish a colony

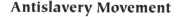
* **charter** written grant from a ruler conferring certain rights and privileges

* **Confederation Congress** legislature established by the Articles of Confederation that governed the United States from 1781 to 1789

Annapolis soon became the leading business and cultural center in Maryland. Products flowed through its river port, bringing great wealth to many of its merchants. The town prospered, and elegant houses and stately public buildings were built. Annapolis received its city charter* in 1708.

At the end of the American Revolution, the Confederation Congress* assembled in Annapolis and approved the treaty of peace between Great Britain and the UNITED STATES. In 1786 the city was the scene of a meeting, the Annapolis Convention, at which delegates from five states discussed the need for changes in the Confederation government. The Annapolis Convention led to a meeting the next year in Philadelphia, where the Constitution of the United States was written. (*See also* **Calvert Family; Governors, Colonial.**)

Antislavery Movement

During the colonial period, SLAVERY spread throughout the North American colonies. Along with it, there arose a movement calling for an end to slavery. While this movement did not achieve its goal at the time, it laid the foundation for a major antislavery crusade in the 1800s.

Native American Slavery. Native Americans were enslaved in America long before black slavery became established. The earliest and most widespread Indian slavery was in the Spanish colonies. The Roman Catholic missionary Bartolomé de LAS CASAS led an attack on this institution in the 1500s. His powerful protest eventually persuaded Spanish authorities to end the enslavement of Indians. To replace the lost labor, Las Casas suggested using Africans instead of Indians. The Spaniards accepted his idea, but Las Casas later regretted that he had proposed an extension of slavery.

The early English colonists also enslaved Native Americans. Roger WILLIAMS and others in New England led protests against Indian slavery in the mid-1600s. They succeeded in persuading most English colonies to abandon it by 1700.

Rising Voices Against Black Slavery. Some writing against African American slavery began to appear in the late 1600s. Samuel Sewall, a Massachusetts judge, wrote the best known of these early antislavery works: *The Selling of Joseph* (1692). But his book provoked others, such as the New England minister Cotton MATHER, to defend the institution. Mather urged slaveholders to convert their slaves to Christianity.

The most prominent voices in the antislavery movement were QUAKERS. In the early years, though, some wealthy Quakers held slaves, and Quakers who opposed slavery were rejected by others of their faith. However, the strong moral principles of Quakerism eventually led more and more believers to conclude that slavery was unjust. By 1758 two prominent antislavery Quakers, John Woolman and Anthony Benezet, persuaded the annual Quaker assembly to express "unanimous concern" over slavery. In 1775 Pennsylvania Quakers established the first organization aimed at ending slavery.

By the 1790s other antislavery societies had formed throughout the British colonies. At that time, the philosophy of the ENLIGHTENMENT, with its emphasis on the natural rights of people, helped spread the idea that slavery was an

Despite the opposition of many colonists, the slave trade continued throughout the 1700s. This watercolor by William L. Breton shows slaves being sold at an auction in Philadelphia.

* **tyranny** unjust use of power

* **abolitionist** person who called for an immediate end to slavery

unjust institution. Some leaders of the American Revolution—including James OTIS, John DICKINSON, and Thomas PAINE—compared the British treatment of the colonists to the slaveholders' tyranny* over slaves. They and other notable Americans urged the ending of slavery in America.

During the 1700s, the goal of the antislavery movement was to bring about a gradual end to slavery. That approach lasted until after the colonial period, and it was most effective in the north. It was not until the 1830s that abolitionists* called for the complete and immediate end to slavery throughout the entire United States.

African American Voices. FREE BLACKS also expressed their opposition to slavery and tried to promote its abolition during the colonial period. In a letter written to the Reverend Samson OCCOM in 1774, African American poet Phillis WHEATLEY wrote movingly of this desire: "In every human breast God has implanted a principle, which we call love of freedom; it is impatient of oppression, and pants for deliverance."

One literary form that arose in the colonial period—the slave narrative—reflected antislavery sentiment. These narratives began as petitions in which a slave described his or her feelings to a slaveholder and requested freedom. Over time these petitions became more complex and were written down. Slave narratives included episodes that highlighted the brutality and injustice of slavery, and they often portrayed the writer's eventual freedom in religious terms. The most famous of these narratives was written by Olaudah EQUIANO, a slave who lived in Virginia in the 1700s.

Legal Actions Against Slavery. By the time of the American Revolution, opposition to the SLAVE TRADE had grown. Even many southern planters

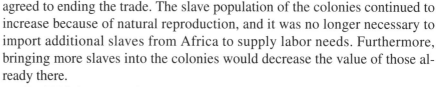

agreed to ending the trade. The slave population of the colonies continued to increase because of natural reproduction, and it was no longer necessary to import additional slaves from Africa to supply labor needs. Furthermore, bringing more slaves into the colonies would decrease the value of those already there.

In 1774 the FIRST CONTINENTAL CONGRESS adopted a Quaker-backed proposal to halt the slave trade. Although most colonists supported the proposal, it was not enforced. Not until 1807, when the colonies had become the United States, was a law passed prohibiting the importation of slaves. Slavery itself was another matter. Between 1777 and 1804, northern states did ban slavery, but the institution remained strong in the South. During the 1800s, the issue of slavery increasingly divided the nation. (*See also* **Slave Resistance.**)

Apache Indians

See second map in Native Americans (vol. 3).

During the colonial period, the Apache Indians lived in the Spanish Borderlands in the area now occupied by Texas, New Mexico, and Arizona. A warlike people, the Apache frequently raided Spanish settlements and camps of other Indian tribes for food and supplies. The name Apache probably comes from a ZUNI word meaning enemy.

The Apache were not one tribe but a group of separate tribes linked by a common language. Two of the better known tribes were the Mescalero and the Chiricahua. Each Apache tribe consisted of a number of smaller groups, or bands, made up of related families. Each band had a headman chosen for his leadership and military skill. The Apache survived largely by hunting animals, gathering wild plants for food, and tending small garden plots along the banks of streams—and by staging raids.

A nomadic people, the Apache had migrated from the north sometime before the arrival of Europeans. After 1600 they began to acquire HORSES, usually by stealing them from the Spanish. The horses enabled the Apache to cover a much larger territory and become an effective fighting force. Mounted Apache warriors, armed with long lances, frequently attacked the settlements of the PUEBLO INDIANS of the region. The Apache also raided the growing Spanish settlements of the area, stealing cattle and other goods as well as horses. They could strike quickly and then disappear almost magically into the rugged wilderness. After attacking, Apache bands sometimes split into smaller groups to make pursuit more difficult. The bands would swiftly turn and ambush their pursuers whenever an opportunity arose.

The Spanish tried to meet the Apache threat by building forts and forming alliances with Native Americans that were enemies of the Apache. A cycle of Apache raids and Spanish revenge continued throughout the 1600s. Despite the constant turmoil, the Apache population actually increased during this period. This happened in part because the Apache often adopted runaways and captives into their bands.

By the late 1700s, a number of small Apache bands had combined into several larger groups. Some eastern tribes made peace with the Spanish, but other tribes would not end their warfare. After Mexico gained its independence

from Spain in 1821, the Mexican government tried—without success—to eliminate the Apache. The fighting continued for many years.

During the 1800s, the Apache increasingly focused their attacks on the American settlers moving into their territory. A series of clashes with Americans, known as the Apache Wars, lasted from the 1850s to 1886. During this time, the United States began setting up reservations for the Apache. While many Indians moved to them voluntarily, others were forcibly removed from their lands. Indian resistance reached a climax under such leaders as Cochise and Geronimo. In the end, however, the United States Army overwhelmed the Apache. (*See also* **Native Americans.**)

Appalachian Mountains

See map in British Colonies (vol. 1).

*T*he Appalachian Mountains are a system of mountain ranges that run north and south through the interior of eastern North America. From the earliest days of English settlement, the Appalachian Mountains formed a physical barrier to westward movement, keeping settlers concentrated along the ATLANTIC COAST. By the end of the colonial period, colonists had begun pushing through the Appalachians to settle in the valleys and lowlands of the interior.

The Appalachian Mountain system runs for over 1,500 miles from Newfoundland in Canada to central Alabama. Included in this system are the White Mountains of New Hampshire, the Green Mountains of Vermont, the Catskill Mountains of New York, the Allegheny Mountains of Pennsylvania, the Blue Ridge Mountains of Virginia and North Carolina, the Great Smoky Mountains of North Carolina and Tennessee, and the Cumberland Mountains of Tennessee. Although not high in elevation, the various ranges of the Appalachians are rugged, densely forested, and difficult to cross.

During the early colonial period, a few hunters, trappers, and explorers did manage to cross these mountains. They made the journey by following gaps, or passes, that cut through the Appalachians—the Mohawk River valley in New York, for example, the Shenandoah River valley in Virginia, and the Cumberland Gap in Tennessee. But few pioneers attempted to get to the other side of the mountains until the mid-1700s.

For a time the Appalachian Mountains formed a political boundary as well as a geographic barrier. In the 1760s, as population increases in the east created a great demand for new land, colonists began pushing westward through the mountains. This led to increased tensions with Native Americans living in the frontier regions. In an effort to reduce the chance of conflict with the Indians, the British government issued the PROCLAMATION OF 1763, which drew a boundary line along the Appalachian Mountains. Colonists were not allowed to advance beyond the line.

The Proclamation of 1763 failed to keep colonists from crossing the Appalachians. Little was done to enforce the boundary, and settlers continued to move westward and claim Indian lands. By the end of the colonial period, the Cumberland Gap and other routes through the Appalachians had become highways for a flood of westbound settlers. (*See also* **Frontier; Ohio River Valley.**)

Apprenticeship

* **artisan** skilled crafts worker

European colonists brought the practice of apprenticeship—on-the-job training—with them to North America. Throughout the colonial period, many young people served as apprentices in occupations ranging from business and law to masonry and barrel making.

Almost all colonial children received a type of informal apprenticeship at home. The sons of farmers learned about crops and livestock by helping on the family farm, and the children of artisans* often learned the craft of their parents. Young girls learned how to manage a home by helping their mothers with sewing, cooking, and other tasks. This informal training provided colonial families with much-needed labor and gave children an opportunity to learn basic skills.

Many colonial children also received formal apprenticeships that involved leaving home and learning a trade from a master crafts worker or professional. Such apprenticeships lasted for a specific period of time and sometimes involved a contract between the youth's parents and the person providing the training. Formal apprenticeship was limited almost exclusively to boys, as most parents expected their daughters to become wives and mothers and to learn housekeeping skills at home.

Apprenticeship Training. Boys generally began an apprenticeship around age 13 or 14. But PURITAN families in New England, who believed hard work to be a religious duty, sometimes sent their children out to apprentice at age 10 or 11.

The period of training for apprentices ranged from three years, for trades requiring easily learned skills, to seven years or more, for occupations involving complex skills and specialized knowledge. Most apprenticeships lasted three or four years and ended by age 21.

Apprentices in the trades typically spent the first year or so performing tasks such as carrying, lifting, cleaning, and errand running. Apprentices in law spent much of their early training copying portions of law books for their masters, since printed books were rare and expensive. They also wrote out wills, deeds, and other documents in longhand. After apprentices proved their commitment to the craft, they were relieved of many lowly tasks, and the master began to teach them the basics of the trade or profession. Legal apprentices read law books and attended court to watch their masters in action.

In addition to work-related training, apprenticeship often included instruction in reading, writing, arithmetic, and religion. Few children, except those from wealthier families, received formal schooling in colonial America. Many parents expected apprenticeship to provide their children with a basic education as well as an occupation.

Role of the Master. The masters who provided training were more than just teachers. They often assumed the role of a parent, providing for the youth's basic needs and sometimes enforcing discipline. The Puritans saw discipline as an important part of apprenticeship. They believed they could maintain better relationships with their children by allowing them to be disciplined by nonfamily members outside the home. Parents in the French colonies, on the other hand, had a strong sense of family solidarity and resented attempts by outsiders to discipline their children. Parents throughout

Orphan Apprentices

Orphans faced a difficult future in colonial America. To relieve the community of the burden of taking care of orphans, many local governments arranged for them to be apprenticed. Although such apprenticeships rarely included basic education in reading, writing, and arithmetic, they did provide training in a trade or craft. Orphan apprentices also learned discipline and proper conduct, skills normally learned from parents. The apprenticeship of orphans helped maintain the stability of the community and ensured that most of its members could provide for themselves and contribute to society.

the colonies would not tolerate abuse, and masters who mistreated their apprentices could be brought to trial and punished.

Contracts and Fees.   Some apprenticeships, often those in which a relative or family friend took charge of a boy's training, were informal arrangements between the parents and teacher. Others involved written contracts that defined the terms of the apprenticeship, including what the boy would learn, how long his instruction would last, and how he would behave. Such contracts also legalized the master's right to act *in loco parentis*—in place of the parent—in matters of basic needs, education, and discipline. In some cases, the agreement also required the master to look after the youth's moral and religious development.

Some apprentices received their training free in exchange for their labor. The master might even provide pocket money in addition to food, clothing, and shelter. However, highly skilled crafts workers, such as silversmiths and gunsmiths, and professionals, such as lawyers and doctors, often expected fees for their instruction.

Of course, not all apprenticeship arrangements proved successful. Children sometimes lacked the talent or temperament to succeed in a particular field. In such cases, the master and the parents of the apprentice would dissolve the agreement, and the family would seek another more suitable occupation.

After completing an apprenticeship, most young men began working to save enough money to set up a business of their own and to marry and start a family. They either worked independently or joined an existing business. The practical experience and training gained from apprenticeship helped many colonial Americans achieve their career goals. (*See also* **Artisans; Childhood and Adolescence; Crafts; Education; Labor; Schools and Schooling.**)

Arapaho Indians

See *Plains Indians.*

Architecture

*I*n the early years of North American colonization, European settlers tended to adapt Native American structures and techniques to build their new communities. In time, the British, Dutch, French, and Spanish colonists created their own styles of building, based on the traditions of their homeland and the materials available in the new land. These various architectural styles remained well defined throughout the colonial period. Gradually, though, as the colonies had more contact with one another, regional differences in North American architecture became less distinct.

British Colonies

The British colonists came to North America with strong views of the kinds of settlements they would create. They believed that neat, well-arranged

Architecture

British colonists in North America had to abandon some traditional styles because they lacked tools and basic materials, such as nails, plaster, and bricks. Wooden houses, such as the Parson Capen House built in 1683 in Topsfield, Massachusetts, became their most common buildings.

towns and buildings were a sign of civilization, and they planned to bring this sense of order to their new environment.

The first settlers, however, found themselves in a wilderness with no manufactured building supplies. They lacked nails, glass, plaster, and bricks. As a result, they examined Native American structures to see how they were built. The colonists discovered that the Indians' homes were similar to the small, rough houses of peasants in England. They also found that some Indian practices—such as building houses without foundations and surrounding villages with palisades*—resembled English methods and could be used with the materials available.

The earliest settlers learned some new techniques as well from Native American buildings. In Virginia, the colonists began imitating the Indian practice of using bark on the outside of their houses and woven reed mats inside. In New England, some early settlers built homes that resembled Indian wigwams—freestanding structures covered with boards or bark. But the colonists soon replaced such buildings with ones that followed English styles and tastes. In Virginia, the JAMESTOWN settlers built houses with thatched roofs and walls made of wattle-and-daub*, similar to those in English villages.

British Colonial Homes. The wooden farmhouse was one of the most common buildings in the British colonies. It had one large main room, often called the "best room," that served as a living, working, and sleeping area. Larger farmhouses might include a parlor, a sleeping and storage room, and a service room, such as a pantry and kitchen. Most farmhouses had just one story. Over the years, many colonists added upper floors and moved service rooms to cellars or to the rear of the house. This development resulted in a roughly symmetrical*, two-story house with an L-shaped extension in the back.

Gradually, different regions developed their own styles of housing. Colonists in Massachusetts and Connecticut built a two-room house with a central chimney, an entry hall, and a storage and work area in the rear. Later they might divide the storage area into a kitchen, a sleeping room, and a storage room. This five-room house—two large rooms in front and three rooms

* *palisade* fence of stakes forming a defense

* *wattle-and-daub* method of construction that interweaves twigs and branches and covers the whole structure with baked mud

* *symmetrical* balanced, matching forms on opposite sides of a structure

40

in back—became known as the Cape Cod house. It appeared throughout New England in the early 1700s, sometimes in a two-story version. Also common during this period were saltboxes—houses having two stories in front and one in back, with a long, sloping rear roof. This style gained its name from a resemblance to wooden boxes used to hold salt.

In New York, New Jersey, and Pennsylvania, houses built by Dutch and German colonists influenced British architecture. A typical German-style home had a kitchen just inside the front door, a square best room, a narrow sleeping chamber, and a small room behind the kitchen. Stairs in the kitchen led to an upper floor, which might be used for storage or sleeping areas. Most Dutch- and German-style houses included cellars.

In the Chesapeake region and the southern colonies, poor settlers usually lived in small, one-room houses. Prosperous southerners often owned two-room houses with a variety of outbuildings. Instead of adding extra rooms to the main house, they put up separate buildings for the kitchens, other service areas, and servants' quarters. This remained the basic design of southern plantations until after the Civil War. One of the most magnificent examples of this style is William Byrd's mansion in Virginia, built in the early 1700s.

Georgian Architecture. In the 1700s, a style known as Georgian—after the reigning kings of Great Britain—became popular in the colonies. Georgian architecture was very symmetrical in appearance and often included decorations such as columns and pediments*. Some Georgian architects based their style on the work of Andrea Palladio, an Italian architect of the 1500s. Palladio's designs reflected his interest in ancient Roman temples and mansions.

The Georgian-style home was generally built of brick and featured a central hall, with two rooms on each side. These rooms, set apart by the hall, provided some privacy and could be used for specific activities such as dining and entertaining. In houses with a second floor, the design followed a similar pattern, with bedrooms or storage rooms off the hall. Only wealthy individuals could afford to build Georgian-style homes in the 1700s, but the design had a significant influence on later American architecture. Some outstanding examples of Georgian architecture can be seen at Colonial Williamsburg, Virginia, including the Wythe House and Bruton Parish Church.

Urban Houses and Public Buildings. Well-to-do residents of colonial cities built houses similar to fine country homes. Poorer urban dwellers lived in narrow row houses connected at the sides. The row houses contained one or two rooms, and many had small additions at the back. Larger houses included upstairs rooms.

Colonial cities and towns had a variety of public buildings. In the early years of settlement, churches and meetinghouses were the most common community buildings. They generally consisted of a large rectangular room with seats facing one of the long walls. A gallery, or balcony, around three sides provided extra space for seating. Beginning in the early 1700s, colonial builders began to adopt a style developed by Christopher Wren, the noted

* *pediment* wide triangular area below a low-pitched roof

Mount Vernon

Mount Vernon, the home of George Washington, reflected the popular Georgian-style architecture of the 1700s. Built in 1743, it was originally a one-story house with a large parlor, a dining room, and two other rooms surrounding a central hall. In the 1770s and 1780s, Washington added a grand dining room and library and extended the house to two and one-half stories. With its separate service buildings and slaves' quarters, Mount Vernon also showed the influence of southern design.

church architect of London. In Wren's design, the seats were placed at right angles to the long walls, with aisles running the length of the room. The new-style churches had steeple towers, soon a familiar sight in towns and villages. The Old North Church in Boston, started in 1723, was the first colonial church to be built in this design.

Most cities had public markets and government buildings as well. In the 1600s and early 1700s, government offices were often housed in the same structure as the market. Although the designs varied, these buildings generally resembled large houses. For example, Independence Hall in Philadelphia, begun in the 1730s, looked like a mansion with a tower. The Colony House, built in Newport, Rhode Island, in the mid-1700s, also followed this style.

Most public buildings of the 1600s were wooden and had to be replaced frequently. In the 1700s, the colonists began to invest in substantial buildings of brick. These more permanent structures reflected the increasing prosperity and economic stability of the British colonies at that time.

Dutch Colony

Dutch colonists drew heavily on the traditions of the Netherlands in building their homes, churches, and other public structures. Like other European colonists, however, they adapted the designs of their homeland to suit the climate and materials found in North America.

Most of the Dutch settled in what is now New York City, the Hudson River valley, Long Island, and New Jersey. The earliest colonists lived in temporary shelters while they cleared and prepared their farmland. They began to construct solid Dutch-style houses in New Amsterdam in the 1630s and around present-day Albany in the 1640s. Although most Dutch colonial buildings have disappeared, historians have learned about them from the few surviving structures and from written descriptions, legal documents, and artwork.

Dutch Farms. Dutch colonial farmhouses usually had two rooms, one used as a kitchen and eating area and the other for sleeping and social occasions. An open attic served as a work space and storage area, and a cellar provided additional storage space. Colonists often added a wing with more rooms.

Materials used for building farms depended on the region and the local resources. Along the upper Hudson and Mohawk rivers, settlers found ample supplies of clay for making bricks and pine trees for lumber. The land west of the Hudson River and south into New Jersey had deposits of limestone and red sandstone, and many farmers built stone houses.

On Long Island, which had forests, Dutch farmers tended to build wooden structures. They used a distinctive low roof, which curved outward and hung over the side walls. Because the roof covered such a wide area, the house could have twice as many rooms as a steep-roofed house. In other areas, Dutch colonists favored the gambrel roof, which featured an upper section with a gentle slope and a lower, more steeply sloped section. Gambrel roofs provided more headroom in the upstairs rooms.

Tall, narrow houses such as this one in Albany, New York, demonstrate the influence of the Netherlands on architecture in the Dutch colony. Of course, the Dutch colonists still had to adapt their designs to the climate and resources available in North America.

* *gable* triangular section of a wall formed by the two slopes of a roof

Dutch-style barns had a large double doorway at each end, a wide center aisle for threshing grain, and side aisles with stalls for animals. Dutch farmers also built hay barracks to store supplies of hay. The barracks roof could be raised or lowered according to the height of the stacked hay. In areas settled by the Dutch, farmers continued to build these structures until the early 1900s. Farmers in the Netherlands still use them today.

Town Houses and Churches. A typical Dutch colonial town house had two rooms, a front room that often served as a shop and a back room for the family's living quarters. The fireplace, often tiled, was usually in the back room, where meals were prepared. The house usually had an entry hall along one side, with doors to the two rooms, and a cellar. The colonists used wood beams for the main structure of the house and bricks between the beams for insulation. Wood shingles covered the roof, and boards covered the outside walls. Gables* faced the street. Town houses also featured divided doors with separate top and bottom sections and a front stoop—stairs and a landing at the front door.

Many of the Dutch colonists were merchants, who needed storage space for their businesses. They usually lived and worked in the same building, using the front room of the ground floor as an office and adding upper levels for warehouse space. Houses of this type, which could have as many as five stories, resembled the tall, narrow buildings found in towns in the Netherlands.

Dutch settlements also included churches in a wide variety of styles. Most churches were decorated simply, with the pulpit occupying a prominent place because of the important role of preaching in the Protestant tradition. An Albany church built in 1715 illustrates one popular style—a square building with a steep-pitched roof and a high, open belfry. On Long Island and in New Jersey, the Dutch built several small eight-sided churches. Both styles closely resembled churches in the Netherlands.

English Influence. After the English captured the colony of New Netherland in 1664, they introduced their own architectural styles. English houses tended to be larger and more symmetrical than the Dutch houses, with a more formal style of decoration. English houses had center halls and separate rooms for eating, sleeping, working, and socializing.

The English style spread slowly from New York City and did not reach Albany until the 1750s. Architectural changes first appeared in public buildings and only gradually replaced the Dutch style in houses, churches, and farm buildings.

French Colonies

The architecture of the French colonies grew out of the cultural traditions of France as well as the climate, environment, and resources of North America. In general, the public buildings represented French traditions, while private homes reflected an attempt to adapt to a new environment.

French Colonial Homes. Early colonists from France brought with them the architectural traditions of various French provinces. The most

* **New France** French colony centered in the St. Lawrence River valley, an area known as Canada; included the Great Lakes region and, until 1713, Acadia (present-day Nova Scotia)

* **eaves** edge of roof

* **facade** front of a building

influential of these was the style of northwestern France: wood-framed walls filled in with dirt, plaster, or other materials. Builders sometimes put sod, pieces of matted grass and dirt, on the outer walls of a home to provide additional insulation. This type of construction dominated French colonial architecture throughout New France*.

The basic frame of the building was made of posts driven into the ground. Boards and beams were attached to the frame to form the walls. These wooden walls lasted only 12 to 15 years. In time, however, colonists learned to use decay-resistant woods, such as oak, cedar, or cypress, to extend the life of their buildings. Stone and brick lasted even longer, but few colonists could afford these materials.

French colonists in the eastern province of Acadia often used rubble or wooden boards to fill in the frames of their houses. In Louisiana the settlers usually packed bricks or a moss-and-clay mixture into the building frame. A whitewash coating of lime and water helped protect the filling from the weather and gave the house a neat and unified appearance. Some houses had a layer of stucco, or plaster, under the whitewash. Dwellings of this sort could be expected to last at least 40 years.

French colonists preferred buildings with a vertical rather than a horizontal appearance. To achieve this look, they built steep roofs that made up half the height of a house or barn. Roof coverings generally consisted of ceramic tiles, wood shingles, or thin wooden boards. People in fishing settlements sometimes covered their roofs with tree bark. Some settlers used thatch on their roofs. But by the 1700s, only barns and other farm buildings had thatched roofs.

The steep roofs of French colonial buildings often had long overhanging eaves* that provided shade in summer. The eaves were supported by posts from raised verandas, or porches. Such verandas were a distinctive feature of French colonial homes from Canada to Louisiana.

The windows in these houses often contained oiled paper instead of glass, which was very expensive. Ground-floor windows generally had shutters to protect and shade the interior. Builders used decorative iron hinges, bolts, and latches to secure windows, shutters, and doors.

In Louisiana, kitchens were often located in separate buildings to keep unnecessary heat from the main house during the warm seasons of the year. In addition, large windows allowed breezes to blow freely through the house. Because of the dampness and flooding, many houses had brick foundations. This helped prevent rotting in the structure's wooden frame. In grander homes, the entire ground floor might be made of brick.

Hallways were rare in French colonial houses. Instead, rooms opened directly onto other rooms. A typical Canadian farmhouse had one large open area for eating and family gatherings and an enclosed sleeping area divided by moveable partitions. An attic sometimes provided additional sleeping space. The house was heated by open hearths on either side of a central chimney. During the 1700s, colonists in the St. Lawrence Valley and Acadia began to heat their homes with iron stoves.

Large towns, such as MONTREAL and QUEBEC, passed various laws regulating house construction. The laws favored stone buildings because stone was more resistant than wood to fire. Regulations also required the facades*

of buildings to line up along the edge of the street. This practice created continuous rows of houses on either side of a street. Courtyards, stables, and small gardens behind the houses gave a rural feeling to the towns.

Public Buildings.   Skilled artisans* from France designed and built many of the churches and other public buildings in New France, and they followed French style. Colonial leaders took great pride in their French heritage and did not wish to change their architectural traditions to suit a new environment.

The typical colonial church in Canada was built of stone. It had a rectangular nave* with a rounded recess at the far end. Large semicircular windows lined the walls, and a circular window was located over the main doorway. The doorway had decorations carved in stone.

Although the outside of the church was quite simple, the interior often had elaborate decorations, with an altar framed by columns, intricate wood carvings, and paintings of saints. Benches near the altar provided seating for the clergy* and notable community members. The rest of the people stood or kneeled on the floor.

Government buildings in the French colonies resembled similar buildings in France. A typical administrative building consisted of a two-story structure with an impressive entrance, surrounded by two single-story wings. These simple yet grand buildings reflected the French desire for order, discipline, and stability.

Spanish Colonies

The architecture of Spanish colonies of North America reflected the tastes of their European builders and the frontier nature of these regions. The Spanish areas did not have many master builders, carpenters, or masons and often used local Indians to help with construction. As a result, complex architectural features such as domes and arches were rare.

Building Materials.   In the Spanish Borderlands*, as in other North American colonies, the materials used for construction depended on available resources. Adobe—dried mud—was common in dry regions such as New Mexico and Arizona. By the time California and Texas were settled, brick had become more widely available in the Spanish empire. Many MISSIONS in California used brick for chimneys or columns. In the wet climate of Florida, wood was plentiful.

The Spaniards built their roofs at a slight angle to permit rainwater to drain. In the simplest type of roof, layers of reeds were stretched over large beams, then topped by grass and earth and covered with plaster. More permanent structures had roofs of thatch or tile. Tile was rare in Florida but common in California.

The only glass factory in NEW SPAIN was in Puebla, Mexico, and it could not produce enough to meet the demand of the Spanish colonies. Windows had to be imported from Europe and were used only in churches. In New Mexico, builders used selenite—a material that light could shine through—as a substitute for glass. In San Antonio, Texas, settlers covered their windows with oil-soaked parchment.

* *artisan* skilled crafts worker

* *nave* long, narrow central hall

* *clergy* ministers, priests, and other church officials

* *Spanish Borderlands* northern part of New Spain, area now occupied by Florida, Texas, New Mexico, Arizona, and California

Architecture

The most distinctly Spanish structure in colonial North America was the mission. Usually built of adobe, missions can be seen today in California, New Mexico, and Arizona. The mission shown here, San Luis Rey de Francia, was built about 1815 just north of San Diego.

Most houses and simple buildings had floors of earth. Some churches covered their floors with stone, and many missions and forts used brick. The floor of the church at San Juan de Capistrano in California was paved with diamond-shaped bricks.

The Spanish settlers generally whitewashed the walls of their buildings to give them a protective finish and to provide a surface for decoration. In Texas, artisans sometimes painted floral designs on a building's entrance or covered the facade with patterns resembling tile. To interior walls, they might add designs such as flowers, chains of coins, cherubs, and coats of arms. At San Xavier del Bac, a mission in Arizona, the wall decorations included pictures enclosed in painted frames and a painting made to look like a door.

Town Planning.   Official building codes regulated the appearance of towns in the Spanish Borderlands. Towns in cold climates were to have wide streets so the sun could warm the streets. Those in hot areas were to have narrow streets so that buildings could provide shade. The center of the town usually consisted of a large plaza with a church and the main government building on opposite sides. Slaughterhouses and fish markets were located at a distance from other buildings.

Towns often required settlers to help with the construction of public buildings. In San Antonio, colonists faced a fine and jail sentence if they failed to do their share of the work. In San Jose, California, some citizens who refused to help with public buildings spent time in prison.

Spanish Colonial Homes.   In St. Augustine, Florida, the earliest houses were simple structures made of wattle-and-daub or cypress wood. Later settlers used a material called tabby, made by adding sand, pebbles, and shells to mortar and pouring the mixture into wooden molds. In the 1700s,

Town Planning

The Spanish tried to plan their colonial towns, but their efforts did not always succeed. In 1797 California ruler Miguel de la Grúa Talamanca y Braciforte decided to build a permanent town that would be named after him. He did not want a "squalid community" like the settlements at Los Angeles and San Jose. He instructed a military engineer to design a square town, with streets crossing at right angles and pastures and irrigated fields surrounding the settlement. In spite of the planning, Braciforte did not prosper. The settlers were poor and lacked the skills to carry out the ambitious plan.

* *loophole* small opening

* *presidio* Spanish fort built to protect mission settlements

See color plate 3, vol. 3.

* *baroque* artistic movement of the 1600s noted for its elaborate decorations

Florida colonists began to use more stone in construction. Glass became popular after the British held St. Augustine for 20 years.

Houses in Florida followed what was later called the "St. Augustine plan." They contained one or two stories with two rooms on each floor. Although the houses were set close to the street, a high fence extending along the street provided privacy. Builders positioned the houses to face the sun in winter and to be shaded in the summer. North walls—with no windows—blocked chilly winter winds.

In New Mexico, homes were usually made of adobe, a technique the Spaniards had used in their homeland. The dwellings of the PUEBLO INDIANS had small rooms because the Indians could not cut large trees for roof beams. Using metal tools to cut large trees and pack animals to haul them, the Spanish obtained the long beams needed to build larger rooms. Settlers who lived in the mountains between SANTA FE and Taos, where wood was plentiful, usually built log houses.

Spanish settlers in New Mexico generally designed their villages to provide defense. The houses enclosed a central plaza that could be used to hold livestock in case of attack, and the outside walls had no windows. Ranch homes—haciendas—were also designed with defense in mind. They consisted of two square buildings connected by a passageway, with barns and storerooms in one square and family living quarters in the other. Surrounding the ranch was a low wall with loopholes* for firing on attackers.

The homes of the early settlers of San Antonio were largely made of wattle-and-daub and often had thatch roofs. Thatch was a fire hazard, and a law passed in 1831 prohibited straw as a roofing material. Over time, skilled artisans moved to the area. As a result, later houses were larger and more elaborate. Some had steep, shingled roofs and large stone fireplaces. Though concerned about Indian attacks, Texas ranchers did not fortify their homes. More commonly, they built a separate, windowless structure with loopholes and a fire-resistant roof.

Public Buildings and Missions. Spanish colonists built missions, forts, and government buildings throughout the Borderlands. Construction of the Castillo de San Marcos in St. Augustine began in the late 1600s. It was the only presidio* built of stone in what is now the United States and took more than 20 years to build. Like other presidios, it contained barracks for officers and men, a chapel, a kitchen, a carpenter's shop, and a blacksmith's forge. It also included the governor's office. A military engineer oversaw the construction, with master carpenters and stonecutters supervising the work.

Missions varied in style from place to place. In Texas, missions had defensive walls. One called San Antonio de Valero achieved fame in the war of Texan independence as the Alamo. California was home to 21 missions, many in the famous "California mission style" of whitewashed adobe and red tile roofs. Others were built of stone. San Carlos Borromeo shows the detailed ornamentation of the baroque* style. San Gabriel looks like the fortress churches built in the early years of Spanish settlement in Mexico. The missionaries at San Juan de Capistrano wanted to built the most important and elaborate church in California, and they had the design plans sent from Mexico. Completed in 1806 but destroyed in an earthquake six years later, the stone church had a domed ceiling, elegant arches, and a bell tower. (*See also* **Cities and Towns; Construction and Building Techniques; Furniture and Furnishings; Housing; Presidios.**)

See map in Missions and Missionaries (vol. 3).

See map in Spanish Borderlands (vol. 4).

During the colonial period, what is now the state of Arizona was part of the SPANISH BORDERLANDS, the northern reaches of Spanish territory in North America. The northern half of Arizona belonged to the Spanish province of NEW MEXICO. The southern half, called Pimería Alta (Land of the Upper Pima Indians), came under the authority of the province of Sonora. Spanish missionaries, miners, soldiers, and ranchers from Mexico created outposts* in this region, where the PIMA and Papago Indians lived.

Explorers, Missionaries, and Miners. The first Spaniard to explore Arizona was Alvar Núñez CABEZA DE VACA in the 1530s. Francisco Vásquez de CORONADO led a large expedition into the area in the 1540s. His men were the first Europeans to see the Grand Canyon. Later Spanish explorers traced the path of the Colorado River and discovered copper and silver deposits in the interior of Arizona. These early expeditions opened the way for two new groups of Spaniards—missionaries and miners.

The missionaries, mostly from the Franciscan order of the Roman Catholic Church, arrived in the 1630s. They intended to convert the Native Americans to Christianity—peaceably if possible, but by force if necessary. The most active missionary was Eusebio Francisco KINO, an Italian JESUIT. Between 1687 and 1711, he traveled thousands of miles on foot and on horseback in an effort to bring Christianity to the Indians of the region. Father Kino founded a number of missions, including San Xavier del Bac near the site of present-day Tucson.

Most of the early Spanish explorers came in search of gold and silver. Mining operations began in the Spanish Borderlands in the early 1600s, primarily in New Mexico. In 1736 prospectors found rich silver deposits in Pimería Alta near a small Pima Indian village called Arizonac (small springs) in the Pima language. The discovery drew attention to the region, which became known as Arizona. Large numbers of miners traveled north from Mexico to try their luck in Arizona, but the mining boom lasted only a short time.

Settlement and Growth. Mining drew some settlers to Arizona. They built their homes with thick walls of adobe, sun-baked clay bricks, which kept interiors cool in summer and warm in winter. The settlers grew wheat and raised cattle with the help of Native American laborers—some of whom were slaves. Trade in Indian slaves existed throughout the Spanish Borderlands. Most of the enslaved Indians were captured in war, often by other Indians, and sold to settlers.

East of Pimería Alta lived the warlike APACHE INDIANS, who frequently raided the ranches and missions of Arizona. To control this threat, the Spanish authorities in Mexico began to establish PRESIDIOS, or forts, in the region. The first one was built in 1752 at Tubac near present-day Nogales. It became the earliest permanent Spanish community in Arizona. The Spanish

Arizona's desert climate made farming difficult. The Spanish were slow to colonize the area, and many open spaces remained untouched throughout the colonial period.

continued to establish presidios, including one at Tucson in 1776. In the late 1700s, soldiers from Sonora moved north with their families to Arizona's presidios. Civilian settlers also came to colonize the region. Almost all settlement took place in Pimería Alta. Small towns grew up around the presidios of Tubac and Tucson, and these developed into the largest population centers of Arizona.

RANCHING and farming became the main economic activities in the region. Introduced by the Spaniards, cattle ranching was concentrated around the missions. But frequent raids by the Apaches in which they killed large numbers of livestock made ranching difficult. In the 1780s, Spanish forces launched a campaign against the Apaches, and succeeded in reducing this threat.

The early missionaries had taught Native Americans in the region to grow wheat and European vegetables as well as their traditional crops of corn and beans. Throughout the colonial period, Indian farmers raised most of the region's agricultural produce. Both ranchers and farmers needed reliable sources of water, a problem in the desert climate of Arizona. The Pima Indians had used irrigation long before the Spanish arrived, and the missionaries taught them new techniques that made better use of the region's scarce water resources. Still, the lack of water led to many disputes, and the issue of water rights remained a constant source of conflict throughout the region.

Spanish colonization of Arizona proceeded slowly, and large areas of the region remained isolated and unsettled except for Native Americans. This was due to both the harshness of the climate and the continuing threat from the Apaches. By the early 1800s, the non-Indian population of Arizona numbered only about 1,000. But even this small group of European settlers brought disaster to the region's Native Americans. During the period of Spanish colonization, the Indian population of Pimería Alta dropped from about 20,000 to 1,000. The rest of the Indians had been wiped out by warfare and European diseases such as smallpox and measles.

Arizona remained under Spanish control until 1821, when Mexico gained its independence from Spain. Mexico ruled Arizona until 1853. At that time, Arizona became part of the New Mexico Territory of the United States, and in 1912 it became a separate state. (*See also* **Agriculture; Encomiendas; Gold; Land Ownership; Silver; Slavery.**)

Armies

See *Military Forces.*

Arnold, Benedict

1741–1801
Revolutionary patriot and traitor

* *militia* army of citizens who may be called into action in a time of emergency

Benedict Arnold, a skilled officer who fought bravely for the Americans in the early years of the Revolutionary War, betrayed his country by giving military secrets to the British. Arnold became one of the most hated men in America, and his name has come to mean "traitor."

Born in Connecticut, Arnold ran away to join British colonial troops fighting France in the FRENCH AND INDIAN WAR when only a teenager. Arnold lost interest in army life and deserted, but he was not punished because of his youth. He later married, had three sons, and became a prosperous businessman and a captain in the Connecticut militia*.

When fighting broke out between the American patriots and the British in 1775, Arnold volunteered to capture the British post of FORT TICONDEROGA. Vermont pioneer Ethan ALLEN had the same idea, and after a dispute about who was in charge the two men captured the fort together. Arnold then took St. Johns, another British fort.

Soon Arnold presented a plan to attack Quebec, and George WASHINGTON, commander in chief of the American forces, approved the plan. Arnold showed great bravery in leading his troops through the Maine forests in winter, but the attack failed. Arnold did succeed, though, in keeping a British fleet on Lake Champlain from retaking Fort Ticonderoga.

Arnold became angry when the Continental Congress promoted five younger, less experienced officers to a rank above his own. Although Arnold eventually received a promotion as well, his resentment did not end. He was further insulted when the congress investigated charges that he had broken rules about private property during the campaign in Canada. Several times Arnold tried to resign from the army, but Washington persuaded him to stay. In 1778 Washington appointed him commander of American military forces at Philadelphia.

Out of bitterness and disappointment, Arnold began sending important military secrets to British headquarters in the summer of 1779. He still felt that the Continental Congress had treated him unfairly, and he desperately needed the money he hoped the British would supply. He later claimed that the Americans' alliance with the French, his old enemies, also played a role in his switch to the British side.

In 1780 Washington put Arnold in command of West Point, an important fort on the Hudson River in New York. Arnold formed a plan to turn the fort over to the British, but the plot was discovered when American soldiers captured a British spy carrying some documents from Arnold. Arnold fled to the British. In 1781 he took his family to Great Britain, where the political leadership soon changed and the new leaders turned against Arnold. He lived out his life in poverty, unhappiness, and disgrace. (*See also* **American Revolution.**)

Art

See
color plate 2,
vol. 2.

* *naturalist* person who studies plants and animals in their natural surroundings

uropean art came to the Americas with the earliest explorers, who often drew pictures of the lands, plants, animals, and people they encountered in their travels. By the mid-1600s, European artists were working throughout colonial North America. These painters and sculptors saw themselves as carrying on their country's artistic traditions. They used the works of European painters as models and often copied details, such as backgrounds or poses, directly from those paintings. Eventually, each colonial area—British, Dutch, French, and Spanish—developed its own artistic traditions, shaped largely by the skills and materials available in the different regions.

After the voyages of Christopher Columbus, people in Europe were eager to know more about the Americas. To satisfy this curiosity, as well as to record their own discoveries, many early explorers made maps, drawings, and watercolor paintings of what they saw.

Some European expeditions included trained artists who could re-create scenes of the place they called the "New World" with great accuracy. In the 1500s, French artist Jacques Le Moyne de Morgues illustrated everyday life in a Florida settlement. Englishman John WHITE made detailed watercolor drawings of Native Americans, Indian dwellings and dances, and plants and animals in the Jamestown colony. Flemish artist Theodore de Bry created prints based on the work of Le Moyne and White. These prints, reproduced in many books, gave Europeans some of the first images of the Americas. Other artist-explorers continued this work in the 1700s. One of the most prominent, the naturalist* Mark Catesby, illustrated birds, plants, and animals in a 1731 book about Carolina, Florida, and the Bahama Islands.

Of course, European-style art was not the only kind of art produced in North America. The Native Americans practiced a wide variety of arts both before and after the arrival of the Europeans. Indian artistry revealed itself in various forms, from baskets to pottery to weaving and leather work. After Europeans began colonizing the continent, some Indians continued to practice their traditional arts, while others adapted their art to suit European tastes and demands.

European Painting and Sculpture

Professional artists began coming to the American colonies in the late 1600s, after colonial societies had been established, towns formed, and practical needs met. The most common art forms in all colonial areas were based on European painting and sculpture. The artists of each colony produced the kinds of works that the residents wanted and expected.

British Colonies. In the British colonies, the portrait was the most popular and important art form. Colonists of the 1600s and 1700s, especially PURITANS and some other groups of Protestants, viewed many types of paintings and statues with suspicion and even hostility. Protestants objected in particular to religious images. Portraits, however, survived this hostile attitude toward art because they fulfilled certain political, social, and family needs. Portraits allowed families to show pride in distinguished ancestors and to remember loved ones who had died. Portraits of public figures—in the view of many colonists—helped reinforce the authority of leaders and provided examples of virtue for others to follow.

The earliest known artworks produced in British America were portraits of adults and children. In these paintings, artists often used common symbols that everyone would understand. For example, if a man wore gloves, that indicated his status* as a gentleman. A fan in a woman's hand showed that she was an upper-class lady. A bird held in the hands of a young boy or girl often represented innocence. In the late 1600s, the artist Thomas Smith painted a self-portrait in which he holds a skull, a common symbol of eternal life after death.

Symbols also played an important role in carved gravestones—the main sculptural work of New England colonists. These carved stones often bore symbols representing heavenly life to help people overcome their fear of death. Common gravestone symbols included angels, trees and birds, flowers growing out of urns, and eagles carrying souls heavenward.

The other major sculpting activity of the colonial period was wood carving. Carvers made figureheads for the bows of ships, decorative boxes for storing Bibles, shop signs, and architectural ornaments for houses and public buildings. Most other sculpture in the British colonies, including elaborate marble tombstones, was either imported from Europe or created by European stone carvers who had moved to the colonies.

Crafts workers in the British colonies also produced fine furniture and silver objects. Artisans* created tables, chairs, chests of drawers, and cupboards with features such as carved shell designs, turned spindles, and gracefully curved legs. Silversmiths used many of the same artistic elements, including decorative patterns taken from nature, in designs for bowls, candlesticks, and teapots.

In the mid-1700s, British ideas about art started to change. Wealthy collectors began displaying the sculpture of ancient Greece and Rome and paintings from the Italian Renaissance*. Many artists now turned to these works, instead of to English artworks, as models. Portraits remained important, but artists began painting more landscapes and other kinds of scenes. Art came to be regarded as a source of national pride, and artists—formerly viewed as crafts workers—acquired new status in social and professional circles.

At the same time, a large number of painters were working in the American colonies, particularly in Boston, New York, and Philadelphia. Indeed, Boston had become the center of artistic life in America. The city's upper class was eager to acquire artworks, and Bostonians' pride in their history encouraged them to collect portraits of family members and civic leaders. Scottish painter John Smibert arrived in Boston in 1729 and opened America's first studio for artists. Smibert's portraits and copies of European

* **status** social position

* **artisan** skilled crafts worker

* **Renaissance** intellectual and artistic movement that began in Italy in the late 1300s and lasted until the 1600s

John Singleton Copley (1738–1815) was the most famous portrait painter in colonial America. He is best known for his portraits of wealthy citizens and their families. Copley painted *Sir William Pepperell and His Family* in 1778.

See
color plate 4,
vol. 3.

paintings served as a "school" for young American artists who studied and copied them. In the 1740s, the American artist Robert Feke enjoyed success as a painter. His portraits were in great demand in cities from Boston to Philadelphia.

Out of the artistic atmosphere of Boston emerged John Singleton COPLEY, the first American artist to gain fame outside the colonies. A portrait painter, Copley broadened the range of his art by incorporating landscapes, seascapes, and other figures into the portraits he painted. His portraits revealed a great deal about life in pre-Revolutionary America. In 1774 Copley moved to London in search of greater artistic opportunities.

Another prominent American artist, Benjamin WEST of Philadelphia, achieved his greatest fame while in Europe. West studied in Italy and later moved to London, where he influenced many young Americans who came to study art. One of his earliest American pupils, Charles Willson Peale, became a famous portrait painter and is remembered for the museum he established in Philadelphia. Benjamin West had a tremendous influence on American art. His work introduced new artistic styles and reflected basic American themes.

By the end of the colonial era, a few wealthy individuals in Virginia, Boston, and Philadelphia had assembled large collections of paintings and other forms of art. These collections introduced European artistic traditions to Americans and helped establish the idea of the value of art. They also laid the foundation for the creation of art museums in American communities.

English artistic traditions had certainly shaped art in the British colonies. Yet by the time the colonies won independence, Americans took great pride

French colonial artists focused on religious subjects. This 1797 wooden statue by François Baillairgé represents St. Elizabeth.

* **New France** French colony centered in the St. Lawrence River valley, an area known as Canada; included the Great Lakes region and, until 1713, Acadia (present-day Nova Scotia)

in the achievements of American-born artists and boasted that their new nation could produce artistic genius equal to that of Europe.

The Dutch Colony. Many settlers in the Dutch colony of New Netherland brought paintings with them from Europe. The artworks included portraits, landscapes, and still lifes that reflected the well-developed artistic traditions of the Netherlands. Dutch settlers also collected the works of colonial painters, whom they called limners (from the Latin *luminare,* meaning "to draw"). Many of the Dutch limners were self-taught artists who traveled from place to place seeking commissions to paint portraits. The limners also produced Scripture paintings—illustrations of events from the New Testament of the Bible. These paintings often occupied a prominent place in Dutch colonial homes of the late 1600s.

A small group of portrait painters who worked in the Dutch communities along the Hudson River became known as patroon painters, after the large landholders of New Netherland called patroons. Between about 1715 and 1730, these artists produced portraits of many prominent colonists of the region.

By this time, however, painting in the former Dutch colony had declined in quality. Compared to the fine work produced by Dutch artists in Europe, colonial Dutch art seemed primitive, dull, and unimaginative. Dutch colonists had kept the tradition of the limner alive for nearly a century, but after the mid-1700s, limners faded from the scene. They were replaced by professional artists who followed English artistic styles and traditions.

French Colonies. As soon as the early French colonists settled in North America, they began producing art to enrich their lives. Some of the paintings and sculptures represented the king, the queen, and public officials. Most French colonial art, however, was religious in nature. Unlike the Protestant English, the Roman Catholic French adorned their churches with religious paintings and statues. In addition, the missionaries in New France* relied on pictures and statues to teach Christianity to the Native Americans.

The art of sculpture developed in the French colonies at an early period. In 1686 a French official brought a bronze head of Louis XIV to New France to show the colonists what their king looked like. This was perhaps the only piece of sculpture imported from France during the colonial era. Because of the weight and the shipping cost, the colonists of New France had to create their own statues. Most sculptures were created for churches. Master stone carvers and wood-carvers, usually trained in France, taught local apprentices the basics of their art. These colonial artists created elaborate altars, carved pulpits, and other ornamental furnishings for the Catholic churches of the French colonies.

Paintings could be shipped to the colonies easily and inexpensively. As a result many early works, particularly those intended for use in churches, were imported from Europe. Most of the paintings that survive, however, are portraits created in New France. Many show local officials and their wives. Some portray notable Indian leaders—such as the Iroquois chief Teganissorens, who had his portrait painted while on a diplomatic mission to

Quebec. In some religious communities, it was customary to have a portrait of a deceased person made just before burial. An artist would come to the deathbed and capture the likeness of the individual, giving the family or community a way of remembering the deceased. Though sometimes rough in style and quality, these deathbed portraits are powerful and emotional works of art.

In the French colony of Louisiana, art sometimes served as propaganda*. A 1720 painting of New Orleans shows a mountain paradise with friendly, gift-bearing Indians studying Christianity, while a lawbreaker is safely put in jail. This attractive image of peace and order was designed to lure new settlers to the rough frontier community. Miniature portraits became a popular art form in Louisiana. The first native-born artist in New Orleans, a woman known only as Madame Prados, painted miniatures in the early 1800s.

propaganda information presented in a way to influence people

Spanish Colonies. Most art in the Spanish Borderlands—the part of the Spanish colonial empire now occupied by Florida and the southwestern region of the United States—had a religious function. Like the French colonists, the Spanish were Roman Catholics who wanted to convert the Native Americans to their faith. They decorated their churches with religious paintings and sculptures and used this art to help teach the Indians about Christianity. Such religious art reached its highest level in New Mexico, the oldest and most densely populated part of the Borderlands.

The central focus—and finest artistic creation—of the Spanish colonial church was its altarpiece, the painted and carved screen framing the altar. An intricate combination of columns, wood carvings, and paintings made up the altarpiece. Seldom the work of one person, most altarpieces in the Borderlands were created by artists from Mexico who had come north in search of work or by local Indians trained to paint and carve in the European style. MISSIONS that lacked the money for large altarpieces substituted murals, or wall paintings, as decoration for church interiors.

Missionaries in the Spanish Borderlands imported oil paintings and carved images of religious figures from Mexico. In return, the missions sent back to Mexico religious paintings on animal hides, a specialty of the Borderlands. Borderlands missions also created life-sized, painted statues of saints and other holy figures. These statues, often adorned with jewels and lavish clothing, were placed in churches and carried through the streets in religious processions on special holy days.

European Prints

The type of artwork available to most American colonists during the 1600s and 1700s was the print, an image reproduced many times from a single source. Three kinds of prints were popular during the colonial period: woodcuts, engravings, and mezzotints. A woodcut is made by carving an image into a block of wood, spreading ink on the image, and pressing paper against the image to make a print of it. Engravings and mezzotints use a similar process. In an engraving, the image is drawn onto a metal plate with a sharp tool or etched into the metal with acid. A mezzotint is an engraved image printed as light lines and shapes against a black background.

Art by Vow

An ancient type of art called ex-voto painting flourished in the French colonies. It involved artworks created for churches or shrines as a result of vows, or promises. A captain who feared losing his ship in a storm might vow to give a painting to his church if his vessel were spared. The church of Sainte-Anne de Beaupré near Quebec had many ex-voto paintings. One dated 1754 showed a group of young people whose rowboats had capsized in the St. Lawrence River. Fear of drowning inspired one member of the group to promise a painting to St. Anne. The vow was only partially successful; two of the five youths drowned.

Printers and booksellers in Europe made thousands of prints in the 1600s and 1700s. Many appeared as illustrations in books. Others were printed individually and bought by people to be framed and hung in homes. Some prints were original images drawn by a painter or engraver. Others were copies of oil paintings—often landscapes, historical scenes, or portraits of important figures. Printed maps and views of cities were also popular. Because prints were far less expensive than original paintings, many people who could not afford paintings or statues could own prints.

Prints became very popular in the colonies. Most early prints came from England or elsewhere in Europe. The first known print made in the English colonies was a 1670 woodcut portrait of the Reverend Richard Mather, a member of a prominent New England family of religious leaders. Almost 60 years later, an engraver printed a portrait of his descendant, the Reverend Increase MATHER, that served as a model for many future portraits of ministers appearing in books.

During the 1700s, many printers in the British colonies began producing their own prints, often using European techniques and following European styles. Portraits were especially popular. Printers adopted the custom of putting a portrait next to the title page of books they published. Publishers used these portraits over and over again—even in works by different authors. Readers expected to see a portrait in books, and any portrait would do.

Colonial printmakers gradually combined portraits with landscapes and other scenes. By the time of the American Revolution, colonial engravers such as Paul REVERE were making prints that illustrated both current and historical events. Prints made in the Revolutionary period also included satiric* portraits and scenes of social and political movements.

In the French and Spanish colonies, saints, biblical scenes, and other religious images were the most common subjects in prints. Many of the prints came from Europe or, in the case of the Spanish Borderlands, from Mexico. Missionaries in the Borderlands had religious prints shipped from Mexico, primarily for teaching Christianity to the Indians. These prints also served as models to the artists who painted altarpieces and church murals.

* **satiric** referring to humor that criticizes or makes fun of something bad or foolish

Native American Art

Native Americans did not have art in the same sense as the Europeans. They created objects to fulfill a function in their society—sometimes practical and sometimes spiritual—not to express artistic ideas or display artistic ability. Nevertheless, many of the baskets, masks, pottery, and other works fashioned by Indians showed great skill in their making and beauty in their appearance.

The lifestyles and cultures of the Indians of North America varied enormously, and the objects they created reflect these differences. Those who lived in the Eastern Woodlands produced quite different forms of art from those living in the deserts of the Southwest. Still, all Native American art had certain common characteristics.

Characteristics of Native American Art.
Native Americans saw close ties between their physical and spiritual lives, and the decorations used

in their art often had spiritual meaning. They employed symbols such as the mandala to connect an object with spiritual powers. The mandala is a circular diagram that usually represents the universe and the balance of spiritual powers within it. Mandalas appeared in sand paintings in the Southwest, on war shields on the Great Plains, and on rock paintings throughout North America. Colors had symbolic meaning as well. Many Indian tribes in North America believed that four colors—black, white, red, and yellow—had sacred significance. They represented the cardinal directions* and other features of the world that could be divided into four parts.

Indians created many objects specifically for spiritual rituals*. Among southwestern tribes, sand paintings were used to accompany religious songs and myth telling and as a part of healing ceremonies. Some Indian tribes wore elaborately decorated masks in ritual dances. Others held painted shields and played painted drums during various ceremonies. Artworks needed to have a function. Native Americans appreciated objects not only for their beauty but also for their usefulness in a particular setting.

In traditional Indian societies, most tasks were divided by gender. This division of labor also applied to the creation of artworks. Women tended to make baskets and pottery and to weave textiles. Men usually carved and painted on wood and stone. However, such gender differences were not universal throughout North America. Women did much of the carving in the Plains region, and men often wove textiles in parts of the Southwest. Both men and women painted tanned animal hides. Men and women generally had different styles of art as well. The paintings done by men tended to be representational*, illustrating personal or historical events, while those done by women were usually abstract* or symbolic.

All Native American art was limited by the technology and materials available. Indians did not have potters' wheels or lathes—turning machines—

* **cardinal directions**   north, south, east, and west

* **ritual**   ceremony that follows a set pattern

See color plate 3, vol. 2.

* **representational**   style of art that attempts to portray the world realistically

* **abstract**   refers to designs or images that do not represent a recognizable person or object

Indians of the Southwest often decorated walls of buildings with murals. This Pueblo Indian painting from about 1500 appears in a kiva—a religious meeting place—in present-day New Mexico.

so they had to shape pottery and wood by hand. Until the arrival of Europeans, they lacked iron tools as well and generally used stone or copper tools to cut and shape objects. The materials Indians used for their art included wood, bone, and ivory for carving; stone and animal hides for painting; reeds for basket making; clay for pottery; and cotton and wool for weaving. Shells were often added for decoration. Even tribes in the interior of the continent worked with shells, obtaining them through trade networks with coastal Indians. The glass beads Europeans brought also became popular items for decoration.

Native Americans in the northeast used strings of shells and glass beads known as WAMPUM as a type of money. Wampum belts—shells or beads woven into strips—often had a ceremonial function, and groups exchanged them at meetings and negotiations. Patterns woven into the belts generally had symbolic meanings.

Regional Characteristics.   Native American art can be divided into regions that had common characteristics of style, subject, technique, or material. For example, pottery produced in the Eastern Woodlands—an area stretching from the Atlantic coast to the Great Plains—generally had geometric patterns cut into the surface of the clay. Many pottery designs included animal symbols. Wood carving was an important activity in the region. The IROQUOIS, for example, created very expressive wooden masks called False Faces. Indians of the region tended to make baskets by plaiting, a technique in which strands of reed or other fiber are braided together into patterns.

Before the introduction of the horse in the 1700s, the Indians of the Great Plains region had little art, except for paintings on rock. With the horse, the lifestyle of the PLAINS INDIANS became more nomadic. They needed objects—including art—that they could carry with them. They painted scenes and symbols on animal hides that represented battles, hunts, and other events. Before the 1800s, Plains Indians tended to paint humans as stick figures. Contact with white artists led to a more realistic style of painting. Plains Indian men often painted their own bodies. Some of these skin paintings had spiritual meaning, representing a man's personal dreams or visions.

In the plateau areas east of the Sierra Nevada, rock painting was the most common type of art. Rock painting was also found west of the Sierra Nevada, in California. In contrast to the red and black colors used in most parts of North America, the rock paintings in California had many colors. In addition, CALIFORNIA INDIANS made baskets and woven blankets decorated with feather designs.

The Indians of the northwestern coast lived in a region with abundant resources. Wealth was important for social position in their complex societies, and artwork—carvings, masks, blankets, and other decorated objects—was one measure of wealth. The great desire for artworks led to a sophisticated artistic tradition and the rise of professional artists, a development unique among North American Indian cultures. Artists of the Pacific Northwest worked with wood, leather, stone, horn, bone, and copper. Among their finest creations were intricately carved masks, including natural-looking

Remember: *Words in small capital letters have separate entries, and the index at the end of Volume 4 will guide you to more information on many topics.*

portraits of individuals. Such masks often had moving parts and were used in dramatic performances that recounted a family's history and achievements. The famous totem poles of the Indians of the Northwest were tall wooden posts carved and painted with figures that symbolized elements of a family and its history. Families had totem poles made to mark their houses or proclaim their heritage at ceremonial gatherings. Some poles honored famous individuals.

The Indians of the Southwest created a distinctive artistic tradition that included wall painting, basketry, weaving, and pottery. They were particularly noted for their weaving of fabrics and blankets in patterns ranging from simple stripes to complex geometric designs. They also dyed, painted, and embroidered designs on cloth. These Indians were best known, though, for their pottery. While Indians of the Eastern Woodlands cut designs into pottery, Indians of the Southwest painted designs on their pottery. They often used red-on-brown or black-on-white color schemes. The designs included abstract shapes and simple representational forms. As Spanish influence spread in the region, Indian artists also painted flower designs and more realistic images of animals on their pottery. (*See also* **African American Culture; Architecture; Artisans; Crafts; Furniture and Furnishings; Roman Catholic Church; Weaving.**)

Artisans

*A*rtisans—workers skilled in handicrafts—played a vital role in the North American colonies. The European settlements that succeeded did so largely because they had artisans who could provide the skills needed to survive in a new land. Part of the early difficulties of the JAMESTOWN COLONY in Virginia resulted from its lack of skilled workers.

Artisans were found in the British, Dutch, French, and Spanish colonies wherever people gathered for trade or settlement. They provided a wide variety of goods and services, ranging from shoes to oceangoing ships. In rural areas, farmers often practiced a craft part-time. Larger communities might have several artisans who provided basic skills, such as carpentry and blacksmithing, and cities generally had a great variety of specialized crafts workers. By 1700 artisans in Boston, New York, and Philadelphia practiced more than 100 different trades and could produce almost any article available from England.

Crafts and the Economy.   Together with agriculture and trade, the work of artisans formed the heart of the colonial economy. Everyone required the services of artisans or used goods made by them. While some families might make their own CLOTHING or perform other handiwork—especially in the earliest days of settlement and on the frontier—they also relied on the specialized skills of shoemakers, glove makers, hatmakers, weavers, bakers, and brewers. Artisans made everything an individual or business might need—from jewelry, FURNITURE, and gravestones to boxes, barrels, and wagons. Even Europeans used the products made by colonial

* **New France** French colony centered in the St. Lawrence River valley, an area known as Canada; included the Great Lakes region and, until 1713, Acadia (present-day Nova Scotia)

* **Spanish Borderlands** northern part of New Spain, area now occupied by Florida, Texas, New Mexico, Arizona, and California

Santeros

Art and religion merged in the Spanish colonies. Artisans known as *santeros* created religious images and figures, representing Roman Catholic saints and holy scenes. *Santos* were paintings on wooden planks; *bultos* were carved wooden statues. Nearly every home in the region had at least one painting or statue. The artisans were usually farmers or livestock herders who made their *santos* or *bultos* during the winter. Despite a lack of artistic training, the *santeros* created some of the most appealing folk art in the North American colonies.

crafts workers. Before the American Revolution, English and Scottish merchants often bought American-made SHIPS because they were less expensive and longer-lasting than the British-made ones.

Some CRAFTS held a special place in particular regions. In New France*, skilled boatbuilders made the CANOES that helped the French explore the interior of North America and dominate the fur trade for 150 years. In the Spanish Borderlands*, artisans concentrated on products needed for military, religious, and trading purposes by the region's missions and forts. The Borderlands were noted for their ironworkers, who produced weapons and armor, metal rims for wagon wheels, and household goods such as skillets and knives. By the mid-1600s, the Spanish had trained some Native Americans in the arts of metalworking and woodworking. Indian weavers, who were highly skilled artisans long before the Spanish arrived, learned to work with Spanish wool as well as locally produced cotton.

Although the great majority of artisans were men, women also played a role in producing handicrafts. They dominated certain trades, particularly the making of women's clothing. In the Spanish Borderlands, women also made pottery and moccasins.

Becoming an Artisan. Artisans were set apart from manual laborers by their possession of a skill, including knowledge of the materials, tools, techniques, and production processes involved. They gained their skills through an APPRENTICESHIP, a period during which they lived with and learned from a master crafts worker. Through apprenticeship, artisans passed their knowledge and skills from one generation to another and helped provide a continuing supply of skilled workers for colonial society.

Many parents apprenticed their children to master artisans to help them secure a solid financial future. The length of apprenticeship varied, usually beginning around age 13 or 14 and lasting from three to seven years. At the end of this period, young people might work for other master crafts workers to perfect their trade and earn enough money to set up their own businesses.

Artisans and the Community. A key element of a colonial artisan's life was independence. Artisans worked for themselves, even when they joined together in large enterprises, such as shipbuilding, that required many crafts workers. They acted independently, negotiating the terms of their work directly with their customers. They were governed only by the need to complete their projects and by the rules of their trade.

Artisans worked hard—often 10 to 12 hours a day in winter and longer in summer. Most toiled in small shops, often attached to their homes. They had their own tools, purchased their own materials, and often relied on the help of family members and apprentices to produce their goods. Yet they also functioned within a tightly knit community in which techniques, work, and credit were commonly shared among those in a trade. These skilled workers relied on their reputations for their livelihood and well-being. Although few became wealthy, most could expect to provide for their family's needs and to live comfortably.

Colonial artisans viewed their livelihood as something more than just work, and they thought of themselves as more than laborers. In practicing their trades, they believed they contributed valuable services to the communities in which they lived. Such attitudes gave artisans a deep feeling of pride, purpose, and responsibility. Having earned a respected place in society, they believed they were entitled to a voice in community affairs. Along with independent farmers, artisans in the British colonies were among the first to demand greater democracy and independence. (*See also* **Blacksmiths; Crafts; Industries; Labor.**)

Asientos de negros

See *Slave Trade.*

Assemblies

Colonial assemblies, or legislatures, formed the cornerstone of representative government in the British colonies of North America. Each of the colonies had an assembly, elected by property owners. Its members represented local interests and defended the rights of the colonists. In the 1760s and 1770s, conflicts between the assemblies and British officials contributed to the Americans' decision to seek independence from Great Britain.

The earliest colonial assembly, the VIRGINIA HOUSE OF BURGESSES, met for the first time in Jamestown in 1619. Attending the opening session were the governor, the six members of the governor's council, and 20 burgesses—delegates elected from the colony's settlements. Similar assemblies, with different names, appeared throughout the English colonies in the years that followed. In time most colonies had two-house legislatures, with the assembly considered the lower of the two houses. The small upper house, generally the governor's council, consisted of individuals chosen by the assembly or appointed by the governor. The large assembly of elected representatives was viewed as more democratic.

At first colonial assemblies had less authority than governors or the governor's councils. By the mid-1700s, however, the assemblies had begun to expand their powers. They claimed the right to meet separately from the council, to choose their own leaders, to establish committees to investigate issues, and to meet on a regular basis. When the British government tried to take charge of governors' salaries—traditionally paid by the assemblies—the assemblies protested. They realized that control of this money gave them some control over the governors' actions.

While colonial assemblies were trying to expand their authority, often claiming powers that had been exercised by royal governors, the British government moved to reassert the power of the governors. The result was a series of clashes between the colonists and Britain. The failure to resolve these disputes contributed to mounting anger and dissatisfaction in the colonies and in time to the AMERICAN REVOLUTION. (*See also* **Colonial Administration; Government, Provincial; Governors, Colonial.**)

Astrology

Colonial almanacs often included an image of the "Man of Signs." It was believed that the planets and stars influenced different body parts.

---

* *mystical* having secret meaning
* *sign of the zodiac* constellation of stars

Astrology is based on the idea that the movements of the planets and stars influence events on earth, particularly the lives of individuals. Like scores of other beliefs and habits of thought, this very ancient idea traveled to North America with the European colonists.

In the 1600s, astrology was closely linked to ASTRONOMY—the scientific study of the heavenly bodies. Records kept by the JESUITS in Canada show that members of this religious order observed astronomical events, such as comets, with great interest. However, along with the scientific observations, the Jesuits also noted the astrological significance of these events—interpreting the passage of a comet, for example, as a sign of certain things to come on earth. The line between science and magical beliefs was sometimes blurred during the colonial period. Some scholars regarded astrology as a form of mystical* science.

Protestant churches, however, condemned astrology. The idea that people could foretell the future through astrology conflicted with the Christian idea that the future unfolds according to God's will and cannot be predicted by humans. Prominent church leaders in Europe and in the American colonies spoke out against astrology and fortune-telling. But despite the churches' opposition, some forms of astrology enjoyed wide popularity throughout the colonial period. Almanacs, publications featuring calendars and practical advice, often included an astrological image called the man of signs. This image related various parts of the human body to particular signs of the zodiac*. Some almanacs contained other bits of astrology and predictions of the future. These simple astrological features remained in use because many people continued to regard them as significant. (*See also* **Magic and Witchcraft.**)

Astronomy

North American colonists were interested in astronomy—the scientific study of heavenly bodies—mainly for practical reasons. These had to do with NAVIGATION and mapmaking. Knowledge of the positions and movements of the moon, stars, and planets helped navigators tell direction, determine their location on the earth's surface, and follow a course on a MAP. Mapmakers, in turn, relied on the observations of heavenly bodies made by navigators and explorers to create their maps of uncharted areas of the globe.

French missionaries of the JESUIT religious order in Canada were among the most accomplished navigators and mapmakers in North America. Some also kept records of astronomical events. During the 1600s Jesuits observed ten lunar eclipses, seven solar eclipses, and several comets. After 1663, the generous resources of France's Royal Academy of Sciences supported astronomical and mapmaking projects in the French colonies.

One of the biggest scientific questions of the 1700s was the size of the solar system. Astronomers knew that in 1761 and 1769 the planet Venus would pass between the sun and the earth and that careful measurements of the timing of this event—known as the transit of Venus—would help them calculate the size of the solar system. In 1761 teams of European scientists spread across the globe but failed to obtain good measurements. They tried again in

1769, when French astronomers went to Baja California in New Spain to make their observations. British colonists also took part. They published their observations in the journal of the newly formed AMERICAN PHILOSOPHICAL SOCIETY, which reported early American scientific achievements. (*See also* **Astrology; Science.**)

Atlantic Coast

See maps in Exploration, Age of (vol. 2).

Much early European exploration of North America took place along the Atlantic coast. These voyages helped Europeans expand their knowledge of the continent and laid the foundations for major territorial claims.

Norse seafarers reached the northern Atlantic coast as early as 1000 and established settlements in Labrador and NEWFOUNDLAND. In the late 1400s and early 1500s, explorers from England, Spain, and France sailed along the coast in search of the fabled NORTHWEST PASSAGE, a direct water channel to Asia. John Cabot explored the shores of Newfoundland for England in 1497. In 1524 Italian mariner Giovanni da Verrazano, working for France, became the first to sail along the Atlantic coast from Georgia to Newfoundland. Ten years later, French explorer Jacques CARTIER surveyed the area around Canada's Gulf of St. Lawrence.

During their explorations of the Atlantic coast, the Europeans had both friendly and unfriendly contacts with Native Americans. They marveled at the abundance of wildlife and forests, but they did not find GOLD—as many of them had hoped. Nor did the explorers discover a water route to Asia. However, many of the MAPS they made in the course of their explorations remained in use for over 100 years.

In the early 1500s, European seafarers began using the rich fishing grounds off the North Atlantic coast. Colonists arrived next, establishing settlements near the coast and on major rivers with access to the coast. By the late 1600s, Europeans had founded colonies along the entire length of the Atlantic coast from Newfoundland to Florida. Although the French and the Spanish established settlements in other regions of North America, the Atlantic coast remained the primary focus of European colonization until the 1700s. (*See also* **Exploration, Age of; Norse Settlements.**)

Attucks, Crispus

ca. 1723–1770
African American patriot

* *casualty* person who is killed or injured

Crispus Attucks was the leader of an angry mob that clashed with British soldiers in colonial Boston on March 5, 1770. The soldiers opened fire, and Attucks and four other men were killed. The incident, now known as the BOSTON MASSACRE, took place during a period of great tension between the citizens of Boston and the British. It was a significant event in the colonists' fight for independence, and Attucks is sometimes called the first casualty* of the AMERICAN REVOLUTION.

Nothing definite is known about Attucks before the event that led to his death and made him famous. He may have served as a sailor on a whaling ship. Boston was an important seaport, and most of the 50 or 60 men involved in the Boston Massacre were sailors. The only physical description of Attucks that survives comes from John ADAMS, who called him "almost a giant in stature." All accounts of Attucks's death agree that he was a man of color—perhaps a runaway slave or a Natick Indian.

Whatever his background, Attucks became the individual most closely associated with the fateful Boston Massacre. Because of his leadership and death in that incident, he is remembered today as an early martyr* for the cause of American independence. In 1888 a statue honoring Crispus Attucks was erected on Boston Common.

* **martyr** someone who suffers or dies for the sake of a cause or principle

Austin, Stephen

See *Texas.*

Backus, Isaac

See *Protestant Churches: Baptist.*

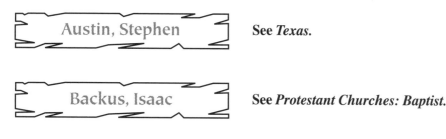

Bacon's Rebellion

* **indentured servant** person who agreed to work a certain length of time in return for passage on a ship to the colonies

Bacon's Rebellion, a revolt of Virginia settlers in 1676, grew out of disagreements over policy toward Native Americans. The rebellion revealed deep-seated divisions in Virginia society between the colonists who owned land and those who wanted to acquire it.

In the 1600s, white settlers in the English colonies lived on uneasy terms with the Indians. The colonial government of VIRGINIA had tried to lessen tensions by granting land north of the York River to the Indians. Some colonists, however, wished to use these lands for settlement. Many former indentured servants*, for example, hoped to acquire their own land. They charged that the wealthy tobacco planters who controlled the government wanted to prevent them from becoming landowners. These divisions between wealthy planters and former servants contributed to the eruption of violence in the 1670s.

In the summer of 1675, some Native Americans on the Virginia frontier killed an English planter who had not paid them for some goods he had purchased. The incident enraged the white settlers. One of their leaders, a young planter named Nathaniel Bacon, demanded that Governor William BERKELEY authorize him to lead troops against the Indians—even friendly ones. When Berkeley denied the request, Bacon acted anyway. With an army of several hundred colonists, Bacon attacked Indian settlements, killing and raiding as he went.

When the governor tried to stop the attacks, Bacon marched his band of followers to the colonial capital at JAMESTOWN and forced the assembly to give him the power he had demanded. As Bacon left to continue his attacks on Indians, Berkeley raised troops of his own. The colony soon found itself engaged in a civil war.

Bacon forced Berkeley to flee Jamestown and then burned the town. For several months Bacon held control in the colony. But when the rebel leader died suddenly of a fever in October, the uprising collapsed. Berkeley struck back, executing some of the rebels and seizing the property of others. Shortly afterward troops arrived from England to help Berkeley regain control. Criticized for these actions, he returned to England in 1677.

Bacon's Rebellion had the greatest effect on Native Americans. Several tribes scattered as a result of the fighting and lost their land to colonists. Future governors of Virginia followed a policy of expansion that cost the Native Americans even more of their land. Some historians argue that the rebellion also produced a change in the colony's labor force. Wealthy planters saw the rebellion as a sign of the difficulty in controlling former indentured servants. They responded by importing more Africans for slave labor, and SLAVERY came to play an even more important role in Virginia's economy. (*See also* **Native Americans.**)

Balboa, Vasco Núñez de

See *Exploration, Age of: Spanish.*

Banking

See *Money and Finance.*

Benjamin Banneker pursued studies in science, math, and astronomy on his own.

Banneker, Benjamin

1731–1806
Inventor, astronomer, and surveyor

*B*enjamin Banneker (also spelled Bannaker) was an African American who made notable contributions to public life immediately after the close of the colonial era. He produced a popular almanac, and he helped survey and plan the new national capital in Washington, D.C.

A FREE BLACK born in Maryland, Banneker attended a private school that was open to black and white students. There he obtained the equivalent of an eighth-grade education. Banneker became a farmer but continued to study science and mathematics and taught himself ASTRONOMY. He was also interested in mechanical devices. With only a pocket watch and a picture of a clock to guide him, he built a wooden clock. This instrument, probably the first clock made entirely of American parts, kept perfect time for several decades.

Using his knowledge of astronomy and mathematics, Banneker predicted the solar eclipse of 1789. Three years later he started publishing an annual almanac, a book that contained tables listing the year's tides and phases of the moon, as well as useful information about crops and medicines and occasional antislavery essays. Banneker sent a copy of his almanac to Thomas JEFFERSON, who courteously acknowledged it.

Banneker is most often remembered for working as a SURVEYOR on the commission that designed the capital of the United States in 1791. He helped select the sites of the White House, the Capitol, the Treasury, and other public buildings. When the head of the commission quit unexpectedly and took away the building plans, Banneker saved the day by reconstructing the plans from memory.

Baptists

See *Protestant Churches.*

Barbados

* **populous** having many inhabitants
* **indigo** plant used to make a blue dye
* **indentured servant** person who agreed to work a certain length of time in return for passage on a ship to the colonies

Barbados, an island in the West Indies, was an English colony that grew prosperous raising sugar. For a while, it was England's most populous* North American colony and its wealthiest. Today Barbados is an independent nation that belongs to the British Commonwealth.

The island was settled in 1625 by the Courteens, a company owned by English and Dutch investors. The investors grew tobacco, cotton, and indigo*, and brought indentured servants* from Europe to work the land. The new workers did not like Barbados. They found the climate difficult, their working conditions harsh, and little land available for settlement in the future. By 1640 the island had about 14,000 indentured servants.

When Barbadians switched to SUGAR production in the 1640s, their need for labor increased enormously, and they imported African slaves to work in the fields. The Dutch had a vital role in this shift. With their experience growing sugar in Brazil, the Dutch supplied the knowledge to launch the sugar industry, the equipment and slaves needed to develop the industry, and the ships to carry the sugar back to Europe.

By the 1650s, the island was a vast sugar plantation, controlled by a small group of wealthy planters and worked by thousands of African slaves. To expand sugar production as much as possible, Barbadians cleared out much of the island's native vegetation, stripping the land of its trees and, in the process, destroying the island's ecology. Then in the 1650s, the English seized Jamaica from the Spaniards and decided to develop the sugar industry there. By the mid-1700s Jamaica had surpassed Barbados in sugar production—and in overall value.

Like the other West Indian colonies, Barbados had a number of important links to the English colonies of mainland North America. It carried on a lively trade with the mainland colonies, exporting sugar, shipping slaves to the southern colonies, and obtaining lumber and food from the northern colonies. In addition, planters from Barbados played an important role in settling SOUTH CAROLINA in the 1670s and opened up a long-lasting connection between the two colonies. (*See also* **Indentured Servants; Slave Trade; West Indies.**)

Barter

See *Money and Finance.*

Bartram, John and William

John	William
1699–1777	1739–1823
Naturalist	Naturalist

* **naturalist** person who studies plants and animals in their natural surroundings

John Bartram and his son William were two of the most prominent naturalists* in British North America. John Bartram achieved fame in the colonies and Europe for his study of plants. William Bartram won wide recognition for a book containing descriptions and illustrations of various species* of plants and animals of the southern colonies.

Raised on a farm in Pennsylvania, John Bartram became interested in botany as a child. He gained a detailed knowledge of plants by collecting different varieties and by reading books. He studied Latin so that he could understand scientific texts on medicinal plants. In 1728 Bartram purchased some land on the banks of the Schuylkill River near Philadelphia and began the first botanical garden in the colonies. The garden included species from throughout the British colonies and from Great Britain. Bartram carried out

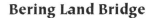

* **species** group of plants or animals with similar characteristics
* **hybridize** to mix different species to produce a new species

some of the earliest experiments in hybridizing* plants there. Many notable people, including George Washington, visited the famous botanical garden. Today it is part of the Philadelphia park system, and some of the trees planted by Bartram can still be seen.

Bartram traveled widely in North America, collecting samples and studying plant, animal, and insect life. He once suggested to his friend Benjamin FRANKLIN that someone should travel west to study that vast unexplored region of North America. Franklin passed the idea to Thomas JEFFERSON, who sent explorers Meriwether Lewis and William Clark on such an expedition after he became President.

Bartram's son William had considerable artistic talent. Accompanying his father on a trip to northeastern Florida, William drew illustrations of the plant and animal species they observed. Some of these sketches reached the hands of an English botanist, who gave William money for further explorations in the Southeast. The American Revolution interrupted William's work, but in 1791 he published an account of his travels. His book gained wide circulation in North America and Europe and influenced writers and scientists.

William continued to study the natural world throughout his life. His studies provided much of the material for a work on medicinal plants, and his drawings were used for a text on the scientific study of plants. He also compiled the first extensive list of native North American birds, numbering 215 species. (*See also* **Science.**)

Beaver

See *Fur Trade; Wildlife.*

Benezet, Anthony

See *Antislavery Movement.*

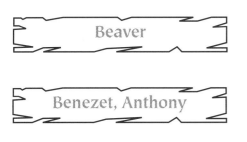

Bering Land Bridge

Asia and North America once were connected by a corridor of land known as the Bering Land Bridge. According to scientific theories, the ancestors of the Native Americans came across this bridge to the Americas from northeastern Asia in many waves over thousands of years.

The Bering Land Bridge linked Alaska and Siberia in Russia from about 100,000 to 15,000 years ago. During that time, great sheets of ice covered sections of the globe. The level of the oceans was lower, exposing land in areas now covered by sea. The Bering Land Bridge, a windy plain with many shallow river valleys, emerged during this period. Today the land is under the waters of the Bering Strait.

Nothing is known of the early peoples who made the crossing from Asia. In all likelihood, they wandered across the plain in search of game animals rather than to find new lands to settle. Their way of life required large hunting territories, and they traveled long distances in search of food.

As they migrated, these peoples joined together to form families and then split up to create new groups. Their descendants gradually spread out and populated all of North and South America, creating many different cultures and languages. By the time Europeans arrived in the Americas in the late 1400s, about 2,000 different native civilizations flourished throughout the Americas, all descended from ancient hunters and gatherers who had traveled across the Bering Land Bridge. (*See also* **Native Americans.**)

Berkeley, Sir William

1606–1677
English colonial governor

*G*overnor of colonial VIRGINIA for over 25 years, Sir William Berkeley was an able but unpopular leader. Although he managed to strengthen the colony's economy and defense, his policies led to discontent and contributed to the uprising known as BACON'S REBELLION.

Berkeley came from a prominent English family. In 1642 King Charles I sent him to Virginia to serve as governor. During his first years in office, Berkeley achieved a number of successes. He reduced conflict among groups of settlers, encouraged farmers to plant a variety of crops, and promoted the development of local textile manufacturing. Berkeley also encouraged exploration of Virginia's western frontiers and, after defeating Native Americans who lived in the region, he forged peace with them. At the same time, however, Berkeley persecuted QUAKERS and PURITANS, forcing many to leave Virginia.

In the 1640s, a civil war erupted in England between the king and groups who wanted to reform the government. After the reformers gained power in 1652, Berkeley lost his position as Virginia's governor. When the monarchy was restored in England in 1660, Berkeley again became governor.

On his return to office, Berkeley established tight control over Virginia's government and took away many of the colonists' rights. Opposition to Berkeley's rule grew. Many colonists resented his policy of setting some lands aside for Native Americans to keep the peace. Some colonists wanted to settle on these undeveloped lands themselves. In 1676 the conflicts came to a head with an uprising known as Bacon's Rebellion. Supported by groups of angry colonists, a young planter named Nathaniel Bacon led raids against the Indians. When Berkeley refused to support Bacon, the rebel leader took control of Jamestown—Virginia's capital—and forced the governor to flee. After Bacon died and the rebellion collapsed, Berkeley regained control. He ordered the execution of many of the rebels and seized the property of others. His harsh actions brought criticism from government officials in England, who ordered him back to England. He died there a short time later. (*See also* **Colonial Administration; Government, Provincial.**)

Bible

*T*he Bible had an enormous influence on colonial life, especially in the British and Dutch colonies founded by Protestants. The Bible shaped the moral and cultural life of the colonists and served as a basic tool in education.

Translations. Until the 1500s, the Bibles used by the Christians of western Europe were written in Latin or Greek. As a result, only the clergy* and well-educated people could read the Holy Scriptures. Then scholars began to

* *clergy* ministers, priests, and other church officials

translate the Bible into German, French, Italian, and English. The Geneva Bible appeared in 1560. It was written by English Protestants who had fled to Geneva, Switzerland, to avoid persecution by the Catholic queen of England. Affordable and small enough to carry, the Geneva Bible became enormously popular. The PURITANS brought it with them to America, and it remained the most common Bible in New England throughout the colonial period.

A new translation that appeared in 1611 became the official Bible of the Anglican Church of England. Known as the King James Version, it began to replace the Geneva Bible in many American colonies. Like the Geneva Bible, the King James Bible was both readable and affordable. Dutch settlers in New Netherland had a version of the Bible in their own language, as did German settlers in Pennsylvania.

Role of the Bible.   The Puritans regarded the Bible as the only true spiritual guide and a model for their behavior and culture. They saw Puritan society as a "city upon a hill," a source of inspiration for other peoples. Their sermons, letters, and other writings often included biblical phrases, characters, and stories. The Puritans believed that their experiences in the colonies were an extension of biblical history and sometimes compared their leaders to biblical figures.

In all the Protestant colonies, the Bible was read regularly in schools and at home. Parents considered the education of their children to be incomplete unless it included moral and spiritual lessons from the Scriptures. This widespread use of the Bible encouraged the spread of LITERACY in the colonies.

The Bible influenced many of the literary works produced in the colonial period—whether diaries, poems, histories, or biographies. Colonial LITERATURE often contained biblical subjects and themes as well as references and comparisons to biblical figures. In many cases, the style reflected the language of the Scriptures. In New England, a form of writing called sermon literature directly expressed biblical beliefs and teachings.

An important religious goal in much of colonial America was to convert the Native Americans to Christianity. Roman Catholics in New France* and the Spanish Borderlands* made great efforts to achieve this end. Although Protestants in the English colonies conducted less missionary activity than the Spanish or French, they did translate the Bible into the Algonquian language spoken by the Indians of Massachusetts. Printed in 1663, this was the first Bible produced in America. The colonists continued to import their own Bibles from Europe, and the first English-language Bible printed in America did not appear until the 1780s. (*See also* **Education; Missions and Missionaries; Protestant Churches; Religious Life in European Colonies; Roman Catholic Church.**)

* *New France* French colony centered in the St. Lawrence River valley, an area known as Canada; included the Great Lakes region and, until 1713, Acadia (present-day Nova Scotia)

* *Spanish Borderlands* northern part of New Spain, area now occupied by Florida, Texas, New Mexico, Arizona, and California

Billings, William

1746–1800
Choirmaster and composer

William Billings was an important figure in early American music. He taught singing, led the choirs of several prominent Boston churches, and wrote numerous hymns and other types of songs that became very popular during his lifetime.

A leather maker by trade, Billings had little schooling and no formal training in music. Nevertheless, his love of music and his belief in his own talent inspired him to write and publish choral music. At the time, church music consisted of a small number of melodies that were used again and again. Billings sang in a church choir and knew that new material was needed. He provided the choirs with five music books, beginning in 1770 with *The New England Psalm-Singer or American Chorister* that included 127 of his own compositions. As one scholar has observed, *The New England Psalm-Singer* was a remarkable document in the history of American music.

A passionate patriot, Billings wrote some songs celebrating the American struggle for independence. In his role as a singing teacher, Billings trained the choirs at several leading churches in Boston. His influence as a choirmaster was wide and long-lasting. The singing school Billings founded in 1774 became the oldest musical society in America. His example also encouraged other Americans to write and publish their own music.

Billings helped transform choral music from merely a part of religious services into a lively and popular art form. Despite his great influence on colonial music, he died forgotten and in poverty. (*See also* **Music and Dance.**)

Blackfoot Indians

See *Plains Indians.*

Blacksmiths

Blacksmiths were important crafts workers in colonial communities. Working with iron and flame, they produced many everyday items.

Blacksmiths, sometimes called smiths, are crafts workers who make tools and other items from iron. During the colonial period, they played a vital role in their communities, producing a great many items that people used in everyday life.

Found in almost every town and city, blacksmiths made metal shoes for oxen and horses and put them on the animals. They produced the metal parts of bridles, saddles, harnesses, and wagons. They also crafted hammers, nails, axes, chisels, and other tools, as well as kitchen utensils, hinges, locks, and latches. In addition, blacksmiths fashioned ice skates, toy wagons, doll carriages, and decorative ironwork for fences and gates.

As colonial economies became more complex, increasing numbers of smiths began to work in specialized fields, such as locksmithing and gunsmithing. Some of the most skilled workers became expert at crafting precise and intricate items for ships. Ships setting out on long voyages often carried their own blacksmiths to make repairs at sea.

Blacksmithing was a physically demanding job, and many smiths were noted for their strength as well as their skill. Their equipment included a forge*, an anvil, hammers, and other metalworking tools. Smiths heated the iron in the forge until it became soft. Then, using tongs, they placed the red-hot iron on the anvil and hammered or cut the metal into shape, reheating it when necessary to keep it workable. Once formed, the metal was left to cool and harden.

The Spanish colonies of North America suffered from a lack of iron ore and a shortage of blacksmiths, and iron hardware had to be brought from Spain or elsewhere. Local blacksmiths learned to reuse everything—melting down old horseshoes to make nails, for example. Spanish missionaries taught blacksmithing to Native Americans, who became quite skillful. (*See also* **Artisans.**)

* *forge* special furnace or fireplace in which metal is heated before it is shaped

Board of Trade

See *Colonial Administration: British; Parliament.*

Books

The early European settlers of North America valued books and reading highly. Many had been persuaded to move to the colonies by publications describing the riches and opportunities that awaited them on the other side of the Atlantic Ocean. Adventure tales and historical novels inspired other Europeans, especially the Spaniards, to seek their fortunes in the Americas. Many colonists carried their BIBLES and prayer books with them. Once settled in their new homes, most made it a priority to teach their children to read.

Printers and Publishers. Spanish missionaries established a printing press in Mexico City in the early 1500s. The first press in the British colonies was brought from England by the Reverend Jose Glover in 1638. Although Glover died during the voyage, his widow set up the press in Cambridge, Massachusetts, with the help of Stephen Day and his son.

Printing and book publishing was usually a family business. Family members, apprentices, and sometimes slaves helped with the work. The printer usually made his home in the same building that housed the printing equipment. In the front was a shop for selling books, NEWSPAPERS, MAGAZINES, and other products. Sometimes a woman took over a printing business on the death of a husband or father. Cornelia Bradford, Ann Franklin, Sarah Updike GODDARD, and Mary Katherine Goddard were among the women who succeeded as printers in colonial times. Besides their regular work, printers often took on the job of local postmaster.

Boston was the first book publishing center, followed by New York and Philadelphia. As settlers moved west, the printing and publishing business moved with them. By the time of the American Revolution, communities throughout the British colonies had their own local printers.

Benjamin FRANKLIN was the best known and most successful printer in the British colonies. After training as an apprentice to his brother in Boston, he started his own printing business in Philadelphia in 1729. Apprentices and employees of Franklin later established printing houses in such places as New York, Charleston, and Antigua in the West Indies.

Colonial Publications. The first materials printed in North America were prepared for churches and governments. Colonial governments needed printers to publish their laws and official documents. Churches wanted religious materials printed. The *Whole Booke of Psalms Faithfully Translated into English Metre,* the earliest book that has survived from the colonial period, is a collection of biblical psalms translated from Hebrew. Printed by the Day family of Cambridge in 1640, it became known as the *Bay Psalm Book.* The first Bible printed in the English colonies, a translation in the Algonquian language of Native Americans, appeared in 1663.

Printers soon began to produce textbooks, almanacs, and works on history, geography, and law, as well as newspapers, magazines, and announcements of all kinds. In the late 1600s, books about the great fire in London and

Colonial Best-Sellers

One of the first books to become a best-seller in the English colonies was the *Bay Psalm Book*, printed in 1640. Mary Rowlandson's 1682 account of her captivity by Indians was another colonial favorite. In the mid-1700s, colonists made Benjamin Franklin's *Poor Richard's Almanack* a best-seller. However, along with the Bible, the *New England Primer* (1687) topped the list of colonial favorites. Combining the alphabet with prayers and moral lessons, the primer sold 3 to 5 million copies.

the eruption of a volcano in Sicily were published in the colonies. Until the 1770s, colonial printers issued mainly pamphlet-sized books. Most of the large books read by the settlers were imported from Britain, where printers had the necessary equipment.

Almanacs were extremely popular in the colonies. At first they were primarily calendars with advice and observations about farming, the weather, and tides. In time, many printers began to use the almanacs to express their views on such topics as politics and religion. Most printers issued at least one almanac a year.

The most famous almanac was Ben Franklin's *Poor Richard's Almanack,* first printed in 1732. Poor Richard, a fictional character created by Franklin, gave shrewd advice in witty maxims, or sayings. For example, "Early to bed, and early to rise, makes a man healthy, wealthy, and wise." (*See also* **Apprenticeship; Education; Libraries and Learned Societies; Literature; Rowlandson, Mary.**)

Boston

Boston—today the capital of the state of MASSACHUSETTS—was one of the first major settlements in British North America. Founded by PURITANS from England who came in search of religious freedom, the settlement quickly grew into an important colonial city. In the mid-1700s, Boston became a center of opposition to British colonial policies and a leader in the movement for American independence.

Founding the City. In 1614 the English adventurer Captain John SMITH explored and mapped the area that became Boston. During the 1620s a group of settlers from the PLYMOUTH COLONY moved to the area, but a new settlement failed to take root. Eventually, only one person remained, a minister named William Blackstone.

* **charter** written grant from a ruler conferring certain rights and privileges

In 1629 King Charles I of England granted a charter* to the Massachusetts Bay Company to establish a colony in New England. By the end of the following year, more than 1,000 Puritans had left England for the Massachusetts Bay colony. One group led by a lawyer named John WINTHROP settled at Charlestown on the Charles River. After discovering that the water supply was inadequate, these colonists moved their settlement to Shawmut Peninsula on the other side of the river. They called their new home Trimountaine because of three hills that dominated the landscape. Several months later, they changed the name to Boston, after a town in England that had been the home of many Puritan leaders. Over the next ten years, thousands of Puritans migrated to the Massachusetts Bay colony from England. Many chose to settle in Boston, and the town grew quickly. It became the capital of the colony in 1632.

Political and Religious Life. The Puritans ruled Boston as a religious community during the early years of its history. They hoped to build what John Winthrop, the colony's first governor, called a "city upon a hill," a community devoted to God and hard work that others would look to as a model and inspiration. They established a government in which only property-owning Puritans could vote, and all government officials had close ties to church leaders. Moreover, the Puritans did not allow religious dissent*. Settlers who

* **dissent** opposition to or disagreement with established beliefs

Faneuil Hall, known as the Cradle of Liberty, was a market and meeting place in the center of Boston. Many colonial protests against unpopular British laws began here.

challenged their religious authority—such as Roger WILLIAMS and Anne HUTCHINSON—had to leave the colony or were banished from it.

In the 1680s, the English monarchy attempted to assert its authority over Boston and the Massachusetts Bay colony. King James II canceled the charter of Massachusetts in 1684 and appointed a royal governor, Sir Edmund ANDROS, for the colony. These actions led to a period of political unrest that ended in 1689, after the king was removed from the throne. Boston citizens then arrested Governor Andros, forced him to leave the colony, and restored the old colonial government. By this time, however, the population of Boston had changed and included many non-Puritans. These colonists now played a much greater role in the city's government.

Commercial Center.   Favored with an excellent harbor, Boston became a leading seaport in the British colonies. Although shipbuilding was one of its major industries, the city also developed into an important commercial center with an economy based on foreign trade. Boston merchants exported fish, furs, and timber products and imported a variety of European goods, such as furniture, books, paper, cloth, sugar, tea, and wine. Some merchants became involved in the SLAVE TRADE.

The city's economic activities helped fuel the growth of its population. In 1700 Boston had about 7,000 residents, making it the largest urban area in the English colonies. Although New York and Philadelphia soon surpassed it in size, Boston remained a vital urban center. Its population had become increasingly diverse, with people of many ethnic backgrounds and occupations. Boston society had distinct class divisions, with wealthy merchants and professionals at the top, artisans* and shopkeepers in the middle, and a large population of laborers at the bottom.

* *artisan* skilled crafts worker

73

* **clergy** ministers, priests, and other church officials

Cultural Center. During the colonial period, Boston became one of the most important intellectual and cultural centers in the British colonies. The first public school in the colonies, the Boston Latin School, was established in 1635. The following year, the city's Puritan leaders founded the first college in the colonies, Harvard College, to train members of the clergy*. Boston claimed a number of other colonial firsts. It had the first colonial post office, opened in 1639, and the first newspaper, the *Boston News-Letter,* which began in 1704.

After the 1720s, Boston became the art center of the British colonies as well. British artists, such as John Smibert, were invited to live and work in the city. Smibert founded an art school in Boston that influenced John Singleton COPLEY, who went on to become one of the most important painters of the colonial period.

Boston also became noted for its ARCHITECTURE. The State House, built in 1713, was an elegant brick structure built to house the government of Massachusetts. The Old North Church (1723) became the first church in North America to include a pointed steeple. Faneuil Hall (1742) held a market in the lower levels with a meeting hall above. Some of these buildings also played a role in the events leading up to American independence.

Opposition to British Rule. Boston became one of the earliest and most fervent centers of opposition to British colonial policies. In 1760 Boston lawyer James OTIS argued passionately against the issuing of writs of assistance—documents that allowed British officials to enter homes and search for smuggled goods. Samuel ADAMS helped organize opposition to the STAMP ACT passed by the British Parliament in 1765, which required people in the colonies to pay taxes on printed documents. The colonists considered this "taxation without representation" because they had no representatives in Parliament to speak on their behalf. Great Britain responded to increasing opposition in Boston by stationing troops in the city. The presence of troops only heightened tensions and led to the BOSTON MASSACRE of 1770, in which British soldiers fired on Boston citizens, killing five people.

A period of quiet followed the Boston Massacre, but opposition flared again when Britain passed the TEA ACT OF 1773. Resistance to the act in Boston led to the BOSTON TEA PARTY, a bold defiance of British authority. Outraged, the British Parliament punished Boston with a series of laws that colonists called the INTOLERABLE ACTS. Although these harsh laws targeted Boston, they also led to increased opposition against Britain throughout the colonies.

The opening events of the AMERICAN REVOLUTION also took place in the area around Boston. A Boston patriot, Paul REVERE, made his famous ride to warn neighboring communities of British troop movements. The Battles of LEXINGTON AND CONCORD occurred a few miles west of the city, and the Battle of BUNKER HILL took place in Charlestown across the Charles River from Boston. British troops occupied Boston in the early months of the war. However, when colonial forces surrounded the city in early 1776, the British troops retreated to Canada. Boston saw no fighting for the remainder of the war, but its leaders continued to play an important political role in colonial affairs. (*See also* **Colonial Administration.**)

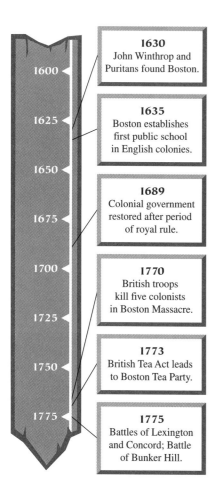

1630
John Winthrop and Puritans found Boston.

1635
Boston establishes first public school in English colonies.

1689
Colonial government restored after period of royal rule.

1770
British troops kill five colonists in Boston Massacre.

1773
British Tea Act leads to Boston Tea Party.

1775
Battles of Lexington and Concord; Battle of Bunker Hill.

1600
1625
1650
1675
1700
1725
1750
1775

Boston Massacre

*T*he Boston Massacre, an incident in which British troops fired into a crowd and killed several colonists, was part of the series of events that led to the American Revolution. This violent clash of 1770 intensified major tensions between Great Britain and the American colonists.

The Boston Massacre came about because British authorities were determined to keep tight control over the economic and political life of the colonies. The colonists, meanwhile, grew increasingly impatient with rules forced on them by officials in London. They began to express their discontent in the 1760s. When Parliament gave customs officials permission to enter colonial homes and warehouses at any time, many colonists protested that their liberty had been violated. James OTIS of Boston, a Massachusetts lawyer and politician, stirred resentment against the British with passionate speeches reminding the colonists that "an Englishman's home is his castle." Responding to these speeches, Massachusetts patriot—and future American President—John ADAMS observed, "Then and there the child independence was born."

Boston became a center of resistance to British rules and regulations, including the hated TOWNSHEND ACTS OF 1767. These laws imposed heavy taxes on imported goods such as paper, paint, lead, and tea. A group of Bostonians that included Samuel ADAMS, John Adams's cousin, began to promote the idea that Britain had no right to claim sovereignty* over the colonies, and they encouraged the public to defy British rules. Many citizens responded by refusing to buy or use the heavily taxed items.

* ***sovereignty*** supreme power or authority

The Boston Massacre—as depicted by Paul Revere's famous engraving of 1770—was a violent demonstration of the growing conflict between the colonists and the British government.

In October 1768, Britain responded to the mounting defiance of the colonists by sending four regiments of troops to Boston to keep its unruly citizens in line. The arrival of these troops only increased the tension and, in the months that followed, friction led to a number of angry clashes between colonists and soldiers.

The situation in Boston came to a head on March 5, 1770. That evening, a crowd of citizens began taunting a soldier guarding the customs house. Seven other British soldiers, led by Captain Thomas Preston, joined the guard. Meanwhile, the crowd became larger and more unruly, and it bombarded the soldiers with snowballs. Unable to disperse the crowd, Preston ordered his men, "Don't fire." The crowd responded by yelling, "Fire and be damned!" In the confusion of the moment, the soldiers fired into the crowd. When the gun smoke cleared, three men lay dead, including the crowd's leader, Crispus ATTUCKS. Two other men died later of their wounds.

Local resistance leaders spread the news of the "Boston Massacre"—as they called it—throughout the colonies. They used the incident to fan the flames of public anger against the British. Samuel Adams led a committee of citizens who demanded that the British remove all troops from Boston. The acting governor, Thomas HUTCHINSON, at first refused but finally agreed to their demands. The British government responded to the crisis by canceling the Townshend taxes, except for the tax on tea.

In October 1770, Captain Preston and the soldiers involved in the incident went on trial for murder. Despite public outrage, colonial officials made every effort to give them a fair trial. John Adams was one of the attorneys who agreed to defend the British troops. Although Adams hated what the soldiers had done, he believed that everyone deserved equal treatment under the law. A Boston jury acquitted Captain Preston and six soldiers. Two other soldiers were found guilty of manslaughter, branded on the hand, and released.

The Boston Massacre contributed to worsening relations between the colonists and the British government. Within two years, the British announced new laws to govern the colonies more tightly. Colonial resistance—fueled by the knowledge that British troops had fired upon unarmed civilians—continued to grow. (*See also* **American Revolution; Boston; Independence Movements.**)

Boston Tea Party

* *sovereignty* supreme power or authority

On the night of December 16, 1773, a group of angry Massachusetts colonists threw a cargo of British tea into Boston harbor. The event, which came to be known as the Boston Tea Party, was a bold gesture of defiance against British authority and a giant step on the road to independence from Great Britain.

Since the 1760s, American colonists had been clashing with Britain over the issues of sovereignty* and taxation. Many Americans wanted greater freedom to run their own affairs, and they objected to British taxes. Britain, meanwhile, remained determined to keep control of the political and economic life of its colonies. Boston became a center of resistance to British authority. Its citizens loudly protested the SUGAR ACT OF 1764, which raised the tax on foreign sugar and imposed restrictions on colonial shipping. They also took a leading role in the STAMP ACT CRISIS of 1765, a protest against taxes on printed documents. Tensions worsened in 1770 when British soldiers shot into a Boston crowd, killing five people. Colonists called the incident the BOSTON MASSACRE.

In an attempt to calm the situation, the British Parliament canceled certain taxes that had angered the colonists. Parliament did maintain the tax on tea, however, partly as a symbol of its right to tax the colonies. Many Americans stopped buying tea in protest, while others bought tea supplied by Dutch smugglers. In 1773 Parliament passed the TEA ACT to help the BRITISH EAST INDIA COMPANY. This trading company was already in serious financial trouble. Although the act did not remove the tea tax, it allowed the East India Company to sell its tea more cheaply than the smuggled Dutch tea.

Both American patriots and merchants had reason to oppose the Tea Act. Merchants worried about losing profits on the reduced price of tea. Patriots feared that if colonists resumed buying the taxed tea, Parliament would take this as confirmation of their right to tax Americans and would impose other new taxes.

When the tea ship *Dartmouth* arrived in Boston harbor on November 28, 1773, American patriots prevented it from unloading its cargo. About 5,000 colonists then met at Boston's Old South Church and passed a resolution demanding that the tea be returned to Britain. The ship's owner agreed. However, Thomas HUTCHINSON, the colony's governor, refused to allow the *Dartmouth*—and two other tea ships that arrived later—to leave the harbor. Hutchinson's decision enraged colonial patriots, and led by Samuel ADAMS they decided to take action. At nightfall on December 16, some 60 men disguised as Indians headed for the waterfront with shouts of: "Boston harbor a tea-pot this night." They boarded the tea ships and threw 342 chests of tea overboard. A large crowd of spectators cheered the action from the docks.

News of the Boston Tea Party soon reached other colonies. In New York and Philadelphia, colonists avoided an open clash by persuading tea ships to return to Britain without unloading their cargoes. But a few other "tea parties" did take place. In April 1774 New Yorkers dumped British tea into their harbor, and patriots in Annapolis, Maryland, forced the destruction of a ship and its cargo of tea.

After the Boston Tea Party, Parliament passed a series of harsh laws that became known in the colonies as the INTOLERABLE ACTS. Though designed primarily to punish Boston, the laws united people throughout the colonies in opposition to Britain. Colonial ASSEMBLIES passed resolutions supporting Massachusetts, and many colonists began to boycott* other British goods. This spirit of unity and defiance widened the gulf between Britain and the colonies and paved the way for the outbreak of the AMERICAN REVOLUTION.

Remember: *Words in small capital letters have separate entries, and the index at the end of Volume 4 will guide you to more information on many topics.*

See color plate 6, vol. 4.

* ***boycott*** refusal to buy goods as a means of protest

Bourbon Reforms

See *Independence Movements; Mexico; Spain.*

Boycotts

See *Trade and Commerce: British.*

Braddock, Edward

1695–1755
British general

* *militia* army of citizens who may be called into action in a time of emergency

A skilled officer of the British army, Edward Braddock came to the North American colonies determined to win a great victory in the FRENCH AND INDIAN WAR, the American part of a larger conflict between Great Britain and France. Instead, Braddock died in a stunning defeat.

At the age of 15, Edward Braddock joined the famous British regiment of the Coldstream Guards, and he rose through the ranks to become a general. He learned the art of war in battles against the French in Europe. Unfortunately, this experience would prove useless in his North American campaign.

The British and the French were wrestling for power in North America. The French controlled the land west of the Appalachian Mountains, but British traders and settlers began to move into this area. In 1754 George WASHINGTON, at the head of a Virginia militia*, tried to force the French to abandon FORT DUQUESNE, located near present-day Pittsburgh. Instead, the Virginians were defeated. The British decided to send Braddock and two regiments from the regular army to fight the French.

Braddock prepared to march west to take Fort Duquesne. Although warned by colonial leaders that fighting the French and their Indian allies in the woods was not the same as a military battle on the plains of Europe, Braddock would not listen. Nor did he pay attention to the Indian scouts who traveled with his forces. Frustrated by Braddock's high-handed treatment, the Indians left his army.

On July 9, 1755, a few miles from Fort Duquesne, French troops accompanied by Canadians and Indians ambushed Braddock's army. The attack turned into an overwhelming defeat for the British, and half the British force died in the fighting. Braddock was fatally wounded and had to be carried away in the retreat. He died four days later.

Bradford, William

ca. 1590–1657
Leader of Plymouth colony

William Bradford was a leader of the PILGRIMS who established PLYMOUTH COLONY, the second English colony in North America. As governor for 30 years, he helped Plymouth survive a difficult beginning. He also wrote a history of the colony's early struggles.

Life in England. Born in northern England, Bradford began to study the Bible in his youth. He joined the SEPARATISTS, a group of English Protestants who chose to separate themselves from the Anglican Church of England. Because of their beliefs, the Separatists faced hostility and even punishment by English authorities.

Bradford and some other Separatists moved to the Netherlands, where they would be free to practice their religion in peace. But after 11 years, they decided to leave. The Separatists had trouble finding work in the Netherlands, and they wanted their children to grow up in an English-speaking society.

One of the Pilgrims on the *Mayflower,* William Bradford helped found the Plymouth colony. He was later elected governor—30 times for one-year terms—and proved to be a capable and well-liked leader.

They obtained financial support from a group of English investors sponsoring settlements in North America. They then received permission to establish a colony on the northern edge of territory claimed by the VIRGINIA COMPANY. Bradford helped in the preparations for the voyage. In September 1620, he set sail from England on the *Mayflower* with 35 Separatists—who became known as Pilgrims—and 66 other passengers who did not share the Separatists' religious views.

Plymouth Colony. When the ship reached North America, Bradford and 40 other passengers signed the MAYFLOWER COMPACT, in which they agreed to accept whatever government would be established for their colony. Not long after their arrival, Bradford's wife died. Despite his grief, Bradford accompanied a group that landed in Massachusetts and chose Plymouth as the place to settle. The location had many advantages. The harbor was deep, the hills had plenty of trees for building and fuel, and a clear stream ran nearby. Because the site had been a Native American village, much of the area was already cleared for farming.

Nevertheless, the Pilgrims faced many problems. They had arrived in the midst of a harsh New England winter. Food was scarce and supplies low, and many people became ill. About half of the settlers died that first winter, including the governor, John Carver. The settlers chose Bradford as their new governor.

The local WAMPANOAG INDIANS helped the Pilgrims survive the first winter by teaching them how to plant corn and catch fish to use for fertilizer. Bradford signed a peace treaty with Massasoit, the Wampanoag chief, and the treaty remained unbroken for many years. Massasoit even warned the Pilgrims when other tribes were preparing to attack.

Despite this aid, the colonists continued to struggle. One reason for their difficulty was the contract they had signed with the English investors who financed the colony. According to this contract, the investors received all the income from the colony. In 1627 Bradford joined a group of Pilgrims and English merchants in buying out the contract. They became owners of all the land, houses, tools, and cattle in Plymouth. Instead of keeping this property, they divided it among all the settlers, including those who were not Pilgrims.

As governor of the colony, Bradford had a great deal of power. He made the laws, enforced them, and acted as judge. The colonists were pleased with his leadership and elected Bradford governor for 30 one-year terms between 1621 and 1656. But Bradford did not receive a salary for this demanding work until 1639.

Later Years. In 1630 the Great Migration began—thousands of PURITANS came from England and settled north of Plymouth, in and around Boston. Their arrival helped the Pilgrims, who sold them food. Bradford welcomed the new settlers, although their leaders often treated him rudely. The Puritans also presented a threat to Plymouth's continued independence. Between 1630 and 1651, Bradford wrote his *History of Plimoth Plantation.* The book describes the struggles of the colony and reveals Bradford's deep faith in God. He tells of crises the colony faced and how these were resolved. Each time,

Bradford writes, "Behold now another providence [blessing] of God." (*See also* **Massachusetts; Protestant Churches.**)

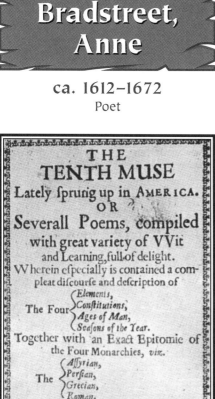

Bradstreet, Anne

ca. 1612–1672
Poet

Anne Bradstreet's poetry was collected in a volume called *The Tenth Muse*. The title refers to Sappho of Lesbos, the first great female poet of European literature.

*A*nne Bradstreet was the first English woman in America to have a book of poetry published. Her letters and other writings give insights into the life of the early settlers in Massachusetts. Much of Bradstreet's work was devoted to nature and the love of God.

The daughter of a prosperous PURITAN family in England, Anne married Simon Bradstreet when she was 16. In 1630 the Bradstreets joined the Puritans who went to America with John WINTHROP. They settled first in Ipswich and then in North Andover. Brought up in a comfortable home in England, Anne Bradstreet was disappointed by the rough conditions of colonial life. She wrote that at first she rebelled against the fate that had brought her to America. "But after I was convinced it was the way of God," she added, "I submitted to it."

"The way of God" was the subject of many of Bradstreet's poems, as it was of much literature of the 1600s. In "Contemplations," now considered her finest work, she described how the beauty of the natural landscape awakens an awareness and love of God. She also dealt with such subjects as the seasons, the history of the world, and the joys of married life. In "To My Dear and Loving Husband," Bradstreet wrote:

> *If ever two were one, then surely we.*
> *If ever man were loved by wife, then thee;*
> *If ever wife was happy in a man,*
> *Compare with me, ye women, if you can.*

She shared the common belief of her time that men were superior to women and that women should submit to male authority. Still, although the literary world was dominated by male writers, Bradstreet claimed that women had the right to express themselves in poetry. She wrote:

> *Men can do best, and women know it well.*
> *Preeminence [superiority] in all and each is yours;*
> *Yet grant some small acknowledgment of ours.*

She collected her early poems into a book called *The Tenth Muse*, published in London in 1650. Bradstreet's poems were widely read and admired. (*See also* **Literature.**)

Brant, Joseph

1742–1807
Mohawk war leader

*J*oseph Brant, a Mohawk Indian chief, fought on the side of the British during the American Revolution. His Indian name was Thayendanegea. Brant's close ties to the British developed because his sister, Molly, was the housekeeper and mistress of Sir William JOHNSON, the British superintendent of Indian affairs. As a teenager, Brant accompanied Johnson on campaigns against the French in the FRENCH AND INDIAN WAR.

Joseph Brant was a Mohawk chief who encouraged the Iroquois Confederacy to fight alongside the British during the American Revolution.

From 1761 to 1762, Brant attended the Reverend Eleazar WHEELOCK's school for Indians in Lebanon, Connecticut. He converted to Christianity and worked as an interpreter and translator for missionaries. When the Ottawa chief PONTIAC led an uprising against the British in 1763, Brant sided with the British. In 1775 Brant went to London, where he met King George III and other British leaders.

Brant returned to America at the outbreak of the Revolution. He urged the powerful IROQUOIS CONFEDERACY, of which the Mohawks were a part, to fight alongside the British against the rebellious Americans. He became the war leader of the pro-British Iroquois in the Mohawk River valley. For five years, Brant and his forces fought battles and attacked American settlements in New York, Pennsylvania, and Ohio—sometimes on their own, sometimes in league with British troops.

At the end of the Revolution, Brant had no desire to remain in the newly independent United States. He and 2,000 other pro-British Indians moved to Canada, where they received from the British government a large tract of land along Ontario's Grand River. Brant spent his remaining years translating Christian texts into Mohawk and urging his followers to become Christians. At the same time, he was proud of his Native American background and tried to help Indians in the United States defend their rights in conflicts with white settlers. (*See also* **American Revolution.**)

Brant, Molly

See *Brant, Joseph; Johnson, Sir William.*

Brent, Margaret

ca. 1601–ca. 1671
Feminist and administrator

* *feminist* person who supports equal rights for women

* *executor* person responsible for carrying out the instructions in a will

Margaret Brent was a strong-willed and capable woman who has been called America's first feminist*. She was the first woman in MARYLAND to own land in her own name. For a short time she played a crucial role in the colony's military and legal affairs.

Born in Gloucester, England, into a large and prosperous Roman Catholic family, Margaret Brent came to Maryland in 1638 with a sister and two brothers. Maryland had been established by the CALVERT FAMILY as a Catholic colony. Through family and political connections, the Brent sisters acquired large grants of land. Margaret Brent called her property "Sisters Freehold" and added to it several times over the years.

During an uprising in Maryland in 1646, Margaret Brent assembled a group of armed volunteers to help Governor Leonard Calvert maintain control of the colony. Calvert showed his respect for Brent by naming her the executor* of his estate. When he died the next year, she became responsible for resolving a crisis. Soldiers who had come from Virginia to assist Calvert during the uprising were demanding pay. Unfortunately, Calvert's estate did not have enough money to pay them.

To avoid a rebellion by the angry soldiers, Brent sold some cattle belonging to Lord Baltimore, Calvert's brother. Lord Baltimore protested, but the Maryland assembly agreed that Brent had done the right thing. "It were better

for the Collony's safety at that time in her hands than in any man's else in the whole Province," declared the assembly. When, however, Brent asked to participate in the assembly and to cast two votes there—one as a landholder and one as the executor of Calvert's estate—she was turned down. Angry at being denied political power, Margaret Brent moved to Virginia.

Brewster, William

See *Pilgrims.*

Britain

See *Great Britain.*

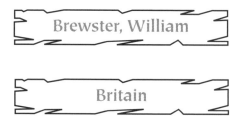

British Colonies

* **Separatists** English Protestants who broke away from the official Church of England

*I*n the early 1500s, English explorers sailed along the east coast of North America looking for the NORTHWEST PASSAGE, a water route to Asia. In the course of their voyages, the explorers claimed new territories for the English crown. At the time, the English took little interest in founding settlements in the New World. By the late 1500s, however, they began to see colonies both as a source of wealth and an opportunity to establish claims for land against French, Spanish, and Dutch rivals.

The first attempts to found English settlements—at Sagadahoc in present-day Maine and ROANOKE ISLAND in present-day North Carolina in the late 1500s—were dismal failures. By the early 1600s, though, the English had established their first permanent settlements in America—at Jamestown and Plymouth. During the next hundred years, the English colonized the entire ATLANTIC COAST of North America from what is now Maine to Georgia.

First Settlements

In 1607 a private trading company, the VIRGINIA COMPANY OF LONDON, established a colony on the James River of VIRGINIA. The JAMESTOWN COLONY overcame serious problems in its early years and in time came to prosper after the colonists started growing tobacco. To attract more settlers, the Virginia Company decided in 1619 to allow colonists to participate in the government. The colonists could elect their own representatives to the VIRGINIA HOUSE OF BURGESSES, the first representative government in North America.

The next English settlement was in New England. In 1620 a group of Separatists* known as PILGRIMS set sail for North America in search of religious freedom. They landed hundreds of miles north of Virginia and founded PLYMOUTH COLONY in what is now Massachusetts. Located in a region beyond the control of the Virginia Company, their colony had no legal standing. The settlers signed a document known as the MAYFLOWER COMPACT, in which they agreed to create a government and obey its rules. Unlike Virginia, Plymouth remained small and relatively poor. In the years that followed, other larger and more prosperous English colonies took root in New

The Naming of Colonies

Five English colonies took their names from kings and queens: Virginia for Elizabeth, the "Virgin Queen"; Maryland for Henrietta Maria, the wife of Charles I; the two Carolinas for King Charles II; and Georgia for King George II. Three other colonies were named in honor of colonial rulers: New York for the Duke of York; Pennsylvania (Latin for "Penn's Woods") for William Penn's father; and Delaware for an early governor of Virginia, the Baron De La Warr. Two other colonies got their names from Indian words—Massachusetts means "near the great hill" and Connecticut means "beside the long tidal river."

The English competed with the Dutch, Spanish, and French for control of land in North America. In 1664 they succeeded in taking the colony of New Netherland from the Dutch and then renamed it New York.

England, overshadowing Plymouth. In 1691 Plymouth was absorbed by the Massachusetts Bay colony.

Growth of British Colonial America

The success of Jamestown and the survival of Plymouth attracted other settlers to North America. By 1733 the British had established 13 colonies along the Atlantic coast. These colonies became a place of opportunity for the British and other Europeans seeking land, jobs, and a better life. For many, the colonies offered shelter from political or religious persecution as well. The governments and societies that developed in these colonies became the foundation for the United States of America.

New England. Soon after the founding of Plymouth, groups of PURITANS made plans to move to New England. In 1630 the first of these settlers established the Massachusetts Bay colony. Over the next ten years, thousands of people voyaged to MASSACHUSETTS in the Great Migration. From the start, the people of the Massachusetts Bay colony enjoyed self-government—but only male church members could vote. These "freemen" elected government officials and held TOWN MEETINGS to decide local issues. At the same time, the Puritans allowed little toleration* for those who disagreed with their religious beliefs. This lack of religious freedom prompted some settlers to leave Massachusetts and form their own colonies.

* *toleration* acceptance of the right of individuals to follow their own religious beliefs

One of these was Roger WILLIAMS, a Puritan minister who called for a complete separation of the church and the government. Expelled from Massachusetts, Williams moved south to Narragansett Bay. In 1636 he purchased land from Native Americans to found a colony of his own, later known as RHODE ISLAND. Williams's colony became a haven for religious dissenters* and independent thinkers.

* *dissenter* person who disagrees with the beliefs and practices of the established church

83

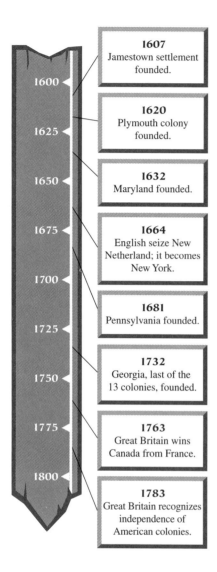

1607
Jamestown settlement founded.

1620
Plymouth colony founded.

1632
Maryland founded.

1664
English seize New Netherland; it becomes New York.

1681
Pennsylvania founded.

1732
Georgia, last of the 13 colonies, founded.

1763
Great Britain wins Canada from France.

1783
Great Britain recognizes independence of American colonies.

Another minister who defied Puritan leaders was Thomas HOOKER. In 1636 he went to the Connecticut River valley with a group of his followers. Other Massachusetts colonists had already moved to the area because of its fertile land, but the migration increased after Hooker established the settlement of Hartford. In 1639 the towns of Hartford, Wethersfield, and Windsor formed the colony of CONNECTICUT and adopted the FUNDAMENTAL ORDERS, establishing a system of self-government. The colony of New Haven joined Connecticut in 1662.

As the population of New England grew and good land became scarce, people moved to settle new lands. Some went north and founded communities in NEW HAMPSHIRE and MAINE, two provinces of Massachusetts. Settlement proceeded slowly. New Hampshire did not become a separate colony until 1679, and Maine remained part of Massachusetts until 1820.

Population growth and the spread of settlement brought New England colonists into increasing conflict with the Native Americans, who resisted attempts to take their land. The first major outbreak of violence occurred in 1636 in the PEQUOT WAR. Some 40 years later, KING PHILIP'S WAR resulted in the destruction of dozens of white settlements and Indian villages and in the deaths of thousands of settlers and Indians. Greatly weakened during the conflict, the Indians never again presented a serious threat to New England colonists.

Middle Colonies. Settlers from the Netherlands moved into the region between Virginia and New England, founding the colony of NEW NETHERLAND in 1624. In the following years, the Dutch and English competed for trade, and their rivalry erupted in a series of wars between 1652 and 1674. The English found the Dutch colony troublesome because it was set between their New England and southern colonies. In 1664 they seized New Netherland. The king of England granted the land and the surrounding area to his brother, the Duke of York, and the new English colony was named NEW YORK.

The Duke of York gave part of his grant to two friends, Lord John Berkeley and Sir George Carteret. They founded the colony of NEW JERSEY. Lord Berkeley sold his portion of New Jersey in 1674, dividing the colony into East Jersey and West Jersey. But the two parts of New Jersey were reunited under the control of the king of England in 1702.

In 1681 William PENN founded the colony of PENNSYLVANIA as a haven for QUAKERS, a religious group persecuted in England. From the beginning Penn encouraged people from many different countries to settle in Pennsylvania, and it became one of the most diverse and tolerant of the English colonies. Penn established a representative assembly with broad powers to make and carry out laws in the colony. He made sure that land occupied by Native Americans was purchased and not simply taken. In 1701 Penn allowed the people in three southern counties to form their own government. This area became the colony of DELAWARE in 1703.

Southern Colonies. The colony of Virginia emerged from the initial settlement of Jamestown and other settlements that grew up around it. As the colony prospered and grew, conflicts arose between the settlers and the Native Americans. Serious fighting broke out in the 1620s and 1640s. To achieve peace, the governor of Virginia decided that certain lands should be reserved

for the Indians. White settlers, who wanted the land for themselves, objected and rose up against the government in 1676. BACON'S REBELLION was defeated, but the Indians were pushed out of Virginia.

In 1632 King Charles I granted Cecil Calvert (the second Lord Baltimore) the charter to establish a new colony near Virginia. Calvert hoped to make his colony of MARYLAND a refuge for Roman Catholics, who were persecuted in England. The first settlers arrived in 1634. After they began to raise tobacco for export to England, Maryland grew and prospered. Calvert appointed a governor and set up an elected assembly. Because the colony had more Protestant than Catholic settlers, Calvert arranged for the assembly to pass an ACT OF TOLERATION in 1649. The law allowed Christians to practice their own form of religion. Puritans later gained control of the government and repealed* the act. Maryland and Virginia are often referred to as the Chesapeake colonies.

In 1663 King Charles II granted eight English noblemen a huge tract of land south of Virginia. Known as Carolina, the area developed into two distinct regions. The northern part attracted settlers from Virginia, who established small farms and remained relatively poor. The southern part was settled by plantation owners from BARBADOS. The planters became wealthy growing rice and using slave labor. In 1712 the two regions were separated into the colonies of NORTH CAROLINA and SOUTH CAROLINA.

The last of the original 13 colonies, GEORGIA, was founded in 1732 by James OGLETHORPE, a wealthy Englishman and reformer. Oglethorpe received a grant of land between South Carolina and the Spanish territory of FLORIDA. He wanted to establish a colony where debtors and poor people could create a new life. The British government hoped the new colony would act as a buffer* between their colonies to the north and Spanish lands.

Great Britain and Its Colonies

From the beginning, the colonies had a great deal of political freedom from England. They established local governments and took charge of many of their own affairs, a development often resisted by English kings. All along, however, the English government kept colonial trade firmly under its control. It believed that the colonies existed to benefit and enrich the economy of England, an economic system known as MERCANTILISM.

Types of Colonies.   Some colonies were run by private companies that had received charters* to establish settlements in North America. Investors bought shares in companies such as the Virginia Company of London and the Massachusetts Bay Company in hopes of making money. Virginia, Massachusetts, Rhode Island, and Connecticut were charter colonies.

Other colonies, known as proprietary colonies, were controlled by an individual, or proprietor, who received a land grant from the king. The Duke of York was proprietor of New York. New Jersey, Maryland, Pennsylvania, and the Carolinas were also proprietary colonies.

Royal colonies were under the control of the reigning monarch. Virginia began as a charter colony but became a royal colony in 1624. As time passed, the English government brought most of the colonies under royal control.

repeal to undo a law

buffer protective barrier between two rivals

charter written grant from a ruler conferring certain rights and privileges

The king appointed a governor, but even in royal colonies the settlers elected representatives to the colonial assemblies.

Challenges to Colonial Authority.   In the 1660s the English Parliament passed a series of laws, the NAVIGATION ACTS, that regulated trade with the colonies. Among other things, the laws aimed to limit trade between the English colonies and the Netherlands and other European countries. The colonists protested the acts, which greatly restricted their trade, but often found ways to get around the laws. However, as Parliament began to exert more control, tensions with the colonies increased.

Another challenge to colonial authority came in 1685, when James II took the throne of England. Wishing to bring order to his empire, he launched

After the French and Indian War, the 13 British colonies along the Atlantic coast were bounded to the west by the Proclamation Line of 1763. This line prevented British colonists from moving across the Appalachian Mountains into Indian territory. British Canada, to the north, had little connection to the eastern colonies.

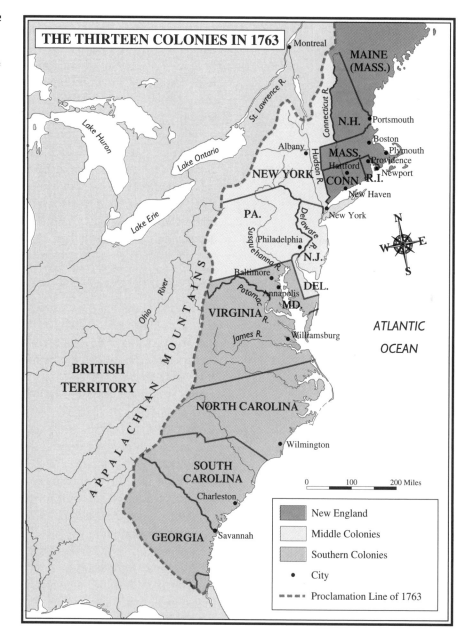

THE THIRTEEN COLONIES IN 1763

a series of measures designed to bring the colonies under firmer royal control. The result was the formation of the DOMINION OF NEW ENGLAND, a union of the New England colonies, New York, and New Jersey. The king appointed one governor to rule the Dominion and abolished the colonial assemblies—much to the displeasure of the colonists. When a revolution in England, known as the GLORIOUS REVOLUTION, overthrew James in 1688, the colonies became separate once again and regained their ability to manage most of their internal affairs.

Rivalry with France.   Throughout much of the colonial period, Great Britain and France competed for power and territory in North America. While the British possessed colonies along the Atlantic coast, the French controlled CANADA, to the north. In addition, France claimed the Ohio and Mississippi River valleys, which blocked the British colonists from moving westward.

The rivalry between England and France, and also England and Spain, led to a series of conflicts—KING WILLIAM'S WAR (1689–1697), QUEEN ANNE'S WAR (1702–1713), KING GEORGE'S WAR (1744–1748), and the FRENCH AND INDIAN WAR (1754–1763). In 1710 the British won NOVA SCOTIA, thus gaining a foothold in French Canada. By the end of the French and Indian War, Great Britain had expelled France from Canada and added the former French territory to its empire.

Road to Independence.   The last of these wars left Britain heavily in debt. Although the French were gone, Indians still threatened settlers who moved to lands west of the Appalachian Mountains. The British decided to station army troops in the colonies and to tax the colonists to raise the money needed to support those troops. From this decision came a series of actions that resulted in a movement for independence in the colonies and the AMERICAN REVOLUTION.

British Canada never became linked with the 13 colonies along the Atlantic coast. The people in Canada—mostly former French subjects and Catholics—had little in common with the colonists to the south, mostly Protestants from the British Isles. Early in the American Revolution, the rebellious colonists tried to capture Canada, but their attempt failed. During and after the fighting, thousands of LOYALISTS—American colonists who wanted to remain British subjects—fled north and settled in Canada. (*See also* **Colonial Administration; Frontier; Government, Provincial; Independence Movements; Taxation; Trade and Commerce.**)

British East India Company

During the colonial period, merchants in Portugal, Great Britain, the Netherlands, and France established trading companies to develop business in Asia. Of these, the British East India Company was the largest and most successful. Although the company had little direct contact with the North American colonies, its great commercial power had an effect on American affairs. This influence was felt most strongly in one significant episode in American colonial history: the BOSTON TEA PARTY.

A group of London merchants founded the British East India Company in 1599 in order to compete with the DUTCH EAST INDIA COMPANY and challenge Dutch control of the Asian spice trade. After receiving a charter* from Queen ELIZABETH in 1600, the British company began making trading voyages to India and other parts of Asia. Failing to gain control of the Dutch spice trade in the East Indies, the company limited its operations to India. Trade with India became immensely profitable, and the company soon grew rich and powerful. By the mid-1700s, the British East India Company had become more than a commercial enterprise. It had also gained political control over much of India and governed the country on behalf of the British crown.

In an effort to strengthen trading ties with China, the British East India Company had bought enormous quantities of Chinese tea. It sold some of this tea in the American colonies. In 1767 the British government imposed a new tax on tea sold in its colonies. To protest what they considered an unfair tax, many Americans stopped buying tea, or they bought tea from Dutch smugglers. Tea piled up in the warehouses of the East India Company, unsold. As its sales of tea fell, the company faced financial ruin. The British government stepped in to help the company by passing the TEA ACT OF 1773. While maintaining the tax on tea, the act made it possible for the company to sell its tea in America at a lower price than the Dutch tea.

Many American colonists opposed the Tea Act. Merchants who sold Dutch tea knew the act would cause them to lose money. Anti-tax colonists worried that if people continued to pay a tax on tea, Britain would think it could impose other taxes. Feelings against the Tea Act reached fever pitch in Boston, New York, and Philadelphia. The British East India Company's agents in New York and Philadelphia decided not to accept shipments of the tea. In BOSTON, however, the agents refused to stop the shipment and sale of the company's tea. Opponents of the Tea Act took matters into their own hands and dumped the East India Company's tea into Boston harbor. This open challenge to British authority became known as the Boston Tea Party.

The British Parliament passed a series of laws intended to punish the colonists. One of them, the Boston Port Act of 1774, closed Boston harbor until the city agreed to pay the East India Company for the tea that had been destroyed. This attempt to crush colonial resistance was a complete failure. Outraged by the new British laws, known in the colonies as the INTOLERABLE ACTS, American colonists moved closer to open rebellion against British rule. In an indirect way, the British East India Company contributed to events that led to the AMERICAN REVOLUTION. (*See also* **European Empires; Independence Movements; Smuggling; Taxation; Trade and Commerce.**)

* *charter* written grant from a ruler conferring certain rights and privileges

See color plate 6, vol. 4.

British Parliament See *Parliament.*

Buffalo

See color plate 2, vol. 2.

jerky dried meat

Buffalo, or American bison, are large, wild grazing animals distantly related to cattle. Buffalo were central to the economic life of a number of Native American peoples. When Europeans began exploring the interior of North America, they discovered the buffalo—and marveled at the shaggy, majestic beasts.

Before the arrival of the Europeans, herds of buffalo roamed over about one-third of North America, from northwestern Canada to northern Mexico and from the Blue Mountains of Oregon to the western parts of New York, Pennsylvania, Virginia, and the Carolinas. Buffalo were most numerous in the Great Plains, between the Missouri River and the Rocky Mountains. The Native Americans who lived in this region built their way of life around the buffalo.

In the spring and fall, hunters of the PLAINS INDIANS followed buffalo herds along their migration trails. They organized buffalo drives, stampeding herds between rows of stones into corrals or over cliffs. Once the buffalo were trapped or injured, the hunters would kill them with spears or arrows.

While the men took charge of hunting the buffalo, the women were responsible for preparing the meat. Buffalo provided feasts of fresh meat as well as supplies of jerky*. The women sometimes mixed jerky with animal fat and berries to form a highly nutritious food called pemmican that could be stored for winter use or traded with other tribes. The Native Americans who hunted buffalo used every part of the animal. They made the hides into clothing and tents, and they fashioned tools and needles from the bones. The Plains Indians attended large gatherings at which tribes from different regions traded goods. The tribes who hunted buffalo might trade hides and jerky for cotton cloth, corn, or pottery produced by Indians of the Southwest.

Some Native Americans hunted the buffalo for food, clothing, and tools made from its bone. A number of tribes built their entire way of life around the buffalo, moving and resettling with the roaming herds. This engraving of a buffalo appeared in a book of the late 1600s.

The hunting methods of the Plains Indians changed dramatically after the Europeans introduced horses to North America in the late 1500s. The Indians quickly became skilled riders who hunted from horseback. The usual technique was to ride as close to the buffalo as possible and fire an arrow down through its ribs into its heart and lungs. Using this method, Indians were able to chase and kill buffalo in all seasons. Buffalo remained central to the Plains Indians' economy and way of life until the mid-1800s, when white hunters almost wiped out the buffalo. During the 1900s, careful management of the remaining buffalo herds brought the animals back from the brink of extinction.

Bunker Hill, Battle of

* *militia* army of citizens who may be called into action in a time of emergency

* *fortification* defensive structure

*T*he Battle of Bunker Hill was the first major battle of the AMERICAN REVOLUTION. Fought on the outskirts of Boston in June 1775, the battle pitted untrained New England militia* against highly trained British troops. Although forced to retreat because of a lack of ammunition, the Americans proved that they could fight effectively against the British.

The American Revolution had started two months earlier, when colonists and British troops clashed at the Battles of LEXINGTON AND CONCORD. Afterward, thousands of colonial militia set up camp near Boston, where the British had stationed their troops. In June the Americans learned that the British general, Sir William HOWE, planned to seize Bunker Hill and Breed's Hill in Charlestown, across the Charles River from Boston. On the night of June 16, the Americans sent Colonel William Prescott and 1,200 soldiers to take Bunker Hill—the higher of the two hills. Instead, Prescott led his forces to nearby Breed's Hill, where they quietly built fortifications*.

The first major battle of the American Revolution was fought between highly trained British troops and recently recruited New England militiamen. The Americans put up a good fight but were eventually forced to retreat. Though not a victory, the battle showed the Americans that they could stand up to the British forces.

At daybreak on June 17, the British discovered the new American fortifications. British warships in the harbor opened fire on Breed's Hill but could do little damage. Meanwhile, Prescott improved American defenses by building a fence of split rails, hay, and stones. His army was reinforced by another 2,000 colonial troops commanded by General Israel Putnam.

In the afternoon, General Howe led 2,400 British soldiers to Charlestown. Splitting his forces into two groups, he ordered attacks on the Breed's Hill fortifications and fence. The first attack on the fence failed, and the British troops were forced to retreat down the hill. Putnam had told his soldiers not to fire on the British troops until they could "see the whites of their eyes." By holding off, the Americans were able to shoot at close range, delivering a round of fire that devastated the British ranks. The British troops regrouped and attacked again—with the same result.

Howe remained determined to seize Breed's Hill in a frontal assault. He brought some cannons into better position and focused on attacking the fortifications. By this time, the Americans had hardly any gunpowder and could offer little resistance. Armed with bayonets*, the British overwhelmed the fort and forced the Americans to retreat. In a battle lasting less than two hours, the British had won the hill—but at a heavy cost. More than 1,000 British soldiers were killed or wounded. The Americans, by contrast, suffered only about 450 casualties*.

The fighting that took place on Breed's Hill is known as the Battle of Bunker Hill. Although the American forces suffered a military defeat there, they won a moral victory. They proved that untrained colonial troops could stand up bravely in the face of heavy British attack.

* **bayonet** short blade attached to the barrel of a gun and used for stabbing

* **casualty** person who is killed or injured

Byrd, William

1674–1744
Virginia plantation owner and writer

An educated and cultured VIRGINIA plantation owner, William Byrd became one of the foremost writers of the colonial period. His lively and witty DIARIES and his other writings have provided historians with a valuable record of the history and culture of colonial Virginia.

The son of a wealthy and prominent Virginia planter, Byrd was educated in England. On the death of his father, Byrd inherited a large estate that he expanded over time to more than 180,000 acres. In 1737 he founded Richmond, the future capital of Virginia, and had the city laid out on a portion of his land. Byrd also became active in politics. He represented Virginia as a colonial agent in Great Britain, and he served in the VIRGINIA HOUSE OF BURGESSES and on the governor's council. In 1728 Byrd took part in a project to survey the boundary between Virginia and North Carolina. His visits to that frontier region provided material for two of his best-known works—*The History of the Dividing Line* and *The Journey to the Land of Eden.*

An enthusiastic reader and individual of many interests, Byrd owned one of the finest libraries in the colonies. His diaries reflect his broad knowledge and his varied interests. Byrd's writings on colonial life—ranging from thoughts on the meaning of life and death to descriptions of popular dances—offer an intimate look at life in early Virginia. (*See also* **Literature.**)

Cabeza de Vaca, Alvar Núñez

ca. 1490–ca. 1560
Spanish explorer

See first map in Exploration, Age of
(vol. 2).

* **shaman** person with spiritual and healing
powers

Cabeza de Vaca explored vast stretches of the Gulf of Mexico coast and the southwestern part of what is now the United States. In his account of an extraordinary cross-country journey, Cabeza de Vaca described the land, its plants and animals, and the many Native American tribes he came to know. His mention of cities of gold created a myth that drew other explorers to the region.

In 1528 the Spaniard Pánfilo de Narváez led an expedition of about 600 men and five ships to FLORIDA. Cabeza de Vaca served as the group's treasurer. Landing near the site of present-day Tampa, the Spaniards left their ships and set out to explore the new land. In their absence, the ships were destroyed by violent storms. The men were stranded in the foreign wilderness.

The Spaniards wandered around for a while, often becoming lost in swamps, but finally made their way back to the coast. There they built crude rafts and set out to sea, hoping to reach Cuba. However, another ferocious storm sank all but one raft. Only four men—Cabeza de Vaca, two other Spaniards, and a black Arab known as ESTEBAN or Estevanico—survived. They were washed ashore on Galveston Island, Texas, without food or clothing. Cabeza de Vaca wrote:

> We were left naked, as we were born. . . . We were in the bitter cold of November, so emaciated [extremely thin] our bones could be counted; we were the figure of death.

A group of Indians found the survivors and clothed and fed them. At first Cabeza de Vaca was fearful of the Indians, but he came to admire them as he learned more about their ways and their culture. Soon the Spaniard became a merchant, trading in local goods with the Indians. At one point, he tended a man who appeared to be dead—and the man recovered. From then on, the Native Americans regarded Cabeza de Vaca as a shaman* and treated him with great respect. His reputation for healing spread.

Cabeza de Vaca and his companions traveled several thousand miles through the American Southwest and Mexico. After eight years, they met a party of Spaniards in the west of Mexico and returned to the world of Europeans.

Cabeza de Vaca wrote an account of his 6,000-mile journey, called *Naufragios* (*Shipwrecks*). Published in 1555, his book contained valuable information on the lifestyles of many different Native American tribes. It also described the geography and the plant and animal life of the regions he visited. The book's greatest impact, though, came from its retelling of stories that Cabeza de Vaca had heard from the Indians about seven golden cities. Although false, the tales inspired later Spanish expeditions to search out these fabled cities of great wealth. (*See also* **Exploration, Age of; Seven Cities of Cíbola.**)

Cabot, John and Sebastian

See *Exploration, Age of: British.*

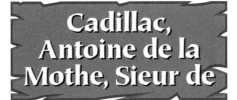

Cadillac, Antoine de la Mothe, Sieur de

ca. 1658–1730
French founder of Detroit

*A*ntoine de la Mothe Cadillac, a leader in France's North American colonies, established a settlement just north of Lake Erie that became the city of Detroit. He also served as governor of the colony of LOUISIANA.

Born in southwestern France, Cadillac entered the French army at an early age and came to North America in 1683. He lived in Port Royal in present-day NOVA SCOTIA and also owned property in what is now Maine. In 1694 Comte de Frontenac, the governor of NEW FRANCE, appointed Cadillac commander of the military post of Mackinac at the crossroads of the upper Great Lakes. Although Cadillac grumbled about the food, the Native Americans, and the climate, his position at Mackinac was an important one. The western posts helped strengthen France's position along the frontier, keeping the English from expanding their activities in the region. Nevertheless, in 1697 the French government closed these western posts because they were so expensive to maintain.

After leaving Mackinac, Cadillac proposed to establish a post on the Detroit River to protect the FUR TRADE from the English. The French crown granted him land, and in the summer of 1701 he founded Fort Ponchartrain du Détroit with 100 soldiers and settlers. He brought his family to join him in Detroit and worked to attract new colonists and Indians to the region.

Cadillac's goal was to make Detroit a fur-trading settlement, military base, and missionary center. His reports on Detroit's prospects were so glowing that the colonial minister in France remarked: "I am glad to be assured that Detroit will become the Paris of New France." Yet despite Cadillac's enthusiasm and ability, his eager pursuit of riches and power earned him enemies. The missionaries of the powerful Jesuit order turned against Cadillac when he lured some of their Indian converts to settle near Detroit.

In 1710 French authorities sent Cadillac to govern the colony of Louisiana. Here, too, Cadillac's conduct led to difficulties. He launched schemes to increase his own wealth and came into conflict with the colonists. He was called back to France in 1716 and then retired. Although Cadillac's rule in Louisiana was a disaster, he is still remembered as the founder of Detroit. In modern times, the city's auto manufacturers have given his name to one of their premium cars.

Cahokia

See *Native Americans: Early Peoples of North America.*

California

*C*alifornia was part of the SPANISH BORDERLANDS, the northern reaches of Spain's empire in the Americas. Although rich in resources, California remained isolated from MEXICO and other Spanish settlements and attracted few colonists until the mid-1700s. California's early history was dominated by the MISSIONS established to bring Christianity to the Native Americans.

See map in Spanish Borderlands (vol. 4).

Geography of California. California's geography contributed to its isolation. On the east, high mountains and a vast desert blocked easy access

California

Spanish resettlement in California began with the construction of a string of missions and forts. One presidio, or fort, was built in San Francisco.

to California. Arrival from the sea was also difficult. The Pacific coastline had few safe landing spots for ships, and strong winds from the northwest and southerly ocean currents made it difficult for ships to sail north along the coast from Mexico.

Although serious physical obstacles discouraged the settlement of California, the region did offer numerous advantages, including a warm and pleasant climate. Valleys in the interior had lush meadows with fertile soil. If rainfall was adequate, the area could produce plentiful crops. In addition, the rolling grasslands were well suited to livestock, and the waters along the coast contained abundant fish and other sea life.

Exploration.   Spanish explorers began inching northward along the west coast of Mexico in the 1530s. In 1535 they discovered a long peninsula, which they called California after a mythical land of great wealth described in a popular Spanish novel of the time. The peninsula later became known as Baja (Lower) California, and it remains a part of Mexico today.

In 1542 João Rodrigues Cabrilho explored farther north along the coast, a region that became known as Alta (Upper) California. In his accounts, Cabrilho described the region as beautiful but also remote and inaccessible. As a result, Alta California received little attention over the next several decades except for occasional voyages of exploration. During one such expedition in 1602–1603, Sebastián Vizcaíno produced the first detailed maps of the Alta California coast. The Spanish authorities decided that the region had little value and prohibited further exploration.

The Spanish began to take an interest in Alta California in the late 1700s. At that time, Russian fur traders were moving south along the Pacific coast from Alaska. The Spanish, fearing that Alta California might fall into Russian hands, decided to colonize the region. In 1769 Captain Gaspar de PORTOLÁ, the governor of Baja California, began an expedition up the coast to establish fortified settlements. These presidios* would help secure Alta California for Spain and provide a foundation for further settlement.

* **presidio** Spanish fort built to protect mission settlements

94

friar member of a religious brotherhood

See map in Missions and Missionaries (vol. 3).

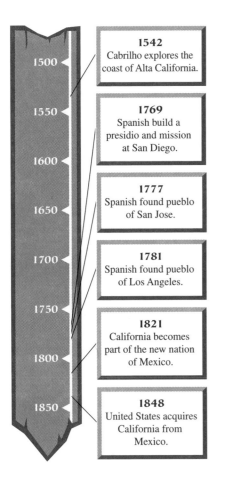

1542
Cabrilho explores the coast of Alta California.

1769
Spanish build a presidio and mission at San Diego.

1777
Spanish found pueblo of San Jose.

1781
Spanish found pueblo of Los Angeles.

1821
California becomes part of the new nation of Mexico.

1848
United States acquires California from Mexico.

Missions and Presidios.   The military and the ROMAN CATHOLIC CHURCH led the way in settling Alta California, as they had done in other parts of the Spanish Borderlands. In 1769 Portolá built a presidio at a place called San Diego. Junípero SERRA, a Franciscan friar*, established a mission nearby. The next year, Portolá and Serra moved farther north to build a presidio and mission at Monterey. Monterey became the capital of the province of Alta California.

Over the following years, the Spanish built two more presidios in the province—one at San Francisco (1776) and one at Santa Barbara (1782). Located at strategic sites along the coast, these fortified settlements discouraged colonization attempts by rival nations and helped control the Indian population of the region. Each presidio served as a government center and marketplace as well as a military establishment. Many soldiers and their families settled on the surrounding lands.

The Spanish also founded 19 additional missions in Alta California. The basic goal of the missions was to convert the Indian population to Christianity and to teach them Spanish culture. But the missions also focused on improving Indian agriculture and encouraging the development of local industries, such as weaving, pottery making, ironworking, and wine making.

Pueblos and Ranchos.   The Spanish had hoped that the missions would grow enough food to feed the soldiers and their families in the presidios. That did not happen. Flood and drought ruined many crops in the early years before the colonists learned how to adjust their farming techniques to the land and climate of the region. In time the missions became fairly self-sufficient, but they still did not produce enough to meet the needs of the presidios. As a result, the presidios had to rely on food shipped from Mexico, and the delivery was unpredictable.

In an effort to increase the food supply, the Spanish decided to create pueblos, towns devoted to agriculture. The pueblos—San Jose, founded in 1777, and Los Angeles, founded in 1781—would also provide civilian government for the region. The Spaniards offered money, food, equipment, and livestock to settlers willing to move to the pueblos. Most settlers came from northern Mexico. Generally quite poor, the new arrivals reflected the mixture of ethnic groups found in the Spanish Borderlands—Spanish, Indian, and black.

Although the pueblos gradually increased their crops, they had difficulty growing enough to meet the needs of the presidios. However, by the late 1700s, the missions were thriving and could sell surplus crops to the presidios. In fact, the missions became the economic backbone of California, producing thousands of bushels of grain and launching new local industries.

Another type of settlement arose in the vicinity of missions and presidios in the late 1700s and early 1800s. Known as ranchos, these landholdings usually developed from private land grants to soldiers and were used to raise livestock, primarily horses, cattle, and sheep. Although the missions controlled most of the better land and had much larger herds of livestock, the ranchos helped provide a steady supply of horses for riding and beef for eating. These landholdings helped soldiers develop strong roots in California and gave them an opportunity to improve their lives.

California Indians

The Russians

The Spanish colonized California to discourage Russian settlement, but the Russians came anyway. In 1812 they established a trading post called Fort Ross north of San Francisco Bay and began a profitable fur trade. They also carried on a lively—and illegal—trade with the Spanish missions, exchanging Russian manufactured goods for food. As the supply of furs declined, Fort Ross became unnecessary. In 1841 Russia sold the land to John Sutter. Eight years later Sutter gained fame when gold was discovered on another part of his land. This launched a "gold rush" that lured thousands of people to California.

* **mestizo** person of mixed Spanish and Indian ancestry

Growing in Isolation. Isolated from other Spanish lands, the colonists of California enjoyed a great deal of political freedom from colonial officials in Mexico. Soldiers and officers organized the presidios to suit their own needs, and local military and civilian authorities ruled with little interference. In addition, weak commercial ties to Mexico resulted in considerable economic independence. Missions carried on trade with the Russians, British, and Americans despite official rules against it.

California's population did not grow very much during the colonial period, and settlement was limited to the coastal areas. In 1779 the province had only 500 Spanish or mestizo* settlers; in 1810 it had about 2,000. California's isolation played a role in the slow growth. In addition, Indian uprisings in ARIZONA closed the overland route to California in the 1780s, curbing the flow of colonists. Meanwhile, the Native American population of the California coast declined dramatically, dropping from about 60,000 in 1769 to 21,000 in 1820. Many Indians had died of European diseases; others had fled to the interior rather than convert to Christianity or serve as manual laborers for the Spanish.

When Mexico won its independence from Spain in 1821, California became a part of the new nation. Reformers in Mexico demanded that the power of the missions be reduced, claiming that they had failed to integrate Indians into society. Many critics also questioned whether the Spanish-born friars would remain loyal to Mexico. In 1834 the Mexican government took control of the missions and sold the land to wealthy ranchers, who became known as Californios. In an effort to increase California's population, Mexican officials granted land to Americans in the 1840s. These new settlers, however, remained loyal to the United States. They eventually took control of California from the Californios and played an important role in acquiring the region for the United States in 1848. (*See also* **Agriculture; California Indians; Colonial Administration; Government, Provincial; Immigration; Presidios; Ranching; Russian Settlements.**)

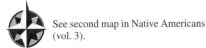

California Indians

See second map in Native Americans (vol. 3).

When European explorers and settlers arrived in what is now California, they found many different Native American groups speaking hundreds of languages and dialects. The rugged California landscape separated these Indians from each other. Mountains and deserts cut them off from the rest of North America. Each of the groups developed its own distinctive way of life, based on the climate, terrain, and resources of the region in which its members lived.

In general, the land provided California Indians with a generous supply of plant and animal life. This abundance helped support a very large population. When the first Europeans arrived to establish settlements in the late 1700s, California had about 300,000 Indians. In the following years, the population declined dramatically as a result of European diseases and mistreatment by settlers. By the late 1800s, fewer than 30,000 Indians remained in California.

Culture and Society. California contains many different environments, and Native Americans lived in all of them. Some inhabited dense forests.

The world of the California Indians changed dramatically with the arrival of the Spanish, who forced many Indians to live and work in missions. The Spaniards introduced Christianity, as well as diseases that devastated the local population.

* *gathering* collecting wild plants, nuts, and berries for food

Others dwelled in the mountains or in river valleys. Still others could be found along the seacoast or in desert regions. Despite the diversity of their environments, all California Indians lived by hunting and gathering*. Agriculture was rare—and largely unnecessary—because the environment supplied a rich variety of food. The Indians hunted deer, rabbit, and other animals. Native Americans in coastal areas also fished, gathered shellfish, and hunted seals and sea otters. Indians throughout California gathered berries, seeds, roots, and other plant foods—especially acorns, an important element in the diet of all California Indians. The acorns were dried and pounded into a flour that could be made into soup or bread. Indians often traded surplus foods with other groups, which helped provide more varied diets.

The California Indians developed styles of living based on the resources they found in their environment. In many areas, they lived in dome-shaped structures made of poles covered with grass or brush. In forested regions in the north, they built homes of wooden planks cut from large trees. Indians throughout California crafted baskets, but each tribe used certain materials and developed unique techniques and designs. The lifestyle of the Hupa and Yurok Indians of northern California, for example, resembled that of the Indians of the Pacific Northwest. These groups placed great emphasis on material possessions and considered them a sign of social rank. The Chumash Indians, a coastal group, were skillful sailors who made boats of wooden planks lashed together with cord. Living in an especially rich environment, the Chumash were among the most prosperous Indians in California.

California did not really have "tribes." Although large numbers of California Indians might share a related language and culture, they usually did not think of themselves as members of a single group. Instead, the California Indians were organized into small subgroups—sometimes referred to as "tribelets"—with distinct dialects and ways of life. These tribelets ranged in size from about 100 to more than 1,000 individuals. Each occupied a well-defined territory with villages in which the members of one or two bands—extended family groups—lived. Heads of households and shamans* shared leadership of the bands. The bands of a tribelet often saw little of each other except when they came together to trade or take part in religious ceremonies.

Most California Indians were relatively peaceful. With abundant natural resources, they had little reason to go to war. Moreover, their separation into small, isolated bands made organizing or waging war against others difficult. The Indians preferred to resolve conflicts through trade and talk. Wars did erupt from time to time, usually in response to theft, trespassing, or suspicions of witchcraft. But the fighting was usually small in scale and finished quickly.

*** shaman** person with spiritual and healing powers

Contact with Europeans.

When the Spanish arrived in the late 1700s, the world of the California Indians began to change. The impact was greatest in the southern and coastal areas of California, where the Spaniards founded MISSIONS to convert the Indians to Christianity and to teach them about European culture.

The Spanish mission system caused great hardship for the Native Americans of California. Some Indians came to the missions voluntarily, but others were rounded up and brought in by Spanish soldiers. Once there, these "Mission Indians" were forced to remain and work as laborers, raising crops and tending cattle. Those who resisted or violated mission rules risked severe punishment. Inadequate food, poor shelter, brutal treatment by Spanish soldiers, and epidemics of measles, cholera, smallpox, and other European DISEASES killed thousands of Indians in mission communities. Diseases spread to other California Indians as well.

The condition of the Mission Indians worsened in the early 1800s, when MEXICO won independence from Spain, and California became part of Mexico. The Mexican government broke up the missions and divided the land among white settlers. Although the Indians were free to leave the missions, they had nowhere to go. The Mexicans had taken their lands and destroyed their villages. Struggling to survive, their numbers declined even further.

Spanish and Mexican rule almost destroyed the Native Americans of southern and coastal California. Between 1769 and 1848, the Indian population of those areas declined by about 90 percent. Many who survived were forced to abandon their traditional ways of living because the agriculture and livestock grazing introduced by the Spanish and Mexicans had changed the natural environment the Indians had relied on for their survival.

The Indians of northern and central California were not really affected by Spanish and Mexican rule. For the most part, their contact with white people in the 1700s was limited to Russian and British fur traders. Some Indians

See color plate 3, vol. 3.

Remember: Consult the index at the end of Volume 4 to find more information on many topics.

worked at Russian trading posts or on ships hunting sea mammals. These small-scale operations had less of an effect on the California Indians than did the missions. However, British traders did introduce European diseases that killed thousands of Indians in northern California.

Impact of Americans. In 1848 California became part of the United States. The next year, gold was discovered in the central part of the state, and thousands of Americans streamed into the area in search of riches. This flood of people had a devastating effect on the Indians of northern and central California. Gold prospectors trespassed on their lands, invaded their villages, and killed defenseless men, women, and children. Settlers captured Indians and forced them to work as slaves. Attempts by the Native Americans to resist were met with force, and the state government organized military campaigns against them. By the late 1800s, fewer than 30,000 Indians remained in all of California. Most of these were living on small reservations, their traditional cultures almost completely destroyed. (*See also* **Native Americans; Russian Settlements.**)

Calvert Family

Founders of
the colony of Maryland

* **charter** written grant from a ruler conferring certain rights and privileges

* **proprietor** person granted land and the right to establish a colony

The Calvert family played a prominent role in the founding of the colony of MARYLAND. George Calvert, born about 1580, held several high governmental positions in England under King James I. After Calvert became a Catholic in 1624, he had to resign many of his posts. England was divided by religious conflict at the time, and feeling against Catholics ran high. Calvert did, however, keep the friendship of King Charles I, who named him Lord Baltimore.

Calvert had a keen interest in the colonization of America. He was a member of the VIRGINIA COMPANY OF LONDON and served on the council of the New England Company, organizations that promoted settlement in North America. Calvert bought some land in NEWFOUNDLAND and received a charter* in 1623 to establish a settlement there. He visited Newfoundland twice, but he found both the weather and the French inhabitants difficult.

Calvert also visited Virginia and had visions of setting up a fur-trading base there. His hopes were disappointed because the Virginia colonists objected to a Catholic proprietor*. In 1632 King Charles granted Calvert lands "not yet cultivated and planted" just north of Virginia on the CHESAPEAKE BAY. These lands would become the colony of Maryland, which was named in honor of Henrietta Maria, the wife of King Charles.

George Calvert died soon afterward. Cecil Calvert, one of his sons and the second Lord Baltimore, received the charter for the new colony and became its first proprietor. Cecil Calvert never visited Maryland, but his brother Leonard arrived in 1634 with settlers for the colony. Leonard Calvert became Maryland's first governor and held that position until his death in 1647.

The early settlers of Maryland included both Protestants and Catholics. But in the 1640s, while civil war raged in England, religious conflicts broke out in Maryland too. To calm the situation, Cecil Calvert proposed an ACT OF TOLERATION in 1649, which was passed by the Maryland assembly. It guaranteed the "free exercise" of religion for Christians in Maryland.

Another generation of Calverts arrived in Maryland in 1661. Cecil sent his son Charles to the colony to serve as governor. When Cecil died in 1675, Charles Calvert succeeded him as proprietor and became the third Lord Baltimore. Charles was not a wise or a popular ruler. He had a dispute with William PENN over Maryland's boundary with Pennsylvania. Charles Calvert returned to England in 1684 to answer various charges against him and never came back to North America. In his absence, Maryland Protestants, now the overwhelming majority in the colony, overthrew the government set up by the old charter. In 1691 the English king established a new government for Maryland, which banned Catholics from holding office. The city of Baltimore, founded in 1729, was named for Cecil Calvert.

Calvinists

*T*he overwhelming majority of the settlers in Britain's North American colonies came from religious groups that followed the views of John Calvin, a Christian religious reformer in Switzerland. The PURITANS and Presbyterians were among those who based their religion on the ideas of Calvin.

Ideas of Calvin. In the late 1520s, Calvin was studying in France to become a priest in the ROMAN CATHOLIC CHURCH. During this time, Europe was in the midst of a religious upheaval. Martin Luther had started a movement to reform the Catholic Church. Calvin went through a form of religious conversion and became committed to developing a simpler, purer form of Christianity. He adopted some of Luther's ideas and added others of his own. In 1536 he collected his thoughts in a book called *The Institutes of the Christian Religion.*

* *damnation* condemned to dwell in hell eternally

Calvin believed in predestination, which meant that people were marked at birth for either eternal salvation or damnation* when they died. According to Calvin, everyone was born a sinner. But God, in his mercy, chose to save some people—called "the elect." However, members of the elect had to fully accept Jesus Christ as their savior in order to be saved. Individuals could not earn salvation through good works—though they were expected to confirm their standing among the elect by performing them.

* *hierarchy* division of society or an institution into groups with higher and lower ranks
* *ritual* ceremony that follows a set pattern

Calvin rejected the complex hierarchy* of the Catholic Church. He simplified church ritual* and emphasized the importance of reading the BIBLE to gain religious understanding. His ideas spread throughout Europe. They were adopted by the HUGUENOTS in France, by the Dutch Reformed Church in the Netherlands, by the German Reformed Church in Germany, by the Presbyterians in Scotland, and by the Puritans in England. Calvinists often suffered persecution for their beliefs. Many thousands moved to North America, hoping to worship in their own way without government interference.

Calvinism in North America. The most prominent Calvinists in North America were the Puritans, who settled in the Massachusetts Bay colony and elsewhere in New England. Baptists in Rhode Island and Virginia followed Calvinist beliefs as well, but less strictly than the Puritans. Many Presbyterians settled in New York, New Jersey, Pennsylvania, and Delaware. The

largest group of Calvinists in New York, though, were Dutch settlers who belonged to the Dutch Reformed Church.

As the colonies grew, the Calvinist churches in America changed. After the English gained control of New Netherland, the Dutch church split. Some believers—mostly wealthy merchants—remained loyal to church leaders in the Netherlands. Others broke away and formed their own institutions. Many French Huguenots eventually joined the Church of England.

* **charter** written grant from a ruler conferring certain rights and privileges

Other changes affected New England Calvinists. The Puritan founders of Massachusetts had allowed only church members who owned property to vote. In 1691 the king of England gave Massachusetts a new charter* granting all property holders—not just church members—the right to vote. As a result, the Puritan leaders lost some of their power in the colony.

By the early 1700s, the strong religious feelings of the early settlers had faded. In many areas, church attendance declined. Some groups became troubled by the Calvinist view of predestination and began to accept instead a view being spread by various preachers—that people could achieve salvation by performing good works. This weakened Calvinism.

In response to the declining church participation, a movement called the GREAT AWAKENING emerged. Ministers—not all of them strict Calvinists—called for a return to religion. Although Calvinist leaders warned Christians that only faith and God's grace could save them, some congregations embraced the new teachings. The Great Awakening revived religious fervor in the colonies, but it lessened the influence of the Calvinist churches. Nevertheless, Calvinism continued to play a role in American life. During the American Revolution, many Americans saw themselves as a people chosen to establish a society in accordance with the will of God, a view that had roots in Calvinist ideals. (*See also* **Edwards, Jonathan; Massachusetts; Protestant Churches.**)

Canada

For more than 200 years, France held an area in North America that included parts of present-day Canada. Great Britain won control of the region in 1763 and ruled it for more than a century. For most of its history, Canada did not exist as a unified political entity. Under both the French and the British, Canada included several distinct provinces that were ruled separately. Moreover, vast stretches of territory to the west were controlled not by a government but by a fur company, the HUDSON'S BAY COMPANY. Not until the mid-1800s did various provinces join together to form the core of the modern nation of Canada.

The French Colonies

Although French explorers claimed much of Canada in the early 1500s, France did not establish a permanent colony there until the founding of QUEBEC in 1608. Other settlements—MONTREAL, PORT ROYAL, and LOUISBOURG—followed, and France's empire in North America, NEW FRANCE, began to take shape.

Under the French, New France eventually stretched from the Atlantic coast in the east to the Great Lakes in the west and included the Ohio and

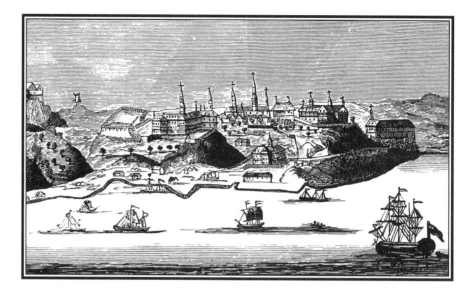

Canada, the region along the St. Lawrence River, was considered the heartland of the colony of New France. The French ruled their colony from the administrative center of Quebec, shown here in a 1740 drawing by Margaret Cecil.

See first map in European Empires (vol. 2).

Mississippi River valleys to the south. The vast colony was divided into five administrative regions ruled from the city of Quebec. Acadia contained modern NOVA SCOTIA and New Brunswick. Labrador covered the north shore of the Gulf of St. Lawrence. The region on both sides of the ST. LAWRENCE RIVER, known as Canada, was the heartland of New France. It included what are now the provinces of Quebec and Ontario. The "upper country" consisted of the upper reaches of the St. Lawrence River, and the "Western Sea" included the area around the Great Lakes and beyond. The French colony of LOUISIANA had its own governor and council independent of Quebec.

The French colonies of North America differed in a number of ways from the British colonies. To begin with, New France had far fewer settlers than the British colonies, and most settlements were concentrated in the regions of Acadia and Canada. On the mattter of religion, the French colonists were predominantly Roman Catholic, while the British were mostly Protestant. As to economic development, New France depended heavily on the FUR TRADE; the British colonists engaged in a variety of economic activities. Concerning relations with the Native Americans, the French were much more successful than the British colonists. These differences between the French and the British had a significant impact on the history of the region.

Transfer of Power

Great Britain and France fought a series of wars in the 1600s and 1700s as part of a struggle for power in Europe and North America. The French emerged from the first of these conflicts, KING WILLIAM'S WAR (1688–1697), with their North American empire undiminished. However, Britain gained ground after QUEEN ANNE'S WAR (1702–1713). Under the terms of the TREATY OF UTRECHT, it won control of the French province of Acadia, and France gave up all rights to NEWFOUNDLAND, an island claimed by both nations.

The FRENCH AND INDIAN WAR (1754–1763), also known as the Seven Years' War, finally ended the rivalry of Britain and France in North America.

See second map in European Empires (vol. 2).

After some early setbacks, the British went on to win a decisive victory over the French. The terms of the TREATY OF PARIS (1763), which ended the war, gave Britain all of New France. Louisiana went to Spain under a separate agreement. Great Britain had gained a vast new territory, and it now faced the challenge of ruling a people with a different culture, language, and religion.

Acadia Under British Rule.   After winning control of Acadia in 1713, the British renamed the region Nova Scotia, Latin for "New Scotland." For the next 40 years, they left the French ACADIANS largely alone. The Acadians had to promise to remain neutral in any future wars between Britain and France. In return, they were allowed to govern themselves and continue their traditional way of life, including practicing their Roman Catholic faith.

When the French and Indian War broke out in 1754, the British had doubts about the loyalty of the Acadians. They believed that these "neutral" inhabitants of Nova Scotia might provide assistance to the French. British officials gave the Acadians a choice: swear an oath of loyalty to Great Britain, or leave their homeland. The Acadians resisted. In what became known as the Great Upheaval, the British forced thousands of Acadians to move to British colonies in the south, to France, or to French islands in the West Indies. Many Acadians fled to Canada or other parts of New France. Several thousand settled in Louisiana, where they became known as Cajuns and developed a unique culture.

In the early 1800s, the former French colony of Canada was divided into two provinces, Lower Canada and Upper Canada. Many Loyalists from the American colonies settled in Upper Canada, which is now part of Ontario. The British provinces of Rupert's Land, Nova Scotia, New Brunswick, and British Columbia were not part of Canada at this time.

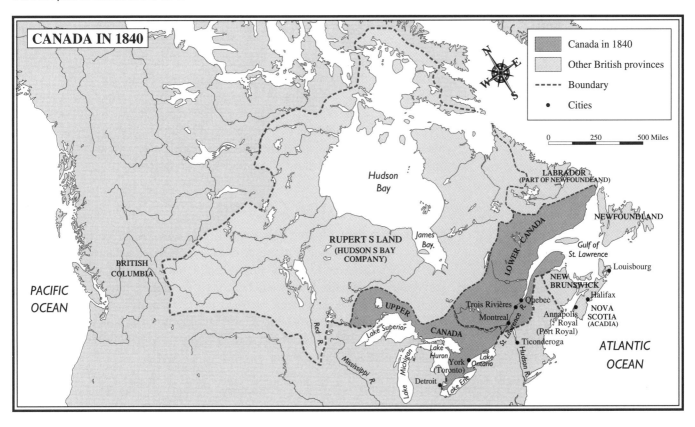

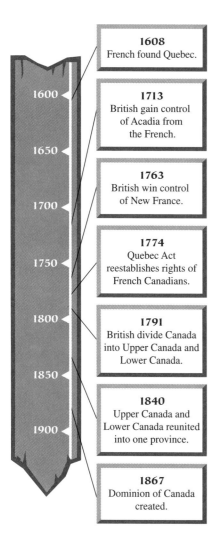

1608
French found Quebec.

1713
British gain control of Acadia from the French.

1763
British win control of New France.

1774
Quebec Act reestablishes rights of French Canadians.

1791
British divide Canada into Upper Canada and Lower Canada.

1840
Upper Canada and Lower Canada reunited into one province.

1867
Dominion of Canada created.

The Catholic Issue.   After winning the rest of New France in 1763, the British faced the serious challenge of governing about 60,000 new subjects, many more than in Acadia. Like the Acadians, the French Canadians were Roman Catholics, and their religion soon presented a problem. The Catholic Church in Quebec needed new priests. But only a bishop could ordain men to the priesthood, and the bishop of Quebec had died. British law would not allow priests or bishops from France to enter British territory. The situation was resolved in 1766, when a priest from Quebec went to France and became a bishop. Upon his return, this bishop ordained new priests for the province. The Roman Catholic Church remained the dominant institution in Quebec, despite the anti-Catholic attitudes of the British.

The Rights of Canadians.   In the PROCLAMATION OF 1763, the British government declared that British laws applied to all Canadians. The proclamation aroused such opposition among French Canadians that the British Parliament passed the QUEBEC ACT in 1774 to pacify their "new subjects." The Quebec Act guaranteed French Canadians the right to practice Roman Catholicism. It also restored the old French civil law and permitted Catholic Canadians to hold public office—even though Catholics in Britain could not hold office. In addition, the Quebec Act extended the authority of officials in Quebec to include the Great Lakes and the Ohio and Mississippi valleys. It did not create a colonial assembly, however, because this would have given the French Canadians—who were in the majority—control of the government.

Canadians generally appreciated the Quebec Act for protecting their rights. However, the act was not well received in the 13 British colonies to the south. By giving control of the Great Lakes region and the Ohio and Mississippi River valleys to Canadians, Britain blocked the American colonists from expanding west of the Appalachian Mountains. American colonists saw the Quebec Act as another indication of Britain's desire to take away their rights. In addition to complaining to British authorities about the act, the American colonists harshly criticized their Catholic neighbors to the north. Britain's protection of Canadian rights in the Quebec Act, combined with the anti-Catholicism of the American colonists, helped cement Canadian loyalty to Great Britain during the AMERICAN REVOLUTION.

Forging a British Canada

After the French and Indian War, many British citizens settled in Canada and began to build lives and communities based on British customs and traditions. When the American Revolution ended, another wave of British immigrants entered Canada. Most were LOYALISTS from the United States who had not wanted to break away from Great Britain. Unhappy with the Revolution and its outcome, about 40,000 Loyalists left their homes and moved to Canada. Increasingly, Canada became a society divided between British- and French-speaking people.

Resolving Differences.   A number of issues separated the new British colonists from the French-speaking residents of Canada—most notably language, law, and representation in government. The British did not understand the French language or French law, which was very different from the British system of law. The British colonists also grew frustrated because they had no representative assemblies in which they could express their views.

In an effort to deal with these issues, the British in 1791 divided Canada into two provinces: Lower Canada (Quebec) and Upper Canada (Ontario). Britain gave each province a separate government that included an elected assembly and a council and governor appointed by the British crown. Although the assemblies had little authority, they did hold the power to tax. Most former Loyalists resettled in Upper Canada, where few French Canadians lived. French inhabitants remained concentrated in Lower Canada. The other provinces of modern Canada were still separate.

Turmoil and Union. British colonists quickly gained control in Upper Canada, dominating its economy, politics, and culture. In Lower Canada, however, power was divided between French- and English-speaking inhabitants. The British controlled the economy and appointive government offices of the province, but French-speaking Canadians dominated the provincial assembly. This led to decades of conflict and turmoil between the two groups.

In the 1830s, tensions between the French and British of Lower Canada erupted in violence. Fighting began when the government tried to arrest leaders of the French political party that controlled the provincial assembly. Clashes in Montreal and the countryside resulted in the destruction of numerous homes and churches. Many French Canadian leaders fled to the United States. Some were hanged or sent to a British prison colony in Australia.

After this outbreak of violence, British authorities began to consider what they could do to end the conflict between French- and English-speaking Canadians. They concluded that it was time to assimilate* French-speaking inhabitants fully into British Canada. In 1840 they united Upper Canada and Lower Canada into a single province, an administrative change that helped reduce tensions between the two groups. Yet French Canadians maintained their own language, institutions, and culture. The division between French- and English-speaking Canadians continues to this day. In the late 1900s, separatist groups in the French-speaking province of Quebec called for independence from Canada.

* *assimilate* to adopt the customs of a society

Relations with the United States

Relations between British Canada and the United States were often strained. During the American Revolution, patriot* leaders tried to get Canada on their side, first through military invasion and then through diplomacy. Neither approach worked, and Canada remained loyal to Great Britain.

When the War of 1812 broke out between the United States and Britain, the United States again tried to seize Canada. Although the Americans gained control of the Great Lakes, invasion attempts failed. The Treaty of Ghent (1814), which ended the war, left various boundary issues unsettled. These issues strained relations between the United States and Canada for several decades.

* *patriot* American colonist who supported independence from Britain

An agreement in 1818 fixed the border between the United States and Canada from the Great Lakes to the Rocky Mountains. However, disputes over boundaries continued to trouble the relations between the two countries. In 1842 the United States and Great Britain signed a treaty that settled the eastern border between Canada and the United States. But the line dividing the two countries from the Rocky Mountains to the Pacific Ocean remained uncertain. As American settlers streamed into the Oregon Territory* in the 1840s, tensions mounted and both the United States and Britain began threatening war. The issue was resolved peacefully in 1846 by a treaty that established the current border.

* **Oregon Territory** northwest region that included the present-day states of Washington, Oregon, Idaho, and parts of Montana, Wyoming, and British Columbia

The Development of Modern Canada

Canada grew steadily during the 1800s. Railroads linked provinces and helped spur growth. Thousands more English-speaking immigrants moved into the area that is now Ontario, and Canada as a whole became more British in outlook. Meanwhile, leaders in Nova Scotia and New Brunswick began to discuss the possibility of uniting with the province of Canada to form a confederation. After considerable debate, the provinces agreed to unite.

The British North America Act of 1867 created the Dominion of Canada, a nation that included the provinces of Ontario and Quebec (separated once again), New Brunswick, and Nova Scotia. Each province had its own government, with an elected assembly. A national government, with its own parliament and power to veto provincial laws, ruled over the entire confederation. In 1873 Prince Edward Island joined the confederation.

The confederation involved only the eastern portion of present-day Canada. In the west, two separate colonies remained—Rupert's Land and British Columbia. Rupert's Land consisted of the area around Hudson Bay and a huge region extending west to the Rocky Mountains. Originally controlled by the Hudson's Bay Company, Rupert's Land came under British rule in 1869.

British Columbia also began as a colony of the Hudson's Bay Company. From the 1740s to early 1800s, Russian fur traders regularly visited the colony's coastal areas, but they failed to establish any permanent settlements. In 1843 the Hudson's Bay Company built Fort Victoria on Vancouver Island. The discovery of gold caused a population boom on the island, which became a separate colony of the Hudson's Bay Company in 1849. The British government established its own colony of British Columbia on the mainland in 1858. The following year, the British took control of Vancouver Island, which they added to their colony of British Columbia in 1866.

Beginning in 1870, new provinces carved from Rupert's Land and British Columbia became part of the Canadian confederation: Manitoba (1870), British Columbia (1871), Alberta (1905), and Saskatchewan (1905). Two other areas—the Yukon Territory and Northwest Territories—have not yet received provincial status and remain territories of Canada. In the east, Newfoundland joined the confederation in 1949. Today Canada continues to have strong ties with Great Britain as a member of the British Commonwealth*.

* **British Commonwealth** group of former colonies linked to Great Britain by common goals and interests

Canoes

The Indians of North America used canoes to travel on the continent's rivers and along its coasts. The canoe, a long, narrow vessel with tapered ends, was so efficient for water travel that many European explorers and colonists adopted it.

Native Americans in different regions developed different types of canoes. In the southeastern region of North America and the Pacific Northwest, the Indians used dugouts, canoes shaped from large logs that were hollowed out by burning or scraping. Arctic people made canoelike boats, called umiaks and kayaks, by stretching animal skins over frames of whalebone or wood.

The canoe that became most familiar and useful to Europeans, though, was the birchbark canoe. Indians in the northeast, the Great Lakes region, and much of Canada were experts in making and using this lightweight, easy-to-guide craft. The birchbark canoe consisted of a wooden frame covered with bark from the white birch tree. It was stitched together with roots and sealed with waterproof tree sap; a layer of thin, flexible wooden strips covered the bark.

The canoeist moved the boat by paddling or, in shallow water, by shoving a pole against the streambed. The canoe was sturdy enough to hold passengers and cargo yet light enough to be carried, or portaged, between bodies of water. Small canoes carried 1 to 3 people, but larger crafts could hold more than 40.

Europeans were quick to see the advantages of the canoe. Travel by land was extremely difficult in much of the forested interior, especially in New France*, with its many interconnected lakes and streams.

The French relied on the birchbark canoe in their pursuit of the FUR TRADE. Trappers and traders in canoes traveled up the St. Lawrence and Ottawa rivers to the Great Lakes. They continued along the Saskatchewan and Missouri rivers to the Rocky Mountains or down the Mississippi River to the Gulf of Mexico. Boatbuilders created ever-larger canoes to carry more goods over longer distances. By 1752 a workshop at Trois-Rivières in Canada was producing canoes 36 feet long, capable of carrying three tons of cargo. The birchbark canoe remained in wide use in Canada throughout the 1700s. (*See also* **Transportation and Travel.**)

* *New France* French colony centered in the St. Lawrence River valley, an area known as Canada; included the Great Lakes region and, until 1713, Acadia (present-day Nova Scotia)

Cartier, Jacques

1491–1557
French explorer of North America

See third map in Exploration, Age of (vol. 2).

Jacques Cartier was the first French explorer of North America. During his three voyages to the continent, Cartier discovered the ST. LAWRENCE RIVER and established France's claim to territory in what is now CANADA.

Born in Saint-Malo, France, Cartier made a voyage to the recently discovered Americas, possibly to Brazil and Newfoundland, in the 1520s. In 1534 the French king, Francis I, sent him on an expedition to North America to secure a share of territory for France. He hoped Cartier would discover a NORTHWEST PASSAGE, a water route to Asia through North America, and riches—as the Spanish had done in Mexico. On his first voyage, Cartier explored and mapped the Gulf of St. Lawrence, with two Huron Indians as guides. He discovered the opening of the St. Lawrence River, but the approach of winter weather forced him to return to France without further investigation.

The next year Cartier returned to the region with three ships to resume his exploration. He sailed up the St. Lawrence River to the site of present-day QUEBEC, where he left some men to set up a winter camp. Cartier then continued up the river to the site of what is now Montreal. Barred from going farther because of rapids, Cartier believed that another great river would be found nearby that might be the Northwest Passage. He and his crew spent the winter of 1535–1536 at the camp near Quebec, where they suffered terribly from the cold and from disease. In the spring, they set sail for France.

From the point of view of France, the two voyages were a notable achievement. Although Cartier had not discovered treasure, he had learned much about the new land and its inhabitants. He had drawn a map of the St. Lawrence River that would remain in use for almost a century and had found a route by which Europeans could get to the heart of North America. Most important, Cartier had established France's claim to a vast territory.

In 1541 Cartier set off on a third voyage to North America, this time to establish a settlement as a base for a French colony. Cartier brought along several hundred men, many recruited from French prisons. A second group of settlers—led by Jean François de La Rocque de Roberval, the newly appointed governor of the colony—was to come later. Cartier began building a settlement at a spot called Cap Rouge, a few miles upriver from Quebec. The settlers had a difficult winter, afflicted by the cold and threatened by hostile Indians. Discouraged and worried about defending the settlement, Cartier packed up the settlers in the spring and set sail for France. On the way, they met Roberval's ships in the Gulf of St. Lawrence. Cartier refused to go back to Canada. Instead he returned to France carrying a load of what he believed to be gold and diamonds. Roberval pressed on to Cap Rouge and tried to establish a colony. By the summer of 1543, Roberval and his settlers had also given up and returned to France.

The French failed in their first attempt to establish an American colony. Moreover, Cartier found neither the Northwest Passage nor the treasures he sought. The "gold and diamonds" he brought back to France after his third voyage proved to be worthless rocks. Nonetheless, Cartier's voyages would serve as the basis for later, more ambitious and successful French colonial ventures in Canada. (*See also* **Exploration, Age of.**)

Catawba Indians

Once a large and powerful Siouan-speaking tribe, the Catawba Indians lived in an area along the border of present-day North and South Carolina. When the English arrived in the region, the Catawba generally welcomed the settlers and the trade goods they brought.

Like other southeastern tribes, the Catawba settled in large permanent villages and had an economy based on agriculture. They built pole-frame houses covered with bark. Although traditional enemies of the CHEROKEE INDIANS, the Catawba also waged war against such tribes as the SHAWNEE, the DELAWARE, and the IROQUOIS.

Remember: *Words in small capital letters have separate entries, and the index at the end of Volume 4 will guide you to more information on many topics.*

See second map in Native Americans (vol. 3).

With the arrival of English colonists in the Carolinas, the lives of the Catawba began to change. Their contact with the colonists turned into misfortune, as epidemics of smallpox and other European diseases ravaged the tribe. Between 1690 and 1760, the population of the tribe fell from approximately 5,000 to fewer than 500. These epidemics left the Catawba greatly weakened and dependent on the colonists for food and other supplies. To survive, they joined other Indian groups that faced similar problems.

When the FRENCH AND INDIAN WAR began in 1754, the Catawba sided with the British against the French. During the war, however, increasing numbers of British colonists moved into their territory, leading to clashes between the Indians and the newcomers. The Catawba went to the colonial authorities to try to resolve this problem. They sought, and received, a reservation within their homeland that was guaranteed to them by British law.

Despite their previous alliance with the British, the Catawba supported the colonists in the American Revolution and fought side by side with American troops to defend South Carolina. Their assistance helped earn the Catawba a reputation as friends of the United States. In the 1800s, the Catawba lost their original reservation and, after several years without a homeland, settled on a smaller tract of land in South Carolina. Members of the Catawba tribe continue to live there today. (*See also* **Diseases and Disorders; Housing; South Carolina.**)

Catholicism

See *Roman Catholic Church.*

Cayuga Indians

See *Iroquois Confederacy.*

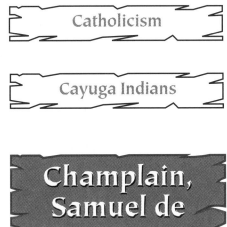

Champlain, Samuel de

ca. 1567–1635
French explorer and founder of Quebec

See third map in Exploration, Age of (vol. 2).

Samuel de Champlain spent half of his life promoting the interests of France in North America. As an explorer, he greatly extended French territorial claims. As a geographer, he added to knowledge of the continent through his writings and excellent maps. As a political leader, Champlain founded and later governed QUEBEC—the first permanent French settlement in North America.

The son of a naval captain, Champlain was born at Brouage on the southwest coast of France. Knowledgeable about navigation and eager to explore the world, the young Frenchman made his first voyage to the Americas in 1599 on a Spanish expedition to the West Indies and Central America. On his return to Europe, Champlain presented a detailed report on NEW SPAIN to the French king, Henry IV. The king rewarded Champlain by granting him a title of nobility and appointing him geographer of a fur-trading expedition about to set sail for North America. During this voyage, which began in 1603, Champlain explored the ST. LAWRENCE RIVER as far as present-day MONTREAL and wrote about the natural features of the region and the Native Americans who lived there.

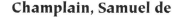

Champlain, Samuel de

As an explorer, geographer, and political leader, Samuel de Champlain made great contributions to French interests in North America. He produced the first accurate maps of the Atlantic coast and founded Quebec, the first permanent French settlement.

·1567· Samuel de Champlain ·1635·

In the years that followed, Champlain made a series of expeditions along the Atlantic coast of North America, traveling as far south as Cape Cod in present-day Massachusetts. He explored more than 1,000 miles of coastline and produced the first accurate maps of the area. The quality and extent of Champlain's work was not matched by any other geographer of the time.

Champlain took part in several attempts to establish French bases on the Atlantic coast. He believed, however, that the St. Lawrence River was a better location for French settlement. After receiving permission from the king, he founded a trading post at a place where the St. Lawrence narrowed. Called Quebec—from an Indian word meaning "narrowing"—this first permanent

Daily Life

Plate 1
The church played a key role in the lives of British colonists. This delightful scene, part of a quilt made by Sarah Furman Warner of Connecticut in about 1800, has the all-important church at the center of the community.

Plate 2
This painting shows the interior of a simple colonial house. Its main room had many functions, serving as a kitchen, dining room, living room, workshop—and even sleeping quarters.

Plate 3
Wealthy planters in the South had indentured servants or slaves to work their land. People with small farms generally plowed their own fields. Ludwig Gottfried von Redeken painted this rural scene near Salem, North Carolina, in 1787.

Plate 4

The well-stocked waters of Nova Scotia and Newfoundland attracted fishing expeditions from France and England. The Europeans established camps along the shores where they cleaned and salted the fish and laid them out to dry. This painting shows Newfoundland harbor about 1760.

Plate 5

In this neighborhood scene of the 1760s, painted by Joseph B. Smith, well-dressed, middle-class families stroll along John Street in New York City. In the background stands Wesley's Methodist Chapel.

Plate 6
This 1788 watercolor of an Indian camp at Point Levy near
Quebec was painted by Thomas Davies, a British military officer.
The artist provides a detailed view of the Indians' life.

Plate 7
This hand-colored engraving of a California mission shows Spanish
soldiers and Indians waiting outside the church for the missionaries.
Between 1769 and 1823, the Spanish built 21 missions in California.

French settlement in North America later became the administrative and economic center of the colony of NEW FRANCE. Champlain became commandant of the colony in 1612.

From his base in Quebec, Champlain explored the region on either side of the St. Lawrence River and lands to the west. In 1609 HURON INDIANS led him to a large lake south of the river, now known as Lake Champlain. The French explorer also visited the GREAT LAKES. Although the region was already known to European fur traders and missionaries, Champlain was the first to describe it in detail and to make maps. He hoped that his expedition through the inland areas would reveal a broad waterway—a NORTHWEST PASSAGE—leading to the Pacific Ocean. Like many other European explorers, though, Champlain failed to discover this shortcut to Asia.

During his explorations, Champlain traveled with Indian companions and became involved in their wars. He took the side of the Huron against the IROQUOIS, who would remain the enemies of France for years. In 1615, while fighting alongside the Huron, Champlain was seriously wounded by an arrow. Thereafter, he focused his attention on promoting the growth of New France. He returned to France several times to gather support and new settlers for the French colony. In Quebec, he often sent men into the wilderness to live with the Indians and learn their languages and their ways. These men helped promote friendly relations and trade with the Indians. At the same time, they extended France's territorial claims and broadened its knowledge of North America.

In 1629 British raiders captured Quebec, sending Champlain and other French colonial officials into exile in Europe. After a treaty restored the area to France in 1632, Champlain returned to Quebec as royal governor of the French colony. He died in Quebec on Christmas Day, 1635, a respected leader who has been called "the father of New France." (*See also* **Exploration, Age of; Fur Trade; Maps and Charts.**)

Charleston, South Carolina

Charleston was the largest and wealthiest city in Great Britain's southern colonies. By the 1770s, this port city of SOUTH CAROLINA ranked fourth in size among American cities after Philadelphia, New York, and Boston. Charleston maintained its importance after the colonial period and became one of the leading commercial centers of the southeastern United States.

Early History. English settlers from BARBADOS in the West Indies arrived in the Carolinas in the 1670s. They were soon joined by settlers from other colonies. In 1680 these colonists founded a town on a peninsula between the mouths of the Ashley and Cooper Rivers. They named it Charles Town in honor of King Charles II of England. The name later became Charleston.

Not too far south of Charleston lay Spanish FLORIDA, and in the early years, the town had to live with the threat of invasion. By 1704 the townspeople had built defensive walls, and Charleston became a powerful rival to the Spanish settlement of ST. AUGUSTINE. After facing an invasion attempt by the Spanish and French in 1706, the inhabitants of Charleston built a fort at the mouth of the city's harbor.

Charleston served as the capital of the Carolinas until 1712, when NORTH CAROLINA became a separate colony, and then as the capital of South Carolina. In 1790 the capital was moved to Columbia in the center of the state, but Charleston remained South Carolina's leading city.

Charleston and Trade.

With a deep harbor opening into the Atlantic Ocean and easy access to the interior, Charleston quickly grew into the most important seaport in the southern colonies. The city's early prosperity came from trade with the CREEK and CHEROKEE INDIANS of the region. Charleston merchants provided the Indians with cloth, guns, tools, and trinkets in exchange for animal skins and furs, which were exported to Europe.

indigo plant used to make a blue dye

Beginning in the 1730s, rice, indigo*, and lumber became the city's major exports. The European demand for rice contributed to the prosperity of Charleston and South Carolina. Using the profits from exports, the city's merchants imported items from Europe, such as fine textiles, glass, furniture, wine, and coffee.

Most of Charleston's international trade was dominated by merchants in Great Britain, who worked through local representatives known as factors. Acting as middlemen, the factors collected agricultural produce in warehouses and arranged for its export to Britain. They also imported British merchandise for local retailers. In time many factors went into business on their own, becoming independent merchants.

cosmopolitan worldly, not provincial and narrow; having wide interests and knowledge

As the SLAVE TRADE developed, Charleston also became a slave-trading center. Blacks brought by traders from Africa and the West Indies were sold as slaves in Charleston to plantation owners from the Carolinas and Georgia. Before the Congress of the United States ended the slave trade in 1808, more than 80,000 African slaves passed through Charleston.

Society and Culture.

Colonial Charleston was a cosmopolitan* city, and its people came from a variety of backgrounds. HUGUENOTS fleeing religious

Charleston was the largest city in Britain's southern colonies. A major seaport, with a population made up of people from diverse backgrounds, Charleston prospered as a center of international trade. This engraving by W. H. Toms shows the city before 1739.

An Exact Prospect of CHARLES TOWN, the Metropolis of the Province of SOUTH CAROLINA.

persecution in France arrived in the late 1600s. ACADIANS who had been expelled from Canada came in the 1750s. Jewish merchants arrived from New York in the early 1700s to take part in the city's growing trade. People from other British colonies and ethnic backgrounds came as well, attracted by the opportunities offered in Charleston. Black slaves added to the cultural mix. By 1776 more than half of the city's residents were slaves.

Despite such diversity, the culture of Charleston was decidedly British. The Charleston library had the latest books from London. Wealthy residents sent their sons to school in Great Britain, built English-style homes, adopted English manners, and became members of organizations such as the Royal Society of London. Many of the finest public buildings in the city, such as the Customs Exchange, resembled public buildings in British cities. Charleston society also resembled society in Britain, with its distinct division into upper, middle, and lower classes.

As a prosperous city, Charleston provided numerous cultural opportunities. The city's many schools offered academic courses with subjects such as Greek, Latin, and history, as well as practical courses with subjects such as surveying, navigation, and accounting. For entertainment, wealthy Charleston residents could attend dances, musical performances, and theatrical productions. Some of the earliest musical theater pieces in America were performed in Charleston.

The American Revolution and After.

The American Revolution and After. Many Charleston residents supported protests against British policies that led to the AMERICAN REVOLUTION. The Charlestonians staged demonstrations during the STAMP ACT CRISIS in 1765, and they later joined the boycott* of British goods to express their opposition to the TOWNSHEND ACTS. In 1774 the city's residents protested against the INTOLERABLE ACTS, which the British Parliament had passed as punishment for the BOSTON TEA PARTY.

During the Revolution, the British twice tried and failed to capture Charleston. They finally succeeded in 1780, and Charleston remained under British control until 1782. After the Revolution, Charleston experienced a new burst of commercial prosperity and growth. It remained the most important port of the South, as well as a center of southern culture and politics. (*See also* **British Colonies; Class Structure in European Colonies; Colonial Administration; Trade and Commerce.**)

* **boycott** refusal to buy goods as a means of protest

Cherokee Indians

* **confederacy** alliance or league of peoples or states

*T*he Cherokee are Native Americans who inhabited large areas of southeastern North America during the colonial period. Their territory included the Appalachian Mountain regions of present-day North and South Carolina, Virginia, West Virginia, Georgia, Kentucky, Tennessee, and Alabama. The large and powerful Cherokee tribe played a significant role in the history of colonial settlement of the Southeast.

The first contact the Cherokee had with Europeans occurred in 1540, when Spanish explorer Hernando DE SOTO arrived in their territory. At that time, the Cherokee had a society based on agriculture. They lived in many independent towns and villages joined in a confederacy*. Leadership in these villages was divided between "white" chiefs, who made decisions in times of peace, and "red" chiefs, who gave advice during wartime.

By the mid-1600s, English traders had established relations with the Cherokee. The two groups gradually developed a steady trade in which the Cherokee exchanged deerskins for English cloth and metal goods. The growing trade brought problems for the Cherokee. Not only did they become dependent on English goods, but European colonists began to arrive and settle on Cherokee land. Contact with Europeans also worsened rivalries between the Cherokee and other Native Americans, leading to periods of intertribal warfare.

Between 1689 and 1763, the Cherokee generally sided with the British in their colonial wars against the French and Spanish. During this period, the Cherokee also warred with various tribes, including the CREEK, CHOCTAW, CHICKASAW, SHAWNEE, and TUSCARORA. In 1721 the Cherokee signed a treaty with their British allies that regulated trade and set a boundary between British settlement and Cherokee territory. Despite the agreement, white settlers continued to move onto Cherokee land, threatening the alliance with the British. In 1760 the Cherokee finally revolted and began raiding white settlements along the frontier. In turn, the British colonists burned Cherokee villages and destroyed crops. When the Cherokee eventually surrendered in 1762, the colonists forced them to sign a peace treaty that ceded* large portions of their territory.

The Cherokee continued to lose land to white settlement in the early 1770s, causing tension between the tribe and the colonists. As a result, most Cherokee fought on the side of the British during the AMERICAN REVOLUTION. When the Cherokee began raiding frontier settlements, American colonists launched devastating attacks on Cherokee villages. By 1777 the Americans had defeated the Cherokee. There followed a series of treaties that forced the Cherokee to give up huge amounts of the territory they still held. The Cherokee were greatly weakened politically, militarily, and economically.

After the colonial period, the Cherokee transformed their society by imitating many aspects of white culture. During the early 1800s, they formed a government modeled on that of the United States and based on a written constitution. Many Cherokee adopted white farming techniques, acquired black slaves, built homes similar to those of white Americans, and learned new crafts. A Cherokee named Sequoya invented an alphabet, which enabled the Cherokee to develop a written language. Soon they began to publish a newspaper. As a result of these changes, the Cherokee became more prosperous than other Indian tribes.

Despite efforts to accept white culture, the Cherokee continued to suffer at the hands of white Americans. In the early 1800s, the Cherokee lost more land to white settlement. Then, in 1835, the U.S. government forced Cherokee leaders to sign a treaty relinquishing all land east of the Mississippi River in exchange for land in Indian Territory (present-day Oklahoma). Many Cherokee refused to accept the treaty. Some managed to remain in their homelands and became the Eastern Band of Cherokee Indians. However, in 1838 U.S. troops evicted thousands of other Cherokee from their homes and forced them to march west. Many Cherokee died on this trip, which became

See second map in Native Americans (vol. 3).

* *cede* to yield or surrender

known as the Trail of Tears. In Indian Territory, different bands of Cherokee merged to form the Cherokee Nation, and they began to rebuild their lives in their new homeland. (*See also* **Economic Systems; Languages; Native Americans.**)

Chesapeake Bay

Chesapeake Bay is a 200-mile inlet of the Atlantic Ocean, bordered by Maryland, Virginia, and Delaware. The bay's name came from an Indian village, Chesepiooc—which meant "on the big river" in Algonquian. In the 1600s, the area became the center of early English settlements in North America.

Forty-eight rivers feed into Chesapeake Bay, including the Susquehanna, the Potomac, the York, and the James. Many of the rivers were deep enough for English colonial ships to navigate, providing easy routes to the interior of the region.

In the years before the Europeans came, numerous Native American tribes lived around Chesapeake Bay. They fished and raised such crops as maize, beans, squash, and TOBACCO. A chief of the Pamunkey tribe named Powhatan united many of the region's tribes in a confederacy*. The large area he ruled included about 12,000 Native Americans.

* *confederacy* alliance or league of peoples or states

In 1607 English colonists founded the JAMESTOWN COLONY on the James River upstream from Chesapeake Bay. This settlement became the center of the colony of Virginia. In 1634 another group of English colonists established St. Mary's City on the Potomac River, the first community of the colony of Maryland. The Chesapeake region provided abundant fish and shellfish, lush forests, and fertile soil. The colonists expanded their settlements and founded two major ports—Norfolk at the mouth of the bay in 1682 and Baltimore in 1729. In time Virginia and Maryland became profitable colonies, with economies based on growing tobacco for export to Europe. (*See also* **Maryland; Powhatan Indians; Virginia.**)

Chesapeake Colonies

See *British Colonies; Maryland; Virginia.*

Cheyenne Indians

See *Plains Indians.*

Chichimec War (1540–1600)

The Chichimec War was a bitter conflict between Indians and Spanish settlers in NEW SPAIN. As the Spaniards gained control of the region that is now MEXICO, they met resistance from groups of Chichimec Indians. The war lasted from the 1540s to about 1600.

The Chichimec. In 1521 Spanish CONQUISTADORS had defeated the Aztec, the strongest Indian power in Mexico. The victory did not give the Spaniards complete control over the region, however. They were blocked to the north by various tribes of fierce nomadic Indians called the Chichimec, meaning "barbarians" in the Aztec language.

These Indians scratched out a living in a harsh, rocky land—the Gran Chichimeca—by hunting and by eating cactus and mesquite, a desert tree with sweet pods. They lived in small groups of a few families. Accustomed to freedom, the Chichimec did not want to be forced to work on the farms, ranches, or in the mines of the Spanish.

In the late 1540s, problems developed between the Chichimec and the Spanish colonists. Silver was discovered in Zacatecas, a few hundred miles north of Mexico City, and Spain soon had a thriving community of mines in the area. Wagon trains from Mexico City carried supplies to the mining area and returned loaded with silver. Conflict was inevitable—the Spanish wagon trains drove right through the Gran Chichimeca. The Spaniards captured many Indians to work on farms or in the mines. The Chichimec responded by burning Spanish settlements and attacking the wagon trains. The area became the battleground of the Chichimec War.

The War.   The Indians proved to be tough opponents. They fought in small bands, often by setting ambushes for the Spanish. They struck quickly, then split up and covered their tracks to avoid pursuit—tactics that many Indian groups would use over the next centuries. They used arrows with obsidian* tips that could easily penetrate the Spaniards' metal armor. Sometimes the Chichimec sent spies into Spanish areas so they could learn of upcoming movements and make their plans accordingly. The Indian women joined with the men in fighting to protect their homes.

The Spanish fought fiercely as well. A 1542 Spanish law banned making slaves of Indians. However, the Spanish declared that the ban did not apply in this case because the Chichimec had burned churches and killed priests. As a result, the Spanish turned the Chichimec they captured into slaves. The Indians responded by taking prisoners too. They forced captured women to become their wives and taught captured children how to fight, gaining new warriors for the conflict.

During the first 20 years of the war, the Chichimec continued to raid Spanish ranches and wagon trains. One Indian raid in 1554 yielded more than 30,000 pesos' worth of silver, clothing, and other goods, including mules to carry it all. By the 1560s, the Chichimec had grown bolder. They began to stage attacks farther south and to carry out larger-scale raids. The Spanish built many presidios* to defend the mines and the wagon routes.

The viceroy* of New Spain decided to try to establish peace with the Chichimec. He banned the taking of Chichimec slaves and freed some slaves captured earlier. He also offered food, clothing, and supplies to the Indians. At the same time, he launched a renewed offensive of Spanish troops and Indian allies against any Chichimec who continued to fight.

In the early 1580s, the conflict began to ease. Disease and warfare had reduced the number of Chichimec who could fight. The lack of unity among Chichimec tribes allowed the Spanish to make peace with individual bands. Offers of supplies and other aid cut resistance. The Spanish also settled some Indian allies in the Chichimec area, hoping that the example of

* **obsidian** volcanic rock that can be shaped into a very sharp point

* **presidio** Spanish fort built to protect mission settlements

* **viceroy** person appointed as a monarch's representative to govern a province or colony

peaceful behavior would be a good influence. By 1600 the Chichimec War had ended.

Chickasaw Indians

See second map in Native Americans (vol. 3).

* *clan* related families

During the colonial period, the Chickasaw Indians lived in what is now northern Mississippi, and their territory included parts of present-day Tennessee, Kentucky, Arkansas, and Alabama. When European powers competed for control of these lands, the Chickasaw became involved in a series of wars involving Spain, France, and Britain, as well as various other groups of Native Americans.

Closely related to the Choctaw Indians in both language and culture, the Chickasaw also had cultural ties to the Creek Indians. The Chickasaw were an agricultural people who raised corn and other crops and lived in fortified villages often built along the banks of rivers. They traded with other Indian groups along the Mississippi River, and their dialect soon became the common language of traders in the region. The principal unit of tribal organization was the clan*, and property and tribal leadership passed through the female members of the clan. A warlike tribe, the Chickasaw dominated much of the lower Mississippi River valley.

The Chickasaw encountered Europeans in the early 1540s, when Spanish explorer Hernando DE SOTO passed through their lands. The Indians welcomed the strangers at first, but the hostile behavior of the Spaniards soon caused the Chickasaw to attack them and drive them away. In the late 1600s, the Chickasaw formed ties with English traders from the Carolinas.

The Chickasaw fought a series of wars with the French. The first one broke out in 1719, when the Indians refused a French order to expel British traders from their territory. They were punished with raids by the French and the Choctaw, traditional enemies of the Chickasaw. The Chickasaw responded by attacking French ships on the Mississippi River. With neither side achieving clear victory, the parties agreed to stop fighting in 1725.

The peace was short-lived. A second war erupted in 1732, when the Chickasaw supported the Natchez Indians in a revolt against French rule. Once again, the French set the Choctaw against the Chickasaw, who responded by blocking French shipping on the Mississippi River. Then, in 1736, an army of almost 2,500 French soldiers and Choctaw Indians invaded Chickasaw territory. Faced with this overwhelming enemy force, the Chickasaw asked for peace.

Not convinced that the Chickasaw would remain peaceful, the French invaded their lands again in 1752. Neither side won a decisive victory in this third war. However, the Chickasaw, now exhausted by the long series of wars, decided to stay out of the French and Indian War between France and Britain.

During the American Revolution, the Chickasaw did not give full support to either the Americans or the British. Some Chickasaw fought on each side, while others remained neutral. In 1786 they signed a treaty with the United States that established territorial boundaries for the tribe. The treaty proved temporary, however. White settlers eventually poured into the region, leading to clashes with the Chickasaw. In the 1830s, the U.S. government forced the Chickasaw, along with the Cherokee Indians and other eastern tribes, to abandon their homelands and move west of the Mississippi to an

area known as Indian Territory (present-day Oklahoma). The Chickasaw land there eventually was opened to white settlement as well.

Childhood and Adolescence

*I*n some ways, growing up in colonial America was much like growing up at any other time or place. Colonial children and adolescents mastered new skills, learned to get along with others, and prepared to enter adulthood. Yet the lives and responsibilities of colonial children differed in many ways from those of American children and teenagers of later generations and today.

Even during the colonial period, the experiences of children varied significantly. Growing up as a boy was quite different from growing up as a girl. In the British colonies, the upbringing of a PURITAN child was not the same as that of a QUAKER child. People from different areas of the world—from Great Britain, France, Spain, the Netherlands, or Africa—brought different ideas about child rearing to North America. In spite of the great diversity, however, the lives of most young people in the colonies shared important features.

Features of Colonial Childhood.   Death was always close at hand during the colonial period. In hot, humid regions where fevers raged, 30 percent of the children died in infancy. Even in the healthiest regions, one out of every ten babies died before his or her first birthday. Many who survived lost siblings* or parents during childhood, so children often lived among stepparents, stepsiblings, and half siblings. Colonial families were generally large. New England families averaged eight children; French colonial families averaged six. As a result, colonial households were busy, crowded places. Children rarely had a room or even a bed of their own. Most had to share space with older siblings. Privacy was a luxury that few could imagine.

Colonial children learned early about the importance of relatives. Related families often lived near each other and relied on each other for help in hard times. Grandparents, aunts and uncles, or other relatives took in orphaned children. Orphans with no relatives found themselves under the guardianship of the courts or, if they had reached adolescence, out in the world on their own.

Colonial parents dressed very young boys and girls alike, in long gowns or buttoned robes. These youngsters had various toys—often homemade—that included dolls, soldiers, and building blocks. As children grew older, they played games such as hide-and-seek and leapfrog. But for colonial children, this period without responsibilities ended early.

At age six or seven, children started to wear miniature versions of adult clothes. They also took on responsibilities for helping in the house or family business or on the farm. Boys gathered eggs, tended livestock, weeded fields, and ran errands. Girls planted and cared for gardens, swept floors, helped cook, and learned domestic skills such as making soap and spinning wool. Girls also helped care for the younger siblings. Many children, especially boys, began learning to read at age six or seven. Most were taught at home by their mothers, with BIBLES for textbooks. Those who went to school often did so for only a few weeks or months at a time.

* *sibling* brother or sister

Children and the Law

Some colonies enacted laws designed especially to keep young people in order. Authorities in Massachusetts and Connecticut could take "rude, stubborn, and unruly" children away from their parents and turn them over to others for disciplining. Children who struck or cursed their parents could be sentenced to death, though no such penalty was ever carried out. Under a 1682 Pennsylvania law, children who hit or threatened their parents could be jailed for as long as the parents thought necessary. This punishment was changed in 1700 to include six months in jail and a public whipping of "thirty-one lashes, well laid on."

In Ammi Phillips's *Portrait of Mary Jane Soggs and her Little Brother, Henry,* both children are shown in long dresses, typical clothing for young children in colonial times. At the age of six or seven, boys and girls would begin to wear garments similar to those of adults.

Between the ages of 7 and 14, many children spent long periods of time away from home. They often lived with grandparents or older siblings who needed assistance with household or farm chores. Children of poor families sometimes worked as servants in wealthy households. Occasionally, well-to-do families sent their children to boarding schools. By age 14 or so, most adolescents were working full-time. Girls who were not needed at home might be hired out as servants. Boys might begin an APPRENTICESHIP, living in the home of a master crafts worker to learn a trade. Only upper-class children, headed for lives of leisure or more advanced schooling, could delay the start of adult responsibilities.

British Colonies.   In some parts of the British colonies, religion played a major role in child rearing. New England Puritans believed that all people were born sinful and that parents had to "break a child's will" to teach godly virtues and ensure a child's spiritual welfare. Although Puritan parents did not lack affection, they practiced stern discipline. Accounts of Puritan childhoods include details of whippings and other harsh punishments. Adolescents often struggled with urges to rebel against parents, while anxiously examining their own feelings of religious faith or doubt.

The Quakers of Pennsylvania also devoted much energy to raising children according to their religious beliefs. Quakers taught the virtues of love and compassion. Unlike the Puritans, they emphasized good examples and discussion as the way to guide their children. If parents did not appear to be doing their duty or their children became troublesome, fellow Quakers might step in to place children in foster homes or apprenticeships.

In the southern colonies, wealthy plantation families developed a style of child rearing that set the pattern for the whole region. Their children enjoyed considerable freedom to make noise, play, and spend time away from adult supervision. Mothers taught their children to read, and the boys of wealthy families might receive additional education from their fathers or from private tutors. Some well-to-do families sent their sons to England for an upper-class education, especially for training in the law. Southern families often had fewer children than northern families. However, because of the region's high death rate, many households took in young cousins and other relatives. Throughout the South, young men and women tended to marry and take on adult roles earlier than adolescents in other colonies.

By the 1640s, communities in New England began establishing schools. A Massachusetts law passed in 1642 required towns to educate local children. Some children attended dame schools, which women held in their homes to teach reading and other basic skills. A few schools were established in Virginia in the mid-1600s, but the scattered population made regular attendance difficult. Throughout the English colonies, religious groups ran informal schools for children of church members.

Most Africans in the British colonies lived as slaves. The experiences of slave children were unlike those of any other group. Very young children might be shielded from the harsh realities of SLAVERY. When they had finished their household chores, they could often play with the children of their white masters. Between the ages of 10 and 14, however, slave children had to assume heavier workloads as household servants or field hands. Some encountered abuse or severe punishment from slaveholders or overseers. Above all, slave children lived with the constant fear that their families would be torn apart. Children might be sold away from parents, or parents from children. African American parents tried to strengthen their children by giving them a sense of kinship with all their relatives. Slave parents also encouraged their children's spiritual growth, in both traditional African and Christian beliefs.

French Colonies. Young people made up a large percentage of the population of NEW FRANCE and LOUISIANA. As a result, children became a powerful economic force in these areas. Their labor in the home or workshop and on the farm was vital to the family's welfare.

Under French colonial law, children remained under the authority of their fathers until they married or reached the age of 25. In reality, however, young people were so numerous and economically important that parents could not always supervise them closely or discipline them. Visitors from France, accustomed to stricter standards, complained that colonial children were rude, disobedient, and lazy.

Children in the French colonies took an important step toward adulthood when they participated in their first Holy Communion, the occasion on which they formally joined the ROMAN CATHOLIC CHURCH. For many young people,

Remember: *Words in small capital letters have separate entries, and the index at the end of Volume 4 will guide you to more information on many topics.*

education began and ended with the religious training they received before this event. A few continued their education in schools run by the church. Some girls attended church schools established by French nuns. As a result, more girls than boys learned to read and write—a highly unusual situation in the North American colonies.

At about the age of 16, many boys entered the colonial militia* or went to work as servants or apprentices. Young women could become apprentices too, but the only trade they could learn or practice was sewing. Although the government favored early marriages to encourage a settled population of families, few young people rushed into marriage before they could afford to set up households.

militia army of citizens who may be called into action in a time of emergency

Dutch Colony. The Dutch colony of NEW NETHERLAND also had a youthful population. Many of the early settlers were young people who worked as laborers or servants. In the 1640s, large numbers of couples arrived in the colony and began raising families.

Dutch colonial parents were not strict about disciplining and supervising their children, and the youngsters enjoyed a great deal of freedom. Records show that most children in the colony enjoyed happy, affectionate relationships with their parents. Peter STUYVESANT, the last governor of New Netherland, complained that the children of the colony were spoiled and often ran wild in the streets.

By the 1650s, schools had become common in New Netherland. Children could study in town schools or with independent schoolmasters in villages. Dutch parents, however, tended to think that preparing children for work was more important than educating them. They preferred to keep their children at home or working and learning in a relative's home. Girls were taught housekeeping. Boys prepared for careers as merchants or craftsmen by working in an office or workshop, generally starting around the time they entered their teens.

Spanish Borderlands. People who settled in the Spanish Borderlands—a region that included present-day California, Texas, New Mexico, and Arizona—followed traditional Spanish customs in raising their children. One custom was *compadrazgo,* in which parents chose friends or neighbors to serve as co-parents for each child. A co-parent was responsible for helping with a child's religious education in the Roman Catholic faith and, if necessary, with other kinds of support as well. *Compadrazgo* gave children security by providing substitute parents who could care for them if their parents died.

In raising children, Spanish colonial parents emphasized obedience to the church, loyalty to the crown, and respect for parents and other adults. The idea of *respeto,* or respect, was especially important in the Spanish colonies. For example, if an adult requested a drink of water, a child had to drop everything, fetch the drink, and wait with arms crossed until the older person had finished drinking.

Tradition and custom gave men and women different roles in Spanish colonial families. Men expected and demanded obedience from women and children. Fathers disciplined children, while mothers took responsibility for their religious training. Parents and the church taught girls to be modest, obedient, and patient. Boys learned the importance of maintaining the family's honor, or good name. Like young people throughout the North American colonies, Spanish children and adolescents modeled themselves on their mothers and fathers as they prepared to enter the adult world of work and marriage. (*See also* **African American Culture; Courtship; Education; Family; Marriage.**)

Chippewa Indians

See *Ojibwa Indians.*

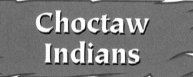

Choctaw Indians

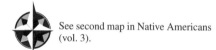

See second map in Native Americans (vol. 3).

During the colonial period, the Choctaw Indians lived mainly in the central and southern parts of present-day Mississippi and Alabama. Some outlying groups of the tribe inhabited areas of what are now Georgia and Louisiana. Related in language and culture to the CHICKASAW and CREEK INDIANS, the Choctaw were one of the largest tribes of the Southeast.

Sometime before the 1500s, the Choctaw moved to the eastern side of the Mississippi River and established farming settlements. Their villages consisted of log homes surrounded by large cornfields and gardens with beans, squash, and other crops. The Choctaw relied primarily on farming, but they also hunted, fished, and gathered wild plants. Each village had a chief and a council of elders who served as advisers. The people of the village had a say in community decisions, though, making the Choctaw more democratic than most southeastern Indian tribes. Conflicts within a village or between villages were often resolved through sport rather than by war. The Indians played a game similar to modern lacrosse in which a leather ball was thrown and caught by sticks with curved and webbed ends. They believed the prayers of their spiritual leaders could influence the outcome of the game.

The Choctaw had an elaborate system of beliefs centered on a sun god, represented by fire. One part of their religious ritual* involved placing people who died on raised platforms so that their bodies could decay naturally under the sun. The tribe believed their spiritual leaders could cure illness and foretell the future.

The Choctaw met Europeans for the first time in the 1540s, when the Spanish explorer Hernando DE SOTO and his soldiers entered their territory. Though their contact was brief, the Europeans introduced DISEASES that killed many Indians. In the late 1600s, the Choctaw began trading with the French. During the 1730s, an attempt by the English to form an alliance with the Choctaw divided the tribe. Some villages supported the French, while others favored the English, causing a civil war. The pro-French villages won, and the Choctaw resumed their alliance with the French.

After the FRENCH AND INDIAN WAR, the Choctaw's lands came under British control. As British colonists began moving into these lands, the Choctaw way of life changed. Some Choctaw women married British settlers,

* **ritual** ceremony that follows a set pattern

and the tribe became dependent on British trade. During the AMERICAN REV-OLUTION, the Choctaw remained largely neutral, although some gave the Americans information about British troop movements in their region. After the Revolution, the Choctaw signed treaties with both the Americans and the Spanish, who controlled areas just to the south.

In the early 1800s, the Choctaw accepted a series of treaties that ceded* portions of their territory to the United States. As their contact with Americans increased, many Choctaw began to adopt white customs. They also established schools to help Indian children become part of white society. Despite their efforts to assimilate*, the Choctaw received harsh treatment at the hands of the American government, which wanted the Indians' land.

In 1830 the United States signed the Treaty of Dancing Rabbit Creek with some Choctaw leaders who did not represent the views of the majority. The agreement gave the United States the remaining Choctaw territory east of the Mississippi River in exchange for land in Indian Territory (present-day Oklahoma). Although a few Choctaw remained in Mississippi, most were forced by the U.S. Army to make the long and difficult journey west. Many Indians died from disease and starvation along the way. Other southeastern tribes, such as the Creek and the CHEROKEE, were also forced to move west over the next decade. Because of the suffering the Indians endured, these migrations became known as the Trail of Tears.

* *cede* to yield or surrender

* *assimilate* to adopt the customs of a society

Chumash Indians

See *California Indians.*

Church and State

*T*he colonization of North America began at a time of religious conflict in Europe. Most European governments established one Christian church as the official state religion and persecuted people who followed other forms of religion. In setting up their colonies, these governments tended to continue the practice of supporting a state religion.

British Colonies. People of many different faiths settled in the British colonies of North America. Some colonies established close ties between church and state. In other colonies the church-state bonds were weak.

In the South, the founders of Virginia made the Church of England (also known as the Anglican Church) the official religion of the colony. Government officials supervised many church activities and tried to prevent the growth of other religions. Maryland was founded as a haven for ROMAN CATHOLICS, but Anglicans soon outnumbered Catholics in the colony. They made Anglicanism the established religion, prevented Catholics from serving in government, and imposed taxes to support the Anglican Church.

In South Carolina, too, Anglicanism became the official religion, but other Protestant churches were allowed. Both North Carolina and Georgia

Church and State

toleration acceptance of the right of individuals to follow their own religious beliefs

dissenter person who disagrees with the beliefs and practices of the established church

proprietor person granted land and the right to establish a colony

supported the Anglican Church. However, the large numbers of settlers of other faiths in those colonies and the lack of religious involvement of government officials promoted religious toleration* and weakened the church-state connection.

In New England, the PURITANS had come to North America to escape persecution for their religious beliefs. Yet the state they established was dominated by their church. In Massachusetts, only members of the Puritan church could vote, and tax money helped to support the churches. Those who protested against the church's dominant role were punished or expelled from the colony. Church-state relations were similar in Connecticut.

The founders of New Hampshire attempted to make Puritanism the official religion of the colony. But the presence of different types of Protestants led to greater religious freedom there than in Massachusetts or Connecticut. Rhode Island was founded by Roger WILLIAMS, a Puritan dissenter* expelled from Massachusetts. The colony became home to a mix of Puritans, QUAKERS, Baptists, and even some JEWS. It had no established church, no taxes for supporting churches, and complete freedom of religion.

A move to separate church and state gained force in England in the late 1600s. In 1689 Parliament passed a law that gave people freedom to practice any Christian faith. This idea was reflected most strongly in the middle colonies—New York, New Jersey, Pennsylvania, and Delaware. After the English took control of New Netherland in 1664, the proprietor* of the colony (now called New York) intended to establish Anglicanism as the official religion. New York's very diverse population protested vigorously, however, and the plan was dropped. In 1693 the Anglican Church did become the official church in the New York City area, but its influence was never very great.

The situation in New Jersey was similar. There were too many different faiths to allow one religion to dominate. In Pennsylvania, founder William PENN, a Quaker, believed in toleration for a great variety of religions. Although Quakers controlled the Pennsylvania legislature for decades, they never tried to exclude any faith.

In the early 1700s, a surge of renewed interest in religion known as the GREAT AWAKENING swept through the British colonies. Some churches gained additional members, and new churches were formed. The great variety of churches provided additional cause for demanding an end to any kind of official religion. The intellectual movement called the ENLIGHTENMENT also played a role in convincing leading colonists that the establishment of an official state religion violated personal rights. When the American colonies gained independence from Great Britain, some states passed laws guaranteeing the separation of church and state.

Dutch Colony. Church-state relations took a different form in the Dutch colony of New Netherland. In general, the Dutch Reformed Church favored a separation between church and state, and the clergy believed that the church should function without political interference. The DUTCH WEST INDIA COMPANY, which governed New Netherland, made the Dutch Reformed Church the official church of the colony. Yet, in practice the company allowed a great deal of religious freedom, largely because of the great diversity of settlers in

In colonial Massachusetts, government and religion were closely related. Boston's Old South Meeting House, for example, was used both as a church and a town meeting hall.

the colony and the need to attract immigrants. People of many different backgrounds and faiths expected and received freedom from commitment to the Dutch Reformed Church.

Spanish Colonies.   Roman Catholicism was the established religion in both Spain and its American colonies. The pope gave the Spanish monarchs broad power over the church, including the right to collect and distribute church revenues and to establish Catholic institutions. The Spanish monarchs exercised this power through colonial governors, district courts, and bishops. The Catholic Church maintained authority over spiritual matters, largely through the Jesuit priests and Franciscan friars* who founded and ran MISSIONS in the colonies. However, because of the close relationship between church and state, the boundaries between spiritual and political issues often became blurred and conflicts arose.

In the Spanish Borderlands*, disputes between government and religious authorities involved two main issues—the role of Native Americans in colonial society and the rights and privileges of the clergy*. The friars controlled huge numbers of Indians and relied on them to help run their missions. However, colonial governors and settlers also wanted to make use of Indian labor in their fields and ranches. Conflicts related to authority over the Indians erupted countless times in the early years in the Spanish colonies. Church and state also clashed over the issue of special privileges. The clergy could not be prosecuted for crimes and could offer protection from government authority to anyone, even rebellious Indians or criminals. Colonial officials and settlers resented these privileges, and they became a source of friction.

In the early 1700s, the Spanish government adopted a series of reforms that weakened the power of the church. The reforms restricted the power of church courts, removed Native Americans from the direct control of the church, and took away some of the clergy's special privileges. After these reforms, colonial governors began seizing missions and giving the land to Spanish settlers. They also allowed the colonists to make use of Indian labor. In California, the missions continued to have considerable power. Elsewhere in the Borderlands, though, the role of the Catholic Church was limited to religious matters by around 1800.

French Colonies.   Like Spain, France was a predominantly Roman Catholic country, and the church played a vital role in its colonies. Besides tending to the religious needs of the settlers, the church performed various other functions, such as keeping birth and death records, running schools, and caring for the poor, the sick, and the aged. As in the Spanish Borderlands, the church and the state were closely connected.

As New France* grew, the French crown took greater control of the colony and limited the power of the church. The bishop of Quebec, the head of the colonial church, could no longer appoint and dismiss members of the colonial council. The church also lost its power to grant land to religious institutions. But the church still received money from the government, primarily to run hospitals and poorhouses. Dependence on this financial support helped ensure that members of the clergy would not cause trouble. Although disputes sometimes arose between the Catholic Church and French authorities, they

* *friar* member of a religious brotherhood

* *Spanish Borderlands* northern part of New Spain, area now occupied by Florida, Texas, New Mexico, Arizona, and California

* *clergy* ministers, priests, and other church officials

* *New France* French colony centered in the St. Lawrence River valley, an area known as Canada; included the Great Lakes region and, until 1713, Acadia (present-day Nova Scotia)

never challenged the basic relationship between church and state. (*See also* **Freedom of Religion; Protestant Churches; Religious Life in European Colonies.**)

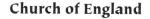

Church of England

See *Protestant Churches: Anglican.*

Cíbola

See *Seven Cities of Cíbola.*

Cities and Towns

The cities and towns of colonial North America were centers of trade, government, and learning. Compared to the cities of Europe, though, they were quite small. In 1700, when London boasted a population of about 500,000, Boston—the largest city in North America—had only 7,000 inhabitants. Still, the influence of colonial cities stretched far beyond their boundaries. The trading activities of major Atlantic seaports connected them with Europe, the West Indies, Africa, and Asia. The ports also served as entry points for new immigrants and ideas.

Colonial cities were centers of change as well, and ideas that emerged in urban areas gradually spread to small towns and the countryside. Cities led the way in economic development. They replaced the barter* system with a commercial economy based on cash transactions and established the first factories, which took the place of small, home-based industries. In addition, city dwellers challenged the old European social order in which everyone had a fixed social position. In its place, they launched a freer society that allowed people to gain status* through their own efforts and accomplishments. As colonial society changed, more and more people expected to have a voice in government. In the British colonies, this resulted in a movement for independence from Great Britain, and the cities became the centers of revolutionary activity.

* ***barter*** exchange of goods and services without using money

* ***status*** social position

British Colonies

In the early days of the British colonies, each city was dominated by a particular group. English Puritans founded Boston, English Quakers established Philadelphia, and Anglican* plantation owners from the West Indies built Charleston. By the early 1700s, however, these and other cities and towns acquired a more diverse population as new immigrants of various religions and national backgrounds arrived. New York City, founded originally as New Amsterdam by Dutch Protestants, came to include a mixture of Dutch, French, English, German, Spanish, and Portuguese settlers.

* ***Anglican*** member of the Church of England

See map in British Colonies (vol. 1).

As the populations of colonial cities grew more varied, their inhabitants became more tolerant, or accepting, of the beliefs and customs of others. The Puritans, for example, regarded a community as a group of believers who shared religious goals, and they did not welcome outsiders. That narrow view

The cities of the British colonies were centers of trade, government, and culture. Philadelphia boasted many fine buildings, such as the Congress Hall and New Theatre on Chestnut Street.

gradually gave way to a broader idea of community—one in which different kinds of people were linked together by trade, employment, and social ties rather than by religion. The idea that people of many backgrounds and beliefs could be united in a single community became the central principle of urban society in the British colonies.

British colonial cities also included slaves who had come from Africa. Between 1720 and 1770, the black population of urban areas grew substantially as the need for labor increased. After 1770, however, the rising ANTISLAVERY MOVEMENT made it more difficult to acquire slaves in the North. Besides, many urban employers preferred to hire free laborers because they did not have to house and feed them. The number of black slaves in northern cities began to decrease, but the population of FREE BLACKS in cities such as New York and Philadelphia increased.

The way that British colonial towns and cities were governed varied from region to region. In New England, local residents held town meetings* to discuss issues, pass laws, and elect officials to take care of daily business. In the Chesapeake and southern colonies, towns were governed by county officials who had both legislative and judicial power. The middle colonies included some governmental systems based on towns and others based on counties. The city of Philadelphia, run by a common council, enjoyed considerable independence.

* **town meeting** assembly of male citizens to discuss and vote on community issues

The Urban Economy. Between 1690 and 1750, many colonists moved inland to find more land for farming and vast forests for timber. The colonists shipped their goods back to coastal cities, which expanded into thriving commercial centers. Although the seaports of Boston, New York City, and Philadelphia grew fastest, the smaller ports of Salem, NEWPORT, ANNAPOLIS, and Norfolk reached populations of about 5,000 inhabitants.

MERCHANTS were leading figures in cities and towns. Their trading activities linked farms in the backcountry with markets in Europe. Merchants operated stores and shops, loaned money, built ships, bought and sold property, and provided jobs for the crafts workers who made barrels, wagons, and ships. They often contributed money to build schools, churches, and other important structures in the community. As a result of their activities, city merchants became among the wealthiest and most influential people of the colonial period.

Crafts workers, or ARTISANS, were far more numerous in cities than merchants. They headed at least half of all urban households. These crafts workers practiced trades ranging from shoe making and carpentry to painting and clock making. Many were self-employed, and they prized their independence. They understood the important role they held in the community. Many artisans were drawn into public and political life during the 1700s. In fact, they provided much of the support and strength in the movement for independence from Britain.

As colonial cities and towns grew, so did urban poverty. Every city had its share of poor widows and orphans, laborers who were sick or unable to find work, and others who could not support themselves and their families. Churches did what they could to help the poor, but communities also had to raise money through special taxes to provide aid for those in need. Some of this money was used for poorhouses, where the needy had to follow a harsh program in exchange for a place to live. To limit the number of people on poor relief, city officials turned away newcomers and used shame to discourage city residents from applying. In New York, anyone who received poor relief had to wear a colored badge.

speculator person who buys land in order to sell it for profit

See color plate 5, vol. 1.

Changes in Urban Life.

In the early days of the British colonies, most settlers became landowners. As the value of urban land increased, however, property ownership became more concentrated in the hands of wealthy merchants, professionals such as lawyers and doctors, and speculators*. Many working people—artisans, sailors, and laborers—could no longer afford to buy property. In 1700 about one in three urban families rented their homes. By 1790 four out of five families had become renters.

In the early days when colonial cities were small, everything was close to the center of town. Wealthy, middle-class, and poor people often lived side by side in the same neighborhoods, and businesses occupied central locations. By about 1750, however, American cities were changing. Wealthy citizens, who had made their fortunes in trade, shipbuilding, and land development, built stately town houses in the center of town. City streets became clogged with horse-drawn carriages, a symbol of prosperity. However, the high cost of urban property forced artisans and laborers to seek land or lodging farther and farther from the city center. Many who had once lived and worked in the same location now had to travel some distance between their homes and their work.

At the end of the colonial era, American cities could still be described as "walking cities." A person could walk from one end of town to the other in a few hours, and people of different classes still lived fairly close to one another. Yet, the geographic, social, and economic gaps between rich and poor had begun to widen. In many cities, the rich dominated the city center, the middle class lived in a ring around the wealthy core, and the poorer working classes lived on the outer edges of the city. This pattern gradually became more extreme, shaping American city life in the years ahead.

Cities in the British colonies flourished during the colonial period. Between 1690 and 1790, Philadelphia expanded from 4,000 to 42,000 inhabitants, making it the largest American city. Although southern cities grew more slowly than northern ones, they did grow. The population of Baltimore soared from about 100 residents in 1750 to 13,500 in 1790. Despite this urban expansion, the new nation of the United States was still a rural, agricultural society. Far more people lived in the country or in small villages than in towns or cities.

Dutch Colony

See map in New Netherland (vol. 3).

The Dutch colony of NEW NETHERLAND—which the English took over in 1664 and renamed New York—had only two cities. Beverwyck, later known as ALBANY, consisted of a fort and a fur-trading post on the upper Hudson River. New Amsterdam, the larger and more important city, was a trading center located on the island of Manhattan. Although it never expanded beyond about 2,000 inhabitants, New Amsterdam had its share of urban problems, including poverty and crime.

The DUTCH WEST INDIA COMPANY, the trading company that founded New Netherland in 1624, established the laws that governed New Amsterdam. Company officials, soldiers, and slave laborers in the city provided a constant reminder of the company's power. Eventually, new immigrants demanded and received more control over New Amsterdam. In 1653 they created a government for the city run by leading citizens called burgomasters, or city masters.

The city government regulated many aspects of economic life in New Amsterdam, setting up market days and appointing officials to inspect and set prices on goods. It also laid down rules governing the disposal of garbage and kept tight control of the city's TAVERNS. Centers of social life, taverns were breeding grounds of drunkenness and disorderly behavior as well. City officials had to deal with fighting caused by drinking and minor violations of the law, but serious crime was rare. Residents who broke laws generally received fines or a whipping as punishment, though serious offenders might be banished from the city.

Life in New Amsterdam followed patterns established in the Netherlands. Although the social system had distinct levels, the gap between rich and poor was not very great. Merchants and government officials occupied the top levels of society. Below them came artisans and laborers. Indentured servants* and slaves were at the bottom of the social order.

Most citizens of New Amsterdam belonged to the Dutch Reformed Church, a Protestant group. They cherished their Bibles and sent their children

*__indentured servant__ person who agreed to work a certain length of time in return for passage on a ship to the colonies

to a school run by the church. A few New Amsterdammers assembled private libraries, wrote poetry, and painted, but the culture of the city never approached the level of Dutch cities in Europe. Above all, the life of New Amsterdam was dedicated to trade and profit. In leisure hours, city residents enjoyed fishing, bowling, golf, and ice-skating in the winter. When the English took control of the city, they adopted many of the rules and practices established by the Dutch burgomasters. These policies formed the basis for the future development of New York City.

French Colonies

See map in New France (vol. 3).

The French colonies of North America had only a few cities, and none of them contained more than 8,000 inhabitants. QUEBEC, the capital of NEW FRANCE and an important seaport, was the most prominent French city. MONTREAL served as the commercial center of the French FUR TRADE. Although little more than military bases and trading posts, the colonial cities of LOUISBOURG in Acadia and NEW ORLEANS in Louisiana were administrative and cultural centers.

palisade fence of stakes forming a defense

Physical Features. French colonial cities seemed more like rural towns than cities. Enclosed within wooden palisades* were houses surrounded by stables, fenced pastures for horses, and gardens. Stray livestock wandered through muddy streets. Many residents were farmers who left each day to work in their fields outside the town walls.

Despite their rural character, these colonial cities also possessed features associated with urban life. The streets were laid out in regular patterns, and the houses, some with two stories, were made of stone or brick. French cities also included impressive government buildings and churches. Quebec boasted a

The leading towns of the colony of New France played different roles. Montreal, shown here in a 1774 engraving, served as the base for French trade, and Quebec was the colony's administrative center.

* **seminary** school that trains individuals for the priesthood

cathedral, seminary*, college, hospital, and poorhouse, as well as various buildings that belonged to the Roman Catholic Church and several that housed the government of New France. Louisbourg and New Orleans possessed similar structures. Montreal, a fur-trading center, had a number of buildings associated with its bustling commercial life.

Maintaining Order.   Royal officials appointed by the French crown were responsible for governing the cities. Urban residents had little role in government. Daily life was regulated by *la police,* French officials with a wide range of duties. *La police* maintained streets and directed traffic. They regulated food markets and set prices for bread and meat to ensure an ample supply of both at fair prices. *La police* also prevented and put out fires, worked to reduce crime and begging, and tried to uphold standards of public morality. Care of the poor, the orphaned, and the aged came under the responsibilities of the Catholic Church rather than the colonial government.

Cities established regulations to control many aspects of urban life. There were rules that closed taverns during church services, required residents to show respect for religion, and punished acts of heresy*. City laws also prohibited dumping garbage in the street and required butchers to dispose of waste products in the rivers. Townspeople used this same river water for drinking and washing. In Montreal and New Orleans, officials tried to prevent violence and disorderly behavior by limiting the number of taverns and restricting entrance to certain taverns to particular social groups or Native Americans.

* **heresy** belief that is contrary to church teachings

Fire Prevention

With wooden buildings everywhere and fire the source of cooking and heating in most homes, fire was a major hazard in French colonial cities and towns. Urban areas made every effort to prevent fires. They had laws requiring home owners to clean chimneys regularly to remove the buildup of soot that could ignite. Other laws regulated the distance between buildings and called for stone construction for houses and slate or metal roofs. Quebec and Montreal even provided citizens with fire-fighting tools and water buckets. Despite all efforts, fires broke out frequently. Quebec, Montreal, and New Orleans all suffered devastating blazes in the 1700s.

Urban Society.   Although small, French colonial cities lacked a sense of community. Urban society was fragmented, and people of different social classes rarely mingled. When townspeople attended church services or community events, they were separated by their social rank. Another factor limiting the sense of community in cities was the mobility of their residents. Many people did not live in towns on a year-round basis. Soldiers were often away for long periods on tours of duty. Fur traders and Native Americans came to trading centers such as Montreal and New Orleans on a seasonal basis, stayed for a short time, and then returned to the forests. The arrival of fishing fleets in Louisbourg caused a sudden expansion in the local population, which decreased again when the fleets left.

The cultural life of the colonial cities was based on the culture of France. Favorite forms of local entertainment varied according to class. Wealthy citizens read books and attended suppers and private balls. Poor residents sang, played cards, drank, and gambled. Theatrical performances were popular with all groups. In the 1690s, however, Catholic officials banned theater in New France on the ground that it was morally dangerous. Church officials also disapproved of men and women dancing together but were unable to prevent it.

Spanish Borderlands

The Spanish created towns throughout their North American empire to provide protection for their widely scattered settlers and to serve as local centers

131

See map in Spanish Borderlands (vol. 4).

presidio Spanish fort built to protect mission settlements

of government. Spanish authorities issued various rules on the planning, building, and administration of colonial towns. In their master plan, the focal point of the town was a plaza, a rectangular open space, surrounded by a government building, a church, and other public structures. The town spread out from the central plaza in an orderly arrangement of streets and house lots that included space for gardens. The area around the town was divided into fields and pasture for grazing livestock.

The Spanish master plan was not always followed strictly in the SPANISH BORDERLANDS, a region that included present-day Florida, Texas, New Mexico, Arizona, and California. Spanish colonists often had to modify the rules to suit local circumstances. In some cases, Spanish soldiers used conquered Indian settlements as the basis for their towns rather than laying out new ones. In addition, many towns grew up around the presidios* and MISSIONS established by the Spanish military and the Catholic Church. The four major towns in the Spanish Borderlands developed according to local needs and followed different patterns.

Major Towns.   ST. AUGUSTINE in Florida was the first town in the Spanish Borderlands. Founded in 1565, it struggled over the years against the threat of Indian, French, and English raids. St. Augustine survived but remained very small, with only about 300 inhabitants. Located on a bay near the Atlantic Ocean, St. Augustine had a fort that guarded the entrance to the harbor. The fort, rather than a plaza, was the town's central point, and the houses were located at some distance from the fort. St. Augustine began to decline after the 1580s, as Spain shifted its attention westward.

In 1610 Don Pedro de Peralta, the governor of New Mexico, established the town of SANTA FE as the province's capital. The town followed the Spanish plan of streets and houses spreading out from a central plaza surrounded by a church and government buildings. In the PUEBLO REVOLT of 1680, the Indians drove the Spanish out of New Mexico. The Spanish returned in 1692 and resettled Santa Fe. Thereafter the city grew slowly but steadily, reaching a population of about 8,000 by the early 1800s.

The most successful Spanish town in Texas was San Antonio, founded in 1731 as San Fernando de Béxar. Built to encourage colonization of the region, the town shared its site—once an Indian village—with a presidio and a mission.

The fourth major town of the Spanish Borderlands, Los Angeles, was in California. Established in 1781 to supply food for a nearby presidio, this was the only town in Spanish California referred to as a city. Los Angeles followed the typical Spanish layout of a plaza, building lots, streets, and fields. The first residents included Native Americans, African Americans, Spaniards, and people of mixed Spanish and Indian ancestry. The town's first mayor was an Indian.

Life in the Towns.   The isolation of Spanish towns and the hardships of frontier life helped forge close ties among town residents. Daily life was shaped by the change of the seasons and the demands of farming and ranching activities. Family gatherings provided the main source of entertainment, and social activities revolved around religious holidays. Various celebrations and dances provided relief from the endless work required on farms and ranches.

At the head of the town government was an official—usually called an *alcalde*—who had judicial and legislative powers. Assisting the *alcalde* were a town council *(cabildo)*, a sheriff, and other minor officials. The town founder usually appointed the first people who held government posts, but later on residents elected their town officials. Government positions usually went to the members of a few prominent families. Although Spanish colonial towns enjoyed self-government, in the end they came under the authority of the royal officials of NEW SPAIN. (*See also* **Architecture; Class Structure in European Colonies; Government, Provincial; Housing; Poverty; Trade and Commerce.**)

Class Structure in European Colonies

*T*he people who colonized North America came from many different European countries and spoke a variety of languages. Each group sought to re-create the society left behind in Europe. In some respects, these British, Dutch, French, and Spanish colonists succeeded. They brought along the cultures and class systems of their homelands. As in Europe, people were divided into classes according to family, wealth, and occupation. Yet the need to adapt to new environments led to significant changes in the class structure of colonial society.

British Colonies

The vast majority of the settlers in the British colonies of North America came from Great Britain. In establishing their communities, these colonists discovered that they needed to make some adjustments in the old social patterns to fit the circumstances of the "New World." The result was the development of a distinct colonial society, recognizably British, yet different from society in Britain.

Class Structure in Great Britain. British society consisted of a rigid class system based on wealth and family. Moving from one social class to another was very difficult. Those at the highest levels of society owned large estates with many tenant farmers* and laborers. Most had hereditary titles of nobility. Rural landowners without titles, known as the gentry, ranked below the nobility. Many belonged to distinguished families with inherited wealth and status*.

Many people considered "middle class" lived in the cities. These individuals—primarily shopkeepers, skilled crafts workers, and some professionals—did not gain wealth, power, and status through inheritance but through their own accomplishments. Britain's lower classes included a broad range of people, from servants to laborers to tenant farmers. Individuals in the lower classes might accumulate some wealth, but they had almost no opportunity to raise their rank in society.

In the early years of colonization, most settlers in the British colonies were farmers, crafts workers, and laborers who sought a better life. Few

* *tenant farmer* person who farms land owned by another and pays rent with a share of the produce or in cash

* *status* social position

133

Class Structure in European Colonies

Just as they had been in Europe, the North American colonists were divided into classes according to social position, wealth, and occupation. This portrait by William Williams shows an upper-class colonial family—that of William Denning—in 1772.

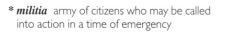
people from the highest ranks of British society migrated to North America. As a result, a hereditary nobility did not take root in the colonies. Although social classes did develop, the opportunity to move up in society was much greater in the colonies than in Britain. There was also more cooperation and interaction among social classes in the colonies than in British society, as well as a much larger middle class.

Rural Societies. Farm communities in New England, New York, Pennsylvania, and New Jersey developed a class structure based on occupation, wealth, and merit. Prosperous merchants and professionals, such as lawyers and doctors, generally held the highest position in the social order. Ministers and church leaders also received a great deal of respect, as did public officials and the heads of colonial militias*. Because most of the people in these farming communities possessed about the same amount of land, age and family status frequently determined their level of prosperity. The young, single, or widowed often had less wealth and status than others. Below them in social rank were those unfortunate laborers, farmers, and others who barely got by and survived from day to day. At the lowest rank in society were indentured servants* and free blacks, who had limited chances to prosper, and slaves, who had no chance of improving their social position.

The society that developed in farming communities of the Chesapeake region and the southern colonies was very different from that of the rural northern colonies. Although there were many small farms in the South, southern agriculture was dominated by wealthy landowners who established plantations on large areas of land, sometimes received from the king. The plantation owners belonged to the highest level of society, along with well-to-do merchants, professionals, and prominent government officials. This upper class possessed most of the wealth and power in these colonies.

The southern and Chesapeake colonies had less of a middle class than other areas of British North America. In plantation society, it was difficult,

though not impossible, for people such as small farmers and crafts workers to improve their position. As in the north, the lowest level of southern society included large numbers of indentured servants and slaves. Although indentured servants might eventually obtain land and move up in the world, it was difficult to do so.

Urban Societies. In the large towns and cities of the British colonies, a complex society emerged. This society was quite different from farming communities and plantations. The top level of urban society consisted of an influential group of prosperous merchants and professionals as well as high-ranking government officials and military officers. The members of this urban upper class had gained their status through personal achievement. Urban society also included a large middle class made up of shopkeepers, innkeepers, crafts workers, and less prosperous professionals. Some members of the urban middle class took leading roles in the community. The lower class consisted of laborers, fishermen, and servants. These colonists rarely lacked food or other essentials, and they generally led more comfortable lives than the lower classes in the cities of Europe. Urban slaves, at the bottom of society, had a better life than slaves on plantations. Most worked as household servants and had a certain amount of freedom in their family and social relationships. Not much better off than urban slaves were free blacks, who lived in small numbers in New York, Philadelphia, and some other cities.

Urban society in the British colonies provided considerable opportunity for social movement. No sharp line divided the upper and middle classes, and middle-class colonists who acquired wealth could move up in society. Although the lower classes could also improve their position, it was more difficult to do so.

Breaking Down Social Differences. Several fundamental institutions in British colonial society brought people together and helped break down social divisions. The most important of these was the church. Although an individual's seat in church was determined by social rank, colonists of all classes worshiped together. Some religious groups, such as the Quakers, Baptists, and Presbyterians, often chose their leaders from among the whole congregation, not just the upper class.

Local government and the court system also helped unite colonial society. Colonists of all social classes served together on juries, as Americans still do today. Court cases involved both the rich and the poor. In addition, local justices might be selected from any level of society in places where upper-class families and college graduates were scarce. Government elections brought people together at the polls to vote. Town meetings*, weddings, funerals, and holidays also offered opportunities for colonists of different classes to socialize. In the later colonial period, various local organizations held community events.

Although the society that developed in the British colonies was less divided than that in Great Britain, class differences remained. In many places, a small upper class controlled most of the power and wealth, and the lower classes were expected to show respect for their superiors. Yet the American

* *town meeting* assembly of male citizens to discuss and vote on community issues

colonists had more freedom to determine their destiny than people living in Britain. The opportunity to succeed or fail because of personal achievement represented a major advance over the class system in Europe and became an important feature of American society.

Dutch Colony

The society that developed in the colony of NEW NETHERLAND reflected its history as the possession of a trading company, the DUTCH WEST INDIA COMPANY. The company's primary goal in founding the colony was to make money for its investors, and it focused on the FUR TRADE as the best way to gain riches. To colonize New Netherland, the company accepted settlers from all over Europe. It also decided to introduce slaves to meet the colony's labor needs. These policies helped create the most diverse society in colonial North America—yet one with a simpler and less rigid class structure than that in other areas. Those who came to New Netherland—whether Dutch, Swedish, English, German, French, Jewish, Catholic, or Protestant—had great opportunities to achieve success and improve their status in society.

Urban Class Structure.   The Dutch West India Company's emphasis on the fur trade led to the prominence of urban rather than rural communities in the colony. The towns of Beverwyck (present-day ALBANY, New York) and NEW AMSTERDAM (now New York City) began as fur-trading posts and soon dominated the colony. Both were busy market towns with colonists from many different European countries.

Of the two towns, Beverwyck had a simpler society. Most residents pursued traditional occupations—as bakers, butchers, blacksmiths, and carpenters—in addition to working in the fur trade during the summer months. Although some residents were richer than others, the distinction between classes was not great.

New Amsterdam had a more complex social structure, based on both occupation and wealth. Dutch West India Company officials and wealthy merchants dominated town affairs and formed the upper class. Below them in social rank came professionals, such as doctors, teachers, and members of the clergy*. The town also had many artisans*, who made up the middle class. The lower class consisted of soldiers, laborers, and indentured servants. African slaves were at the bottom of the class structure.

Great extremes of wealth and poverty did not exist in these Dutch colonial towns. Certain families, such as the Schuylers and Van Cortlandts, began to accumulate wealth and property that later would form the basis for great fortunes. Although some of these families lived on a grander scale than their artisan neighbors, differences were not as sharp as those in other colonial areas.

Rural Class Structure.   Most rural communities in New Netherland consisted of small villages of family-run farms. Residents raised food for themselves and sold small surpluses in the cities. Such farming communities often included several crafts workers as well as a handful of slaves held by the more prosperous farmers. Although some rural residents owned more

* *clergy* ministers, priests, and other church officials

* *artisan* skilled crafts worker

136

land and livestock than others did, the differences in wealth and social status were not important.

The patroon system brought greater differences in wealth and social position. A patroon was a well-to-do individual who received a large piece of property from the Dutch West India Company in return for promising to bring 50 people from Europe to settle the land and farm it. The patroons had powers similar to those of European lords, including the right to make laws governing the people on their estates and to appoint local officials. Small communities grew up around a patroon's estate and attracted various crafts workers.

French Colonies

The colony of NEW FRANCE covered a vast area of North America, but by 1760 its European population amounted to only about 85,000. These settlers, mostly rural farmers and fur traders, had come from France, Scotland, Ireland, England, Spain, and Germany. The population also included métis, individuals of mixed French and Native American parentage.

Despite the diversity of national origins, New France developed a class structure similar to that of France. All colonists, regardless of their background, held a specific rank in society, and colonial laws protected the privileges of those at the top. People who belonged to the lower classes were expected to show proper respect for their superiors in the upper classes.

Class Structure. In the early years, the colonists of New France enjoyed greater freedom than people in France. Moreover, the changes they made to

The French government gave large grants of land to lords known as seigneurs. The farmers who worked the land were required to pay dues to their seigneur every year, as shown in this illustration by C. W. Jefferys.

adapt to the American environment and their contact with Native Americans led to the development of new values and attitudes. Yet the French colonists did not consider equality or democracy to be goals of their society. In this respect, they followed the custom of their homeland, where a small upper class held almost all wealth and power. In addition, the French government introduced institutions and policies that encouraged the development of a colonial society similar to French society.

The class structure of New France was based on such factors as family, wealth, and occupation. Although not as rigid as the class structure of France, it provided few opportunities for people to move from one social class to another. The gap between rich and poor was smaller than in France, and people in the middle and lower classes generally enjoyed a better standard of living than similar groups in Europe.

A pattern of landholding known as the SEIGNEURIAL SYSTEM played an important role in the class structure of New France. Under this system, the French government or a trading company granted land to an individual known as a seigneur, who divided the land into lots for tenants to farm. The seigneur governed those living on his property according to a code of specific rights and obligations. His position resembled that of a feudal* lord of the Middle Ages. The seigneurial system helped preserve a class structure that had existed in France for hundreds of years.

*__feudal__ relating to an economic and political system in which individuals give service to a landowner in return for protection and the use of land

The Upper Classes.

The highest level of society in New France consisted of the nobility and members of the clergy. The colonial nobility included descendants of French nobles and well-to-do landowners, many of them seigneurs. Many of the clergy also came from the nobility. Members of the upper class enjoyed special privileges in New France that were protected by laws and the court system. Despite their high status, not all nobles were wealthy. Some had lives similar to those of the members of the middle class.

The ROMAN CATHOLIC CHURCH and its clergy had great power in New France. Churches were at the center of colonial life, and members of the clergy often assumed leadership roles in the community. The vast landholdings of the church brought it considerable income. By the mid-1700s, about one-third of the colony's population lived on church-owned land and paid rents to the church.

The church used its authority and activities to maintain traditional social patterns. In church services, for example, local seigneurs had the most prominent seats, and the remaining seats were assigned according to wealth and social position. Seigneurs also received the sacraments—holy ceremonies of the church—before others in the community.

The Middle and Lower Classes.

The middle class, or bourgeoisie, consisted of merchants, nonnoble seigneurs, and people involved in various business activities. Most of the middle class resided in towns. They frequently invested in business enterprises such as the fur trade, shipbuilding, exports, and small industries. Some took positions in government. Many members of the urban middle class envied the nobility and tried to adopt an aristocratic way of life. A few very wealthy members of the bourgeoisie actually managed to gain noble status through marriage.

The lower classes of colonial society, sometimes referred to as the "third estate," included minor government officials, shopkeepers, artisans, laborers, farmers, and soldiers. Although subject to control by the upper class, most of these people enjoyed a great deal of independence. Unlike similar groups in France, they could change their occupations and places of residence freely. On the other hand, people in the lower classes were expected to know their place and show proper respect to their superiors. They had little opportunity to receive an education or to improve their status in society.

As in the other colonies, slaves occupied the lowest level of the class structure. In certain regions, such as CANADA and NOVA SCOTIA, slaves usually worked as domestic servants. In the colony of LOUISIANA and in the Mississippi Valley, they served mainly as agricultural laborers on farms and plantations. New France had LAWS that regulated the relations between slaveholder and slaves. The laws encouraged slaves to marry among themselves, discouraged the breakup of slave families, prohibited interracial marriages, and allowed slaves to take their masters to court if the laws were violated. This system provided more protection for slaves than the system in the British colonies.

Spanish Borderlands

The SPANISH BORDERLANDS—an area that included parts of present-day California, Arizona, New Mexico, Texas, and Florida—developed social patterns quite different from those of other Spanish colonial areas. In Central and South America, Spanish society had a rigid class system based on race and wealth. The structure of Borderland societies was much less rigid.

Social Classes.   The Spaniards developed an elaborate social hierarchy* that classified people according to race. The main categories were *peninsulares,* European-born Spaniards; CREOLES, American-born Spaniards; mestizos, individuals of mixed Spanish and Indian parentage; mulattoes, people of mixed Spanish and African parentage; blacks; and Indians. Over time, as racial mixing increased, the distinction between these groups became blurred.

Creoles and racially mixed individuals made up the two largest groups in colonial society. The proportion of European-born Spaniards was small. Often Indians were not considered part of the colonial society because some of them remained outside Spanish control.

Racial groupings played an important role in politics and the economy. *Peninsulares* generally held the highest administrative positions, serving as viceroys*, military generals, high court justices, or Catholic bishops. Creoles often had middle-level positions as regional governors, city mayors, or district officials. In many cases, Creoles also controlled town councils, militias, and church parishes. Racially mixed individuals usually found it difficult to gain administrative posts.

Race, while influential, did not by itself determine a person's place in society. It was socially desirable to be classified as a Spaniard—but no guarantee of economic success. Although European-born Spaniards enjoyed a high status, most belonged to the working classes. Moreover, aside from the top level of noble families, movement between social classes was quite common.

* *hierarchy* division of society or an institution into groups with higher and lower ranks

* *viceroy* person appointed as a monarch's representative to govern a province or colony

139

Characteristics of Borderland Society.   *Peninsulares* controlled most of the trade between the colonies and Spain, while Creoles dominated manufacturing and agriculture. In addition, Creoles provided most of the artisans and professionals of the Borderlands. People of racially mixed parentage often worked as laborers in mining, manufacturing, and farming or had their own small farms. Most Indians and blacks served as temporary laborers.

The military role of the Borderlands affected its social structure. From Florida to California, soldiers and their families made up the bulk of the non-Indian population. Although only European-born Spaniards and Creoles could legally serve in the military, colonial officials often enlisted mestizos, mulattoes, and blacks to fill shortages in the ranks. Soldiers who performed well and could read and write had the chance of rising to the level of an officer. Military service offered a way of moving up in society. In most areas, military officials also served as community leaders, often becoming the wealthiest and most prominent residents of a region.

Farming and ranching, the most common occupations in the Borderlands, provided the greatest opportunity for prosperity. Most farmers and ranchers had small, family-run operations. Although members of all racial groups could own land, most large landowners were Spaniards. Farm laborers and ranch hands came from all racial backgrounds. Many were former slaves or the poor relatives of more prosperous farmers and ranchers. Professionals, such as doctors and artisans, were not likely to get rich—or gain high social status—because the Spanish Borderlands did not have enough people who needed their services.

Regional Variations.   Each region of the Spanish Borderlands had certain distinct social characteristics. In the later years of the colonial period, Florida had a society marked by great diversity. Spanish officials shared the top ranks of society with merchants and planters from other countries, including Britain and Italy.

In New Mexico, the upper class consisted primarily of a small group of families who controlled large estates known as ENCOMIENDAS. Most of the other colonists made a living as small farmers and ranchers. Indians generally worked as servants or artisans. New Mexico had a more varied economy than other Borderland colonies, with large numbers of artisans in the middle and lower ranks of society.

Society in Texas, Arizona, and California centered around military posts known as PRESIDIOS. Spanish-born and Creole military officers often occupied the higher ranks of society, along with wealthy farmers or ranchers. The majority of the population consisted of lower-class Spanish, people of mixed blood, and Indian farmworkers and ranch hands.

Breaking Down Social Divisions.   Several institutions and factors helped bring together the many different elements of society in the Spanish Borderlands. MISSIONS introduced Native Americans to Spanish culture and customs. Presidios served as magnets for settlers, and the military employed men of all racial categories. Ranches provided a shared workplace for people from diverse backgrounds. Finally, the Roman Catholic Church united people of various social classes and racial categories in a single faith. With these important institutions, Spain was able to create a common culture throughout its vast colonial territory in the Americas. (*See also* **Colonial Administration; Economic Systems; Land Ownership; Race Relations; Social Conflict in European Colonies.**)

Climate

* *moderate* not severe, avoiding extremes

Climate refers to the average weather conditions of a region, measured over the course of many years or even centuries. Weather is the short-term pattern of atmospheric conditions that occurs over days, weeks, or months. The factors that determine the climate of a region include its elevation above sea level, its distance from the equator, the winds and ocean currents of the region, and landforms such as mountains and rivers. With its vast size and greatly varied landscape, the North American continent contains many different types of climates. These climates shaped the lives of Native Americans and the Europeans who colonized North America.

North American Climates. The continent has two major mountain chains: the Rocky Mountains in the west and the APPALACHIAN MOUNTAINS in the east. Both follow a north-south direction. The lack of an important east-west mountain barrier in North America means that air masses can flow freely between the Arctic Ocean in the north and the Gulf of Mexico in the south. The shifts and collisions of cold air masses from the north and warm ones from the south create dramatic temperature changes across most of the continent. However, the west coast is shielded from these air masses by the Cascade and Sierra Nevada mountain ranges. The west coast's moderate* climate, with less variation in temperatures than other parts of the continent, comes largely from air masses from the Pacific Ocean.

Meteorologists, scientists who study climate and weather, have identified dozens of different kinds of climate in North America. In general, the northerly part of the continent—from Alaska in the west to the St. Lawrence area of Canada and New England in the east—has a climate marked by extreme variations in temperature. The northern region also receives less precipitation than southerly or coastal regions. Winters in the north are long and severe, with rivers frozen and the ground often covered with snow for months at a time. In contrast, summers can be very hot and humid. This climate of extreme conditions poses a great challenge to animal and human life.

The southern part of North America—from the coastal areas of the east to the Southwest—enjoys mild winters and long spring, summer, and fall seasons. The summers tend to be hot and humid, except in the southwest, which has a dry, desert climate. Cut off from the interior of the continent by mountains, the west coast also has a fairly mild climate. Plants, animals, and humans find the moderate climates of the southeast, southwest, and west coast hospitable. The regions have long growing seasons, and less energy is required to keep warm than in northern climates.

Moisture is as important as temperature in shaping a climate. Throughout much of North America, the amount of precipitation increases from

Remember: *Consult the index at the end of Volume 4 to find more information on many topics.*

north to south. Most of the continent receives adequate moisture to support plant life. There is little water, however, in the desert and semidesert areas of the Southwest and the Great Basin region of Utah. As a result, vegetation is sparse, and the lack of water and vegetation makes human and animal life in these areas difficult. The wettest region of North America is the Pacific Northwest. The coastal areas of the Gulf of Mexico also receive a great deal of precipitation.

These variations in climate have a major influence on the types of plants and animals that are native to each region. However, other factors—such as type of soil and terrain—also affect plant and animal life. These and other factors combine to give each region its distinctive identity.

Climate and People. When Europeans arrived in North America, they encountered Native Americans who had developed a variety of lifestyles suited to the great range of climates and environments on the continent. The tools, customs, and diets of different groups of Indians were tailored to the specific environments in which they lived. The Native Americans of the far north knew how to make temporary snow shelters and warm clothing, and they ate fish and sea mammals rich in fat to help keep warm in the cold climate. Native Americans of the dry Southwest built homes of thick clay bricks to keep out the heat of the day. They also became skilled at building irrigation systems to make the best use of their precious water supply and enable them to raise their crops of beans, corn, and squash.

The Europeans who settled in North America also had to learn to live in a variety of climates. Some features of the climate helped the colonists. The dependable rainfall of the east coast allowed the French, Dutch, and British who established the colonies in the region to grow adequate supplies of food. Climate also determined what kinds of crops the colonists could raise. Apples and vegetables did well in the cool climate of the northeast, while rice and tobacco thrived in the warmer climate and rich soil of the southern colonies.

Climate could work against the colonists as well. British colonists considered New England the healthiest region. They believed that its cool climate helped prevent the "bad air" found in the warm, swampy regions of the southern colonies. According to the colonists, this bad air promoted malaria, yellow fever, and other deadly DISEASES. Of course, people learned later that such diseases were really caused by microscopic organisms carried by mosquitoes that bred in southern swamps. Nevertheless, the colonists were right to recognize that certain climates were unhealthy, even though they did not know why.

In the late 1600s and 1700s, scientific societies in the colonies began to take a great interest in the climate of North America. As new, more accurate tools for measuring temperature, humidity, and other features of climate became available, people started to study the climate in a systematic manner. Benjamin FRANKLIN and Thomas JEFFERSON, two of the leading scientific thinkers of the British colonies, kept detailed weather records over long periods of time. The data they and other scientists collected helped identify the basic patterns of climate in the North American colonies. (*See also* **Geography of North America.**)

Clothing

status social position

tunic simple slip-on upper garment, belted at the waist

American Indians dressed in breechcloths, leggings, tunics, and robes. They made their clothing from animal hides, furs, and cloth of grass, tree bark, or cotton. Colonist John White made several sketches and paintings of the Indians of coastal Virginia; this picture is based on one he drew in 1585.

Clothing in the North American colonies was more than a covering for the body and a protection against the weather. Clothing provided information about identity and status*, indicating a person's place in society. It also served as a link with European tradition and style. The settlers who founded the British, Dutch, French, and Spanish colonies wore clothes just like those worn in their home countries. During the 1600s and 1700s, colonists continued to copy European fashions, but they also developed new styles that suited life in the colonies and used local materials.

Materials and Manufacture. Early settlers bound for North America took the most complete wardrobe they could afford, knowing that clothing would be difficult to replace. As trade with the parent countries became more regular, colonists were able to buy both fabric and ready-made garments from Europe. Prosperous colonists had their clothes custom-made by tailors. The very wealthiest bought their clothes during visits to Europe or ordered them from European tailors. Most people, though, wore clothing made at home.

Nearly all colonial girls learned to sew, and even in well-to-do households, women made a good part of the family's clothing. They produced the fabric as well. To make woolen cloth, the women had to clean the wool sheared from sheep before spinning it into yarn to weave or knit. For lighter-weight fabric, they spun fibers gathered from flax plants into thread and wove the thread into linen cloth. A similar operation produced COTTON cloth, which came into use in the late 1700s. Many colonial garments were made of linsey-woolsey, a sturdy blend of linen and wool.

The other important material used for clothing was leather. Backcountry families made leather from the hides of animals they killed. In settled communities, tanners took over the job of turning raw hides into leather. Crafts workers then fashioned the leather into boots, shoes, pants, aprons, and other garments. Because shoes were expensive, poor people in warm regions tended to go barefoot when possible.

The average colonist's wardrobe probably included both plain, homemade garments for everyday wear and some finer, tailor-made clothes for special occasions. A prized item such as a woman's satin gown or a man's velvet jacket might be saved for weddings and funerals. Families passed such garments from one generation to the next, with many repairs and alterations to fit new owners.

Native Americans. European colonists learned much about dressing for the rugged conditions they faced in North America from Native Americans. Depending on climate and available resources, Indians wore clothing made of animal hides and furs and of cloth woven from grass, animal fur, or tree-bark fiber. The basic garment of Native American men was the breechcloth, a square of material like a small apron that hung from a belt. In some tribes, women wore a skirtlike version of the breechcloth. Indians might also wear leggings, loose pullover tunics*, cloaks or robes, and moccasins.

Native Americans acquired wool and linen when they began trading with Europeans. They received thousands of wool blankets, for example, in exchange for furs. Most of the time the Indians adapted European materials to their own style of dress, substituting a blanket for a hide cloak or wearing a linen shirt over leggings like a tunic.

European settlers borrowed some items of clothing from Native Americans, especially moccasins, which were widely worn throughout the colonies. For traveling or working in forest underbrush, colonists copied the Indians' long-lasting leather leggings. In rural areas of Canada, French settlers fastened their heavy cloaks with sashes, imitating a style of the local Indians.

The Europeans who penetrated farthest into the wilderness and spent much time among the Native Americans often dressed like them. In New France, for example, the voyageurs (river traders) and COUREURS DE BOIS (woods runners) wore leggings, capes, and moccasins made of hides. The outfits of frontiersmen in the British colonies included leggings, fringed leather shirts or jackets, fur hats, and moccasins.

British Colonists.   In the English colonies of the 1600s, clothing reflected a person's status in society. The gentry* could be recognized immediately by their manner of dress. Only gentlemen wore collars trimmed with fancy lace or jackets with gold or silver buttons. The quality of fabric reflected status as well. The garments of upper-class colonists were made of smooth, tightly woven wool and linen in rich colors. Ordinary people wore coarser fabrics in plainer colors.

The basic outfit of a well-dressed man included breeches*; a linen shirt; a long, scarflike collar over the shirt; shoes and stockings held in place by garters; a vest; a jacket; and perhaps a hat and cape. A woman's outfit began with a loose, knee-length shift that served as both undergarment and nightgown. Over this she put on one or more skirts or petticoats; a bodice or waistcoat, which were snug-fitting, shirtlike garments; an apron; and a cap—uncovered hair was

* *gentry* people of high social position

* *breeches* loose, knee-length pants

See color plates 4 and 5, vol. 3.

This painting by Joseph Beekman Smith shows British colonists in John Street, New York City, in 1768. Men of this time typically dressed in a shirt, vest, jacket, breeches, and stockings. Women wore a bodice and several layers of skirts over a simple underdress called a shift and covered their heads with a cap.

Long-Lasting Fashions

When the English took over New Netherland in 1664, many Dutch colonists remained. Some of them—especially members of the upper classes and city dwellers—started wearing English-style clothes. But in rural areas, Dutch colonists and their descendants clung to their traditional garb. For 150 years they ignored changes in fashion, continuing to wear the same styles. In 1794 a traveler in New York State observed:

> The women in their external appearance are the perfect copies of their ancestors. . . . Exactly such figures may be seen in old Dutch paintings.

* **aristocratic** referring to people of the highest social class, often nobility

considered immodest. Upper-class women often wore one-piece dresses, known in colonial times as gowns.

The clothing of laborers and farmers was usually made of dull-colored, homemade fabrics. The men wore loose trousers rather than breeches, and the women's skirts were shorter than those of the upper classes. Slaves wore rough, ready-made clothes of cheap fabric.

Colonists, especially PURITANS, are often shown in black, but many of their garments were tan or brown. Women of all classes wore red petticoats, green stockings, and green or blue aprons. In the southern colonies, many women favored lighter, brighter clothes or even patterned fabrics. Although men generally dressed in blue, gray, or black, one account describes an upper-class gentleman in a stylish orange suit.

Dutch Colonists.   Everyone in the Dutch colony of New Netherland wore the same basic outfits. As in the British colonies, however, the garments of the gentry were made of better-quality materials.

Dutch colonial women dressed in black or red skirts topped with shirts and jackets. Their loose, hip-length jackets came in a variety of bright colors and had removable sleeves. Wearers could attach short or long sleeves made of silk, wool, or linen. Women covered their outfits with sheer white linen aprons that hung to their ankles and white linen headdresses or caps.

The men of New Netherland dressed in black, tan, or gray knee breeches and jackets and white shirts. Around their necks, they wore stiff, pleated collars, called ruffs, or long lace or linen scarves tied in bows. Many men had a large collection of hats and caps, with special headgear for sleeping, keeping warm, or riding horseback. Most of them chose plain black hats for everyday business, but local officials and prosperous merchants added gold lace and other decoration to their hats.

French Colonists.   The most stylish clothes in New France belonged to the aristocratic* families who settled there. These nobles did their best to keep up with changes in French fashion and spent lavish sums on elegant clothing. The wardrobe of a noblewoman might cost as much as a small house. Aristocratic women favored long gowns, cut low in front. The finest were made of silk or velvet. Under their dresses, women wore chemises—which were similar to shifts—as well as corsets and petticoats.

Men wore underdrawers or used their long shirttails as underwear. Over these came stockings and breeches. The most fashionable men dressed in "petticoat breeches," which were full and decorated with ribbons. In the 1600s, they wore short jackets, but longer, coatlike jackets came into fashion later on. Fine garments were made of wool, or perhaps velvet, with gold and silver buttons or braid. The dressing gown, a long robe worn over a shirt and breeches, was popular for relaxing at home.

Country women dressed in snug shirts, skirts that reached to mid-calf, neckerchiefs, aprons, and short capes. Rural and working-class men wore loose breeches and dark-colored jackets. During the cold Canadian winters, the most important garment was the capote, a long, heavy, dark-blue cloak with a hood.

Different styles developed in the French colony of Louisiana, where Spanish, African, and Native American traditions mingled with European

Colonists in North America used clothing as a form of identity and expression. A person's position in society could often be determined simply by what he or she wore. This French woman is wearing a finely tailored dress and matching hat, indicating that she is of the upper class.

fashion. Louisianans added bright colors such as scarlet to the usual black, white, and gray clothing. Their hot, humid climate led them to favor lightweight cotton and linen fabrics. Some people went barefoot in the summer.

Spanish Colonists.   Most of the people who settled in the Spanish Borderlands—in present-day Texas, New Mexico, Arizona, and California—came from Mexico. The men dressed in breeches, jackets, and capes. The women wore skirts and fitted tops or dresses, with high-collared cloaks or hooded capes.

Upper-class men and women of Mexico wore fashionable attire from Europe that was made of colorful, luxurious fabrics. Settlers in the Borderlands were not so well dressed. Any clothing they received from Mexico depended on the arrival of travelers or new colonists. Only in California, where Spanish ships docked regularly, could the upper classes dress with style.

Colonists of mixed Spanish and Indian ancestry had some garments inspired by traditional Native American dress. Women wore a shawl called a rebozo, and men wore the serape, a blanketlike cloak with a hole for the head. Both items were adapted from Indian clothing. In this way, the people of the Borderlands created a distinct style that was Spanish American.

Clothing and Change.   In the early colonial period, a basic principle of social organization was that people knew their place in society and acted accordingly. Because clothing was an important sign of status, people were expected to dress at all times in a style appropriate to their class. The colonies of Massachusetts and Connecticut had specific rules, called sumptuary laws, that spelled out the kind and amount of finery each class could wear. For example, a 1651 Massachusetts law said that only upper-class women could wear silk hoods and new fashions and only upper-class men could wear high boots.

Sumptuary laws, which had a long history in Europe, lost their force in the colonies in the late 1600s. The development of trade and the rise of the middle class meant that more and more people of simple origins were becoming wealthy through their own efforts. Prosperous merchants and their families could afford to dress like the upper classes—and did so—often ignoring the sumptuary laws.

During the 1700s, class distinctions began to break down. The way that colonists dressed was no longer determined by their position in society but by what they could afford. The rich and the poor continued to dress much as they always had, but some members of the new middle class adopted the fine clothes that had once been available only to the upper classes. (*See also* **Class Structure in European Colonies.**)

Coercive Acts

See *Intolerable Acts (1774).*

Coins

See *Money and Finance.*

Colden, Cadwallader

1688–1776
Physician, scientist, public official

effigy dummy of a person

*C*adwallader Colden was a physician and scientist who became a high government official in NEW YORK. In addition to having a long career in public affairs, he published works in history, botany, medicine, philosophy, and physics.

Colden grew up in Scotland, attended the University of Edinburgh, and then studied medicine in London. Following the advice of his aunt, Colden migrated to Philadelphia in 1710. In the 1720s, he became surveyor general for the colony of New York and served on the Governor's Council. In 1761 he became the lieutenant governor of New York, a post he held for 15 years.

Colden's government positions did not prevent him from pursuing his many other interests. He was an exceptionally determined man with a curious mind. He developed a new method of printing, known as stereotyping. He studied and classified the native plants around his home in the Hudson River valley and passed his love and knowledge of botany on to his daughter Jane. He produced *The History of the Five Indian Nations Depending on the Province of New York,* a dry but widely read description of the Native Americans of New York. Colden also wrote medical articles about yellow fever and cancer and pamphlets about physics and the movement of the planets.

A staunchly loyal official of the British government, Colden refused to join the colonists' protests against the STAMP ACT of 1765. His insistence on enforcing the hated law in New York led a group of angry colonists to burn him in effigy*. When the AMERICAN REVOLUTION began, challenging British authority in the colonies, Colden retired to his estate on Long Island. (*See also* **Colden, Jane.**)

Colden, Jane

1724–1766
Botanist

naturalist person who studies plants and animals in their natural surroundings

genus group of closely related plants or animals

*J*ane Colden was the first woman botanist in North America. She spent much of her life studying and classifying local plants near her home in the Hudson River valley.

Colden's parents had come to the British colonies from Scotland in the early 1700s. Her father, Cadwallader COLDEN, was a physician and distinguished scientist with a keen interest in botany. He moved his family to a large estate near Newburgh, New York, where he could pursue his study of plants. When he noticed that his daughter shared his love of botany, he decided to give her a thorough education in the field. He taught her how to make impressions of leaves using ink and how to sketch detailed drawings of plants. Using these techniques, Jane Colden developed a catalog of about 400 local plants.

Cadwallader Colden introduced his daughter to many of the prominent naturalists* of the day. Because few colonial women received the education needed to pursue an intellectual career, Jane Colden's achievements made her somewhat of a celebrity in the scientific community. Her work was well respected, and there was even some discussion of naming a new genus* of plant after her.

Jane Colden married a New York City physician in 1759 and probably stopped her work in botany at that time. She died seven years later.

Colleges

*E*uropean colonists wanted to preserve their cultural heritage when they moved to the wilderness of North America. This goal led to the establishment of colonial colleges. While primary and secondary schools taught children such basic skills as reading and math, colleges prepared men for public and professional careers. The colleges also sought to provide an education that would pass on the values and ideas of Western culture.

In the French colonies, religious groups took charge of most higher education. The JESUITS, a Roman Catholic religious order, established a school in Quebec to train pilots, navigators, and mapmakers. The Spanish Borderlands had no colleges. Instead, well-to-do individuals sent their sons to Europe, Mexico, or the West Indies for training as priests, lawyers, and doctors. The colonists of New Netherland also shipped their children to Great Britain for higher education. Although some wealthy British colonists looked to Europe for their children's education, British settlers made an effort to create institutions of higher learning in their own colonies.

The Early Colonial Period. Early colonial leaders were expected to be men of learning. This generally meant that they would have some knowledge of Latin and Greek and familiarity with the writings of ancient philosophers and other great European thinkers. Such learning was considered the foundation of professional training. In fact, most educated men in the 1600s did not learn professions in college but acquired the necessary skills on their own after their formal schooling. Women seldom received instruction beyond the basics of reading and writing, considered sufficient for their role as homemakers. Women could not go to college, and those educated by their families often kept their knowledge a secret. Colonial society disapproved of "overly educated" women.

European colonists established three colleges in North America during the 1600s: Quebec College in New France, Harvard College in Massachusetts, and the College of William and Mary in Virginia. Quebec College was founded in 1663 to educate the upper classes of French colonial society. Its curriculum* included Latin, geography and history, mathematics, science, and philosophy*. The college also exposed students to drama, allowing them to perform in several plays.

The first college in the English colonies was Harvard College, founded in 1636. Harvard began as an institution to train ministers and civic leaders for the PURITAN church. The curriculum included Greek and Latin, mathematics, logic, history, and religion. Although Harvard's charter* called for educating Indian youth, only four Indians attended the college in the 1600s.

The College of William and Mary, founded in the 1690s, did not begin college-level education until the 1720s because of a lack of qualified teachers. William and Mary had three basic aims: to train ministers, to provide a religious-based education for the colony's leaders, and to convert Indians to Christianity. Virginia colonists also hoped that the college would stimulate the local economy and add to the reputation of the colony. During its early years, many students failed to obtain degrees. Nevertheless, attending the college gave students political and social contacts that helped them become leaders in the colony.

* *curriculum* course of study

* *philosophy* study related to ideas, the laws of nature, and the pursuit of truth

* *charter* document stating the principles of an organization

The first college founded in the British colonies was Boston's Harvard College. It was established to train ministers and leaders for the Puritan church.

In the late 1600s, some New England colonists believed that Harvard College was drifting away from its original purpose. In 1701 a group of church officials in Connecticut decided to found their own institution, Yale College. In its early years, Yale lacked a building, and students had to follow their teachers from place to place. The college finally began construction on a building of its own in the town of New Haven in 1717.

The Later Colonial Period.   During the 1700s, the population of the British colonies grew dramatically and became more diverse as immigrants arrived from various parts of Europe. At the same time, the colonies experienced a religious revival known as the GREAT AWAKENING, which led to divisions in PROTESTANT CHURCHES. Some Protestant groups did not approve of the religious training of colleges run by other churches. The social and religious diversity of the colonies led to the founding of more colleges.

A split in the ranks of Presbyterian Protestants led to the creation of the College of New Jersey (later Princeton University) in 1746. The college accepted students from all religious backgrounds. Its curriculum included courses similar to those of other colleges.

In 1749 the College and Academy of Philadelphia (now the University of Pennsylvania) was established as a nonreligious institution. The curriculum of the college differed from that of earlier colleges. In addition to offering such traditional courses as mathematics and philosophy, it also trained students in agriculture and other practical subjects and prepared them for professional careers in law and medicine.

In 1754 New Yorkers decided to establish a college of their own. Although founded by Anglicans*, King's College (later Columbia University) was open to people of many faiths and backgrounds. In 1766 Dutch Reformed Protestants in New Jersey established Queens College (later Rutgers University) in order to have their own institution for training ministers. Another goal of the college was to teach Dutch-speaking colonists the English language.

The Baptists, one of the few major Protestant groups without a college, opened the College of Rhode Island (later Brown University) in Providence,

* *Anglican* member of the Church of England

Rhode Island, in 1764. Although controlled by Baptists, the college prohibited religious discrimination of any sort. Most of its students came from other colonies.

The last institution of higher education founded in the colonial period was Dartmouth College in New Hampshire. Dartmouth was created in 1769 to train missionaries to work among the Indians, but most of its graduates entered other professions.

During the 1700s, the curriculum of colonial colleges went through some changes. Occupational preparation became more specialized to meet the need for increasing numbers of doctors, lawyers, ministers, teachers, and public officials. Yet the colleges continued to focus on traditional subjects and to provide Christian religious education. Some colonists saw education as a way to lessen the differences between people of various backgrounds. Others saw it as a way to develop good citizens and reform society.

* *status* social position

Throughout the colonial period, wealth and status* were the keys to obtaining a college education. College was expensive, and few could afford to attend. A college education probably added little to the social and economic position of students from the upper class. For others, however, it helped provide access to profitable careers and leadership positions in colonial society. (*See also* **Education; Schools and Schooling.**)

Colonial Administration

*A*fter establishing colonies in North America, European powers had to find ways of managing them. It was a task for which they were not well prepared. Over time, however, European nations developed various procedures and institutions for administering the political and economic life of their colonies. The European governments formed colonial policy at home and sent officials to the colonies to carry out their plans. Yet because of the distance, control was difficult, and the colonists enjoyed a great deal of freedom.

British Colonies

British colonial administration gradually changed from loose supervision of a few scattered settlements to complex arrangements for governing the 13 North American colonies. For many years, Britain enjoyed good relations with its colonies. Beginning in the mid-1700s, however, the British government took steps to strengthen control of its growing, economically valuable possessions. These actions stirred resentment among the colonists, contributing eventually to a movement for independence.

* *charter* written grant from a ruler conferring certain rights and privileges

* *proprietor* person granted land and the right to establish a colony

First Settlements to 1696. The earliest English settlements—the JAMESTOWN COLONY, the PLYMOUTH COLONY, and the Massachusetts Bay colony—were founded on the basis of royal charters*. These charters granted trading companies and proprietors* the right to create a colony and establish its government. In return, the English monarchs claimed a share of the profits made in the colonies.

See map in British Colonies (vol. 1).

Throughout the early and mid-1600s, the colonies managed their affairs with little interference from English authorities. Trading companies—such as the VIRGINIA COMPANY—and proprietors—such as Lord Baltimore, the founder of MARYLAND—were generally free to rule their colonies in their own way. However, when the Virginia Company lost its charter in 1624 as a result of financial difficulties, King JAMES I declared VIRGINIA a royal colony. He appointed a royal governor to oversee its affairs, putting the colony under the direct authority of the English crown.

Under King Charles I, the Privy Council—a group of the king's close advisers—administered the colonies. In 1634 Charles created an organization called the Commission of Plantations to gain greater control over the colonies. PARLIAMENT later created its own Committee on Plantations to oversee colonial affairs. But these councils had little effect. At the time, the king and Parliament were locked in a bitter struggle for power that erupted in the English Civil War in 1642. During the conflict, England paid little attention to the colonies. Parliament won the struggle—and beheaded the king—but its main concern continued to be the situation in England. The colonies remained on their own.

The monarchy was restored in England in 1660. For the next 15 years, King Charles II relied on councils of advisers to govern the colonies. These advisory councils, large and unmanageable, had little success in their mission. In 1675 they were replaced by a single organization called the Lords of Trade, which helped bring some stability to colonial administration.

At about this time, England began to take a greater interest in North America. The colonial population was growing rapidly, new colonies were being formed, and trade with England was expanding. For England, this trade became particularly important because the taxes on goods shipped to the colonies provided a major share of government funds. The king and Parliament made a greater effort to bring the colonies under their supervision.

The colonists—left alone for so many years—rebelled against tighter control of their affairs. Colonial merchants broke English trade laws by shipping goods wherever they wished. Colonial ASSEMBLIES delayed sending agents to England and refused to approve the funds needed to pay the salaries of royal governors. Defying a request to send legislation to England for approval, the colonists passed laws that remained in effect for too brief a time to allow English authorities to review them.

Major Changes in Colonial Administration. Determined to improve colonial administration, the king and Parliament took a series of steps in 1696. Parliament passed a law that tightened English control of colonial trade. It established courts to enforce trade policies, created a system for collecting taxes on trade goods, and required that all colonial laws be sent to England for review. Meanwhile, William III created a new, more powerful council called the Board of Trade. The board was responsible for regulating colonial trade, ensuring that the colonies' laws followed English law, recommending new members of colonial councils, helping non-English people settle in the colonies, issuing instructions to royal governors, and supervising colonial administration.

Colonial Agents

The British colonies employed agents to represent their interests in Britain and to explain the colonial point of view to members of the government. These agents could be summoned to appear before the Board of Trade. Sometimes they testified in Parliament, as Benjamin Franklin did during debate over the Stamp Act. Although many agents were born and raised in the colonies, some were English. The colonies preferred agents with good connections, such as Richard Jackson, a secretary to the British prime minister and a member of Parliament.

Colonial Administration

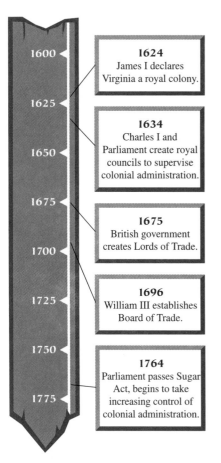

1624
James I declares Virginia a royal colony.

1634
Charles I and Parliament create royal councils to supervise colonial administration.

1675
British government creates Lords of Trade.

1696
William III establishes Board of Trade.

1764
Parliament passes Sugar Act, begins to take increasing control of colonial administration.

* Anglican of the Church of England

Other changes took place in colonial government. By 1732 nine of the colonies had come under the direct control of the king. Each had a royal governor, appointed by the king, who followed instructions from the Board of Trade. The royal governor was the king's representative in the colony, with wide-ranging authority over the legal system, the courts, military defense, and trade. The governors also oversaw officials such as the collectors of quitrents, who collected fees from the colonists for the use of the land. These royal colonies also had appointed councils answerable to the king and his advisers. Only CONNECTICUT and RHODE ISLAND kept their original charters, which gave them the right to choose their own governors and colonial councils. However, even these two colonies were expected to send their laws to Britain for review.

For the next few decades, British colonial administration worked quite well. The Board of Trade was responsible for most of the work of running the colonies. Parliament had the power to make policy concerning colonial trade, manufacturing, and citizenship. The king and his advisers directed foreign policy that affected the colonies.

Stable Relations with the Colonies.   Unlike earlier efforts to increase control over the colonies, the reforms by the king and Parliament met little resistance. Loyalty to Britain and its institutions played a role in colonial acceptance. Moreover, Britain's stability and prosperity inspired American colonists to cooperate. Compared to the 1600s, with the bitter conflict between the king and Parliament, the 1700s were relatively peaceful.

The main reason colonists accepted British control more willingly, though, had to do with an improved system of administration. British officials had better information about the colonies and could make fairly intelligent decisions. At the same time, the colonists had more opportunity to influence British policies. Colonial governors, judges, and trade officials could send information to the Board of Trade. British churches, merchant organizations, and other groups formed ties with colonists and helped communicate their views to British officials. For example, the bishop of London, responsible for the Anglican* churches in the colonies, was also a member of the Board of Trade, where he could support policies favorable to the churches. Finally, the colonies had agents who voiced colonial concerns directly to the Board of Trade. This access to the Board of Trade gave the colonists a voice in decision making, which made them more cooperative.

In this spirit of cooperation, colonial assemblies generally followed the course set by the British government. When royal governors arrived in the colonies from Britain, they had no local support and little political influence. They needed the assemblies to approve their salaries and to pass legislation to put the instructions of the Board of Trade into effect. To achieve these goals, governors sometimes had to give some of their power to the assemblies. Meanwhile, colonial assemblies were becoming stronger for other reasons. Increasingly, colonists went to their representatives in the assemblies—not to royal officials—to resolve problems. The assemblies began using new approaches to get their work done. They formed committees, chose more effective speakers, and kept better records. They also consulted more often with the people they represented before deciding an issue. This expansion of the assemblies' role further weakened the governors.

Parliament Takes Control.   The relationship between the colonies and Britain changed during and after the FRENCH AND INDIAN WAR, the conflict in which Britain and France struggled for control of North America. The British won the war, but the victory and its aftermath were costly, both financially and in terms of their relations with the colonies.

The French and Indian War left Britain in enormous debt. In addition, the continued threat of Indian resistance on the colonial frontiers forced Britain to station troops in North America on a permanent basis, an expensive undertaking. The colonists' lack of support during the war frustrated the British. After all, the British believed that they had fought the war largely for the benefit of the colonists. Parliament wanted to have the colonies share the financial burden of the war and to become dutiful citizens of the British Empire.

Meanwhile, the structure of British colonial administration was changing. The Board of Trade had grown weaker, and Parliament began to assume a greater role in colonial administration. The colonists did not like this change. For years, they had enjoyed a role in shaping the decisions of the Board of Trade, but Parliament was much more difficult to influence. The result was a growing hostility toward British rule in the colonies. Beginning with the SUGAR ACT OF 1764, Parliament passed a series of laws aimed at raising money from the colonies. When the colonists resisted, Parliament passed other laws that punished them. The situation worsened and led to a movement for independence from Britain.

Citizens of Boston protested a British law by throwing a shipload of tea into Boston harbor. The incident was just one of many conflicts between colonists and the British government that eventually led to the American Revolution.

See map in New Netherland (vol. 3).

Dutch Colony

In establishing the colony of NEW NETHERLAND, the Amsterdam division of the DUTCH WEST INDIA COMPANY had only one goal: to make money for its investors. In 1624 the company decided to send 30 families to the colony. The new colonists had to agree to follow the rules of the company and to carry out its orders. However, the colony's commander had instructions to form a council made up of settlers, which would have a role in governing the colony.

The West India Company believed that the most profitable activity for the colony would be to develop a FUR TRADE. It promised to pay settlers "reasonable" prices for the furs they supplied. The colonists were also encouraged to search for "mines of gold, silver, copper or any other metals." Because the company established the colony as a business, the settlers dealt with the company as both their government and their employer.

In 1629 the Amsterdam division of the company tried another approach to attract colonists. It agreed to the plan of Kiliaen Van Rensselaer, one of its investors, to allow landowners to establish large feudal* estates in New Netherland. Each patroon—as the landowners were called—could hold large tracts of land and the rights to all the resources on them. The patroons could rent their land to tenants, who would farm it and pay the owner in money, goods, and services. The plan gave the patroons enormous powers over everyone living on their property. They could impose taxes or fees, appoint officers of the law, and run the courts. As the rulers of their estates, the patroons even had the power of life and death over their tenants.

The patroon system did not succeed in increasing colonization and was largely abandoned by 1640. The West India Company then began offering

* ***feudal*** relating to an economic and political system in which individuals give service to a landowner in return for protection and the use of land

It was from this beautiful building on Haarlem Street in Amsterdam that the Dutch West India Company administered its North American colony.

* **_monopoly_** exclusive right to engage in a certain kind of business

200 acres of free land to any colonist who would settle in New Netherland with five family members or servants. The company also ended its monopoly* on furs, opening the fur trade to any Dutch citizen. It did, however, continue to tax certain imports and exports. These changes came about because of the company's financial problems and the desire of Amsterdam merchants to keep New Netherland alive. Although the West India Company loosened its hold over the colony's economy, it kept full control of its government.

Beginning in the 1640s, hundreds of English families migrated to New Netherland from New England. Thousands of Dutch, Scandinavian, German, and French settlers streamed into the colony as well. This flood of new colonists led to changes in colonial administration. Most of the non-Dutch settlers resented the rules of the Dutch West India Company and pressured colonial officials to give them greater control over their affairs. The company agreed to grant charters allowing self-government to towns throughout the colony, including towns of Dutch colonists. But the large number of settlers of different national backgrounds made Dutch control of New Netherland increasingly difficult. When an English fleet appeared off NEW AMSTERDAM in 1664, Director General Peter STUYVESANT failed to rally enough support to defend the colony. Powerless to meet this threat, the Dutch West India Company surrendered the colony to the English.

French Colonies

See map in New France (vol. 3).

Like the British and Dutch colonies, the French colonies began as business ventures established by groups of private investors. In the mid-1600s, however, the French government took over these colonies and maintained tight control of them for the remainder of their existence.

Company Rule.   From the early attempts at settlement in the 1540s until 1663, the French colonies were controlled by a series of private trading companies. Because their focus was on business, primarily the fur trade, these companies did little to encourage large-scale colonization. As a result, few French settlers came to North America before the 1600s.

Real efforts at colonization began with the explorer Samuel de CHAMPLAIN. In 1608 he founded QUEBEC, France's first permanent settlement in North America. The town later became the administrative center of NEW FRANCE. Then, in 1627, a powerful French government official led a group of investors to form the COMPANY OF ONE HUNDRED ASSOCIATES, which was committed to boosting the settlement of New France. The company recruited colonists and set up an administration to govern the colony. By the mid-1600s, however, conflicts with Native Americans had interrupted the fur trade, hurting the colony's economy. Almost bankrupt and unable to defend New France, the Company of One Hundred Associates gave control of the colony to the French crown in 1663.

One factor that played a role in the decision of French king Louis XIV to take over the colony was the idea of MERCANTILISM. According to this theory, colonies could bring great wealth and power to their parent countries. The

Colonial Administration

Contact with France

Communication between France and New France could take many, many months. The distance across the Atlantic Ocean and Canada's cold climate both played a role in the slowness. Quebec, the capital of New France, was icebound for seven months of the year. Each July or August, ships from France arrived at the city with supplies—and with instructions from royal officials. In late October or early November, these ships left for France loaded with furs and carrying letters from colonial officials to their superiors in France. In the following weeks, the waterways of Quebec froze, and colonial officials would not receive answers to their correspondence until the following summer.

* *bureaucracy* large departmental organization within a government

* *heresy* belief that is contrary to church teachings

colonies could provide important raw materials for European companies to turn into manufactured goods, which goods could then be sold throughout Europe and back to the colonies. From the point of view of mercantilists, New France did not hold out much promise. Furs were its only valuable resource, and its population was too small to provide a significant market for French goods. Nevertheless, France took over the colony and integrated it into the royal administration. For a brief period, the colony was run by the FRENCH WEST INDIES COMPANY. But by 1670, royal officials had regained control.

Government Control.   Under royal administration, New France had two main government officials—the governor-general and the intendant, both appointed and supervised by French authorities. The governor-general had overall authority for the colony, but his primary concern was with military and diplomatic matters. The intendant held the real administrative power. He supervised the collection of taxes, coordinated economic policy, and administered justice. The intendant also had responsibility for the settlement of colonists, land grants, the prices of basic goods, and the colonial bureaucracy*.

Colonial officials were supposed to have all their policy decisions approved in France. Yet the slowness of communications between France and North America meant that they often had a great deal of freedom in governing. If they did not like the instructions received from France, the administrators could delay putting them into effect by sending a letter of protest. During the months that it took to receive a reply, they could follow their own course. Colonial officials could control policy in another way as well. Their correspondence with French officials reported on conditions in the colony. By presenting information that supported their views, the colonial administrators could promote their own policies. Officials in France had the final word, though, and colonial administrators eventually had to obey their decisions.

Unlike the British colonies, the French colonies had a tightly centralized administration based in France. In general, local officials in the various regions of New France and in the colony of LOUISIANA received the same instructions from French authorities and responded to them uniformly. One area of frequent disagreement, though, was the colonial budget. Each year, the governor-general and the intendant drew up a budget that projected the financial needs of the colony and sent the budget to France for approval. Inevitably, royal authorities decided to send less money than the colonies had requested. The colonies, however, needed the funds to pay military and government salaries, build and maintain fortifications, buy supplies, and purchase gifts to help maintain friendly relations with the Indians. These expenses were related to survival, so the colonies usually spent more than the royal officials had approved. Colonial finances became a source of great controversy, and French authorities complained bitterly about the cost of maintaining the colonies.

CHURCH AND STATE were closely linked in France, and French colonial officials were expected to promote the ROMAN CATHOLIC CHURCH. Authorities had the power to punish religious crimes, such as heresy*, and they took

156

steps to uphold the dignity of church officials and to restrict other religions. The Company of One Hundred Associates had prohibited the settlement of Protestants in New France. Some Protestants managed to come anyway, but they could not practice their religion in public. The ban on Protestants was relaxed in the 1700s. Although the bishop had direct control over religious administration, the state kept a close watch on church affairs. Church officials served the government directly by publicizing laws, drafting legal documents, and running hospitals and schools.

State and Society. Despite the control that France had over its colonies, the enforcement of French policies was seldom automatic. Colonial administrators often did things in their own way. Yet they were public servants whose careers depended on the support of royal authorities in France. North America was not considered a desirable location—in spite of the possibility of gaining wealth from the fur trade—and colonial governors and intendants looked forward to obtaining better positions in France. For this reason, they did not stray too far from the instructions they received from royal authorities.

In the colonies, families, military officers, wealthy merchants, and high church officials all had close ties with colonial officials. These relationships helped them gain some influence in colonial administration. Many prominent citizens also maintained connections with authorities in France.

The majority of French colonists, however, had few contacts with colonial or French officials and little interest in the activities of the colonial administration and the French government. This lack of interest on the part of ordinary settlers, along with the desire of prominent colonists to maintain close ties with France, helps explain why an independence movement never arose in the French colonies.

Spanish Colonies

After establishing colonies in the Americas, the Spanish monarchs moved quickly to organize colonial administration. Like the French, they created a tightly controlled, centralized administration. Yet colonial officials gradually gained a great deal of freedom to deal with local issues.

Early Administration. In 1503 the Spanish monarchy set up an organization called the House of Trade to administer its overseas investments. Based in Seville, the House of Trade was responsible for regulating trade and organizing the voyages that brought settlers and supplies to the Americas. Royal councils, also based in Spain, handled colonial political administration and appointed governors to rule the colonies.

In 1524 Charles V of Spain combined political and economic control of the colonies in the Council of the Indies. The members of this council, all Spaniards of high rank, advised the king and acted on his behalf. The king created a new position, viceroy, to replace the governors as head of colonial government. Only men close to the monarch and of proven loyalty were chosen to fill this important post. The viceroy presided over the

> **Remember:** Consult the index at the end of Volume 4 to find more information on many topics.

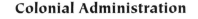

viceroyalty region governed by a viceroy

See map in Spanish Borderlands (vol. 4).

Seven Years' War series of conflicts in Europe, North America, Africa, and Asia that involved two struggles—one between Austria and Prussia and the other between Britain and France; the American part of the conflict, the French and Indian War, ended in 1763 with Britain defeating France and its ally Spain

cede to yield or surrender

courts, managed colonial finances, enforced the law, and played a role in church administration. Although this official enjoyed considerable freedom in interpreting laws and putting them into effect, all his decisions had to be approved by the Council of the Indies. Communication between the colonies and Spain took time, so colonial government moved slowly and inefficiently.

The center of Spanish colonial administration in North America was Mexico City, the capital of the viceroyalty* of NEW SPAIN. New Spain consisted of an assortment of provinces and administrative units. Among these were the SPANISH BORDERLANDS, an area including present-day FLORIDA and the southwestern part of the United States. Lightly settled and far from the core of Spanish America, these frontier regions faced special problems of defense against Indian attack and the ambitions of the British and French.

Florida. People from New Spain moved north to settle and govern most of the Borderlands. Florida, however, was colonized directly from Spain and administered by government officials in the WEST INDIES.

Spain established its colony in Florida for purposes of defense. When the French began showing interest in creating colonies in the Southeast, the Spanish became alarmed. The presence of the French would threaten the Spanish treasure fleets that sailed for Spain laden with gold and silver. The ships sailed along the east coast of Florida, so the Spanish decided to establish several forts there in the 1560s. The colony of Florida remained fairly small and poor, but its location was crucial. The Spanish crown took direct control of the colony and ordered New Spain to provide the funds needed to support forts, missionaries, and settlers.

Spanish policy in Florida changed in the late 1600s, largely as a result of growing competition with the English. English traders from South Carolina gained influence with local Indians. The Spaniards in Florida could not compete for trade because of their poverty, and they abandoned coastal areas north of St. Augustine in the 1680s.

In the 1700s, policies made in Spain began to affect Florida directly because Spain and Britain were at war. In 1703 and 1704, English forces invaded Florida and destroyed many settlements. Then, in 1763, Spain lost Florida to Britain as a result of the Seven Years' War*. Spain regained Florida 20 years later, but the colony remained small, and Spanish administration focused on trying to settle growing border disputes with the new United States. Spain finally ceded* Florida to the United States in 1819.

The Western Borderlands. In the western part of the Spanish Borderlands—the area from TEXAS to CALIFORNIA—Spanish settlement was largely the result of actions taken in Mexico City. Although royal officials in Spain directed the effort, colonial officials in Mexico City made the many decisions that put Spanish policies into effect. Moreover, money from New Spain supported the colonization efforts of the soldiers, missionaries, and others who planted settlements in the Borderlands. As a result, officials in New Spain played a significant role in the administration of this northern territory.

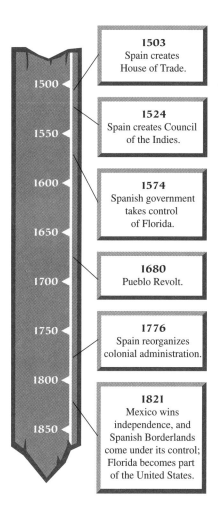

1503
Spain creates
House of Trade.

1524
Spain creates Council
of the Indies.

1574
Spanish government
takes control
of Florida.

1680
Pueblo Revolt.

1776
Spain reorganizes
colonial administration.

1821
Mexico wins
independence, and
Spanish Borderlands
come under its control;
Florida becomes part
of the United States.

* outpost frontier settlement or military base

* tribute payment made to a dominant power

These trends continued from the late 1500s to 1763, when Spain's defeat in the Seven Years' War led to some changes. To avoid further losses, Spain sought to exercise greater control over its colonies—even the remote Borderlands—to ensure their defense. A new Indian policy called for increased trade and financial support for tribes, including those that had previously been hostile. That policy, combined with stronger military forces, was aimed at bringing peace to the frontier.

Spain also pursued a more aggressive policy toward other nations in the late 1700s. Fearing a growing Russian presence in California, it launched a program to plant MISSIONS and forts in that region. Spanish authorities also strengthened their defenses along the border between Texas and the United States.

In the early 1800s, civil war broke out in MEXICO as some groups there sought independence from Spain. Mexico won its independence in 1821. Florida became part of the United States, while the western section of the Borderlands became the northernmost provinces of the new nation of Mexico.

Administrative Issues. Administration of the Spanish Borderlands had three main issues to address: the need for frontier defense, policies towards Indian labor, and the power of the missions and missionaries. Florida and the northern Borderlands were frontier outposts*, created as defensive zones to protect the main body of the Spanish empire. Texas, NEW MEXICO, and ARIZONA provided a shield primarily against attacks by Indians. Florida and California helped halt the advances of other European powers. To carry out their policy, officials in New Spain built PRESIDIOS, or forts, throughout the Borderlands region. They usually established presidios near new missions or in areas threatened by Indian attack. By 1787 the Borderlands had 22 presidios with more than 3,000 officers and soldiers.

After the Seven Years' War, Spain changed its frontier defenses. Some presidios were closed and others moved south toward the central areas of New Spain. The need for a more coordinated frontier defense led Spain to reorganize its colonial administration in 1776, combining the Borderland provinces as the Interior Provinces of the North. Although still officially a part of the viceroyalty of New Spain, the new provinces gained a measure of independence and were under the control of veteran soldiers.

Spain hoped to promote the economic development of the Borderlands by using Indian labor. Colonists had brought a system from New Spain called the *ENCOMIENDA,* which forced Indians to pay them tribute* and to become their permanent workforce. Spain feared the *encomienda* would lead to the emergence of a powerful colonial aristocracy that would challenge Spanish rule. In the mid-1500s, Spanish authorities introduced regulations to restrict the *encomienda.* The system did decline, but mostly because European diseases caused a dramatic drop in the Indian population. Spain introduced a new system, *repartimiento,* which allowed colonists to use Indian labor only at important times, such as during planting and harvesting.

Both the *encomienda* and *repartimiento* were used in Florida, New Mexico, and Arizona. In New Mexico, Indian resentment over the practices led to the Pueblo Revolt in 1680. By the time Texas and California were settled, the forced labor systems had been abandoned. However, Indian labor still played a major role in those colonies through another important Spanish colonial institution—the missions.

The Roman Catholic Church held a central position in the administration of Spain's colonies. Spanish monarchs controlled the Spanish Catholic Church, and the church in New Spain formed part of the colonial government. The establishment and operation of missions, then, involved both church and colonial authorities. Officials in Mexico City approved the creation of each mission, granted the necessary land and water rights, and provided enough money to keep it going. Missionaries had spiritual authority over the Indians who lived on the missions and also served as their legal guardians.

Spanish plans called for gradually converting the missions into self-governing towns and dividing mission land among the Indians. This rarely occurred. In most cases, the missionaries kept control of mission property, agricultural products, and Indian labor. Tensions often arose among missionaries, settlers, and soldiers at the presidios that had been built to protect the missions. Missionaries sometimes challenged the authority of government officials, and major conflicts often arose over the economic power of the missions and their control of Indian labor.

In the early 1800s, Spain wanted to close the Borderland missions or at least limit their power. Little was accomplished, however, because the colonial officials who controlled the missions refused to act. Their ability to ignore instructions revealed Spain's lack of control over colonial administration. It was not until after Mexico gained its independence in 1821 that Mexican officials ended the mission system. (*See also* **British Colonies; Church and State; Government, Provincial; Independence Movements.**)

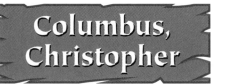

Columbian Exchange

See *Environmental Impact of Colonization.*

Columbus, Christopher

ca. 1451–1506
Explorer

*C*hristopher Columbus's life is surrounded by myth. Many people still think of Columbus as the first European to reach the Americas. Some assume that he was one of the few people of his day to claim the world was round. However, historians have established that Vikings from Scandinavia visited present-day Canada in the 1000s, and they also know that most educated people of the late 1400s believed the world was round. Furthermore, Columbus made an error in calculating the size of the earth, which led him to conclude—incorrectly—that he had achieved his goal of sailing to Asia.

Although many stories about Columbus are myths, his voyages were still enormously important. Few people of his time knew about the Viking expeditions and discoveries. Columbus's voyages launched a time of contact between the peoples of Europe and the Americas, changing the course of history on both sides of the Atlantic Ocean.

Early Years. Born in Genoa, Italy, Columbus was the son of a wool weaver and merchant. He went to sea at an early age and took part in voyages to the northern Atlantic, possibly sailing as far as Iceland, and to Africa. Settling in Portugal with his younger brother, Bartolomeo, Columbus married an Italian-Portuguese woman. Through her, he gained some wealth and connections to the Portuguese royal court. He also began to read geography texts and accounts of sea voyages. The idea of finding a new trade route to Asia fascinated Columbus.

For centuries, European merchants had traded with Asian countries for such luxurious goods as silks and spices. The only known route to Asia— over land—was long, expensive, and dangerous. Europeans wanted to find an alternate route. The Portuguese were exploring the Atlantic coast of Africa, hoping they could sail around Africa to reach Asia.

The Columbus brothers had a different idea. Their plan was to reach Asia by sailing west from Europe. While educated people knew the world was round, they did not know its exact size—or that large landmasses lay to the west between Europe and Asia. For years, scholars thought that about 11,500 miles separated Europe and Asia. In 1474 an Italian scholar claimed that the distance was only half that. Columbus and his brother believed the distance to be even less—only about 2,700 miles. If their estimate was correct, the ships of the time would be capable of making the voyage.

Promoting the Plan. For almost 10 years, the Columbus brothers tried to convince European rulers to finance an expedition to Asia. They presented their idea for a voyage to the Indies—meaning Asia—to King John II of Portugal. He turned them down on the advice of a group of experts who thought they were mistaken about the length of the journey.

Columbus then tried Queen Isabella and King Ferdinand of Spain. While the Spanish monarchs found his proposal attractive, they were busy fighting the Muslims. They said that they might support him but made no commitment. Columbus also presented his plan to King Henry VII of England and to the ruler of France. Both turned him down.

In 1492 the Spanish monarchs finally agreed to finance Columbus's expedition. Along with financial support, Queen Isabella gave Columbus a number of honorary titles and granted him power to rule as viceroy* over any lands he might discover.

* *viceroy* person appointed as a monarch's representative to govern a province or colony

The First Voyage. Columbus sailed from Spain on August 3, 1492, in the *Santa Maria.* Two smaller ships—the *Niña* and the *Pinta*—were also part of the expedition. After stopping in the Canary Islands for fresh supplies, the ships set sail on September 6 and headed west to the Caribbean. Had Columbus maintained a straight westerly course, he would have reached present-day Florida. Instead, he turned southwest and on October 12 sighted one of the Bahama Islands. He named it San Salvador—"the holy savior"—and claimed it for Spain. He called the native people who greeted his arrival "Indians," believing he had landed in the East Indies.

The three ships continued to explore the Caribbean, reaching Cuba by the end of October. On December 24 disaster struck. The *Santa Maria* ran aground and sank off the island called HISPANIOLA. Columbus left 39 men in a settlement on the island and returned to Europe in the remaining ships. Slowed by bad weather and unfavorable winds, he did not reach Spain until March 1493.

Columbus believed that he had reached the Indies. As proof of his success, he brought back several natives to Spain. He presented them to Isabella and Ferdinand and easily won approval of another voyage. The queen instructed him to treat the natives well and convert them to Christianity.

Remaining Voyages. In September 1493, Columbus sailed off on his second voyage with a large fleet of 17 ships and 1,200 Spaniards who hoped to settle in the "New World." On arriving, he discovered that the men he had left behind on Hispaniola had been killed by the Indians. After establishing a new colony, Columbus set off to explore Cuba and left his brother Diego in charge. Soon his brother Bartolomeo arrived as well. The Columbus brothers made several bad decisions, and many of the colonists were dissatisfied with their leadership. In addition, the native population had begun rebelling because of harsh treatment by the Europeans. The complaints of colonists who had returned to Spain led the queen and king to send an investigator. In 1496 Columbus sailed back to Spain to defend himself and his brothers against charges of poor administration.

Isabella and Ferdinand gave the explorer their support and agreed to send him on a third voyage in 1498. This time Columbus sailed along the coast of

In this 1590 engraving of the "discovery" of America, artist Thomas de Bry shows Columbus and his men being greeted by Indians bearing gold and other gifts. From illustrations such as this, Europeans got the impression that the Americas were filled with riches waiting to be claimed.

present-day Venezuela and became convinced that he had finally reached the mainland of Asia. When he returned to Hispaniola, though, he found the colony in revolt against the rule of his brothers. Columbus tried to pacify the settlers by allowing them to enslave the Indians to work their land. The Spanish crown sent another agent to investigate the charges of incompetent rule. The official arrested Columbus and his brothers and shipped them back to Spain—in chains. From that time on, the Spanish crown took control of its colonies in the Americas.

Although Queen Isabella refused to have Columbus punished, she delayed approving another voyage. She finally granted permission for a fourth trip in 1502, but Columbus was forbidden to return to Hispaniola. On this voyage, he explored the coast of Central America around modern-day Honduras. He had hoped to find the rich cities of Asia, but his ships began leaking, forcing him to land on Jamaica. Columbus and his crew were marooned on the island for over a year.

Columbus returned to Spain in 1504. In spite of his wealth and the presence of his family and friends, Columbus's last years were difficult. His health was poor and he felt betrayed by the Spanish crown, which had taken away many of his titles. Columbus died two years later. In 1507 a German cartographer* published a map that included a continent west of Europe. Columbus had brought this landmass to Europe's attention, but the cartographer did not name it for him. Instead, he called it America in honor of another Italian sailor—Amerigo Vespucci—who had recognized that this continent was not Asia but a *mundus novus* (new world). (*See also* **European Empires; Exploration, Age of.**)

* cartographer mapmaker

Comanche Indians

See second map in Native Americans (vol. 3).

The Comanche were Native Americans who roamed the buffalo-rich grasslands of the southern Great Plains. They were among the first Indians to use HORSES, which were unknown in North America until Spanish explorers introduced them. The Comanche quickly gained a reputation as skilled riders. During the colonial period, they often fought with Spanish settlers and bands of APACHE INDIANS.

In the early 1700s the Comanche settled in what is now southwestern Kansas. Several other tribes living in the area had obtained guns from the French, and they drove the Comanche southwest into the hunting grounds of the eastern Apache. The arrival of the Comanche led to increased tension between these two tribes.

The Comanche Indians were organized into about a dozen tribes that remained independent. Their life revolved around the horse and the BUFFALO. The Indians taught their children to ride at the age of four or five. They bred and trained large herds of horses, supplementing their stock through raids and trade. The horses allowed the Comanche to travel long distances in search of buffalo, which they depended on for food and to make tepees and clothing. They also used buffalo hides to trade for European goods. Because of their nomadic lifestyle, they acquired very few possessions, keeping only practical items such as iron tools and blankets.

Fierce fighters, the Comanche practiced the PLAINS INDIAN custom of counting coups (blows), in which a warrior won honor for touching an enemy. They reserved the highest honor, however, for those who killed an enemy. Bands of Comanche frequently raided their Spanish neighbors for guns, cloth, iron tools, and blankets, as well as horses and human captives. They adopted some of these captives, particularly women, and traded others back to European settlements.

Indian attacks on Spanish colonists hindered settlement in New Mexico and Texas for many years. In the late 1700s, Spanish authorities recognized the need to make peace with local Indian tribes. Although they viewed the Apache as ignorant savages who did not keep their word, they admired the bravery and honesty of the Comanche and entered into a series of negotiations with them. As part of the peace process, the Comanche agreed to join the Spanish in the fight against their common enemy—the Apache. The Comanche and the settlers also engaged in a thriving trade. Each year the Indians brought deerskins and buffalo hides to a trade fair at Taos, New Mexico. Relations between Spanish colonists and the Comanche Indians remained relatively peaceful until Mexico achieved independence from Spain in 1821. Under Mexican and later American rule, the Comanche renewed their attacks as more and more settlers moved into their territory.

Committees of Correspondence

Committees of correspondence were groups formed in the British colonies in the early 1770s to exchange information and organize resistance to British policies. These committees played a vital role in building public support for independence from Great Britain. Later, during the period when the colonies were breaking away from Britain, the committees took over some functions of government.

Formation of the Committees. In November 1772, Samuel ADAMS persuaded the Boston town government to form a committee of correspondence. The committee had two goals: to send a statement of the colonists' rights and grievances to other towns in the colony and to urge those towns to set up committees of their own. Within three months, more than 80 Massachusetts towns had established similar groups.

The following March, Virginia's legislature, the House of Burgesses, created a committee of correspondence that represented the entire colony. By 1774, all the colonies except Pennsylvania and North Carolina had formed similar organizations.

Actions of the Committees. In 1773 the British government passed the TEA ACT, which allowed the BRITISH EAST INDIA COMPANY to sell tea in the colonies at a price that was likely to give it a monopoly on the tea trade. The colonial merchants were outraged, and the committees of correspondence sprang into action. The committees of five Massachusetts towns, including Boston, decided to prevent the East India Company from unloading or selling tea. Soon after, Samuel Adams inspired a group of rebellious

colonists to board a British merchant vessel and dump chests of the company's tea into Boston harbor. News of this BOSTON TEA PARTY quickly spread to other seaports, and they staged similar protests.

When Boston refused to pay the East India Company for the destroyed tea, the British PARLIAMENT punished Massachusetts residents by passing a set of laws known as the INTOLERABLE ACTS. The Boston committee of correspondence urged other colonies to protest the acts by joining in a boycott* of British goods. To coordinate their resistance, colonial leaders agreed to meet in Philadelphia in the FIRST CONTINENTAL CONGRESS.

* **boycott** refusal to buy goods as a means of protest

New Governments. As colonial opposition to British rule grew, patriots* began to ignore the official colonial governments, which supported British policy. In several colonies new committees of correspondence, later known as committees of safety, began taking over government functions. In July 1775, the SECOND CONTINENTAL CONGRESS urged all colonies to form such committees to assume the duties of government.

* **patriot** American colonist who supported independence from Britain

With the approval of the congress, the committees began to recruit soldiers for the army, capture and punish Loyalists*, and take control of colonial affairs. Gradually, each state adopted a new constitution and chose a new government to replace the committees of correspondence. Only in New Hampshire and Connecticut did the committees last throughout the war. (*See also* **American Revolution; Constitutions, Colonial; Patriots.**)

* **Loyalist** American colonist who remained faithful to Britain during the American Revolution

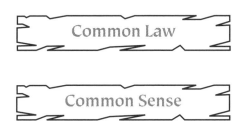

Common Law

See *Laws and Legal Systems: British Colonies.*

Common Sense

See *Paine, Thomas.*

Company of One Hundred Associates

* **monopoly** exclusive right to engage in a certain kind of business

The Company of One Hundred Associates was a private French company established in 1627 to develop French settlements in North America. Inspired by the success of British and Dutch trading companies, the company's investors agreed to send colonists to NEW FRANCE. The company would also provide for the colonists' defense and convert the Indians to Christianity. In return, it received political power over the colony, control of land, and a monopoly* on all trade except fishing.

The company was formed by Cardinal Richelieu, the most powerful official in the court of King Louis XIII. Its investors—government officials, merchants, nobles, church officials, and other wealthy individuals—received large grants of land in New France called seigneuries. The investors were responsible for recruiting and sponsoring colonists to work on their estates. Hoping to avoid tensions between Catholics and Protestants, the company banned HUGUENOTS—French Protestants—from settling in the colony.

The French king gave the company, also known as the Company of New France, authority over all the territory in North America north of present-day Florida. However, parts of this land had already been claimed or occupied by the English and the Dutch, so the company focused its efforts on the region around the St. Lawrence River and Acadia in what is now Canada.

For about 35 years, the company brought a steady trickle of settlers to the region, but it did not attract enough people to make the colony successful. Heavily in debt, the company gave up control of New France in 1663. The French crown took over the colony's administration and transferred control of the FUR TRADE to the FRENCH WEST INDIES COMPANY. (*See also* **British East India Company; Dutch East India Company; European Empires; Seigneurial System.**)

Congregationalists

See *Protestant Churches.*

Connecticut

One of the earliest British colonies in North America, Connecticut shared a PURITAN heritage with its neighbor MASSACHUSETTS. The rich, fertile soil of the Connecticut River valley contributed to a thriving agricultural economy, and Connecticut developed into a prosperous colony.

The Dutch arrived first. Explorer Adriaen Block, the first European to visit the region, sailed up the Connecticut River in 1614. The Dutch built a fort at the site of present-day Hartford in 1633, but the English arrived and established a trading post the same year. Soon English settlers pushed out the Dutch.

Early Settlement.   In the mid-1630s, settlers in Massachusetts decided that their colony was becoming too crowded. Complaining that they did not have sufficient pasture for grazing their cattle, some colonists moved to the Connecticut River valley. The group included many single males who hoped to establish farms for themselves.

Other colonists moved to the Connecticut River area from Massachusetts because of disputes with Puritan leaders. In 1635 one group of dissatisfied Puritans settled at Windsor, and another group founded Wethersfield. The next year Puritan clergyman Thomas HOOKER left his church in Newtown, Massachusetts, with about 100 members of his congregation, to establish the town of Hartford.

Meanwhile, a group of English nobles led by the Earl of Warwick received a grant from the king for much of the land held by the settlers from Massachusetts. In 1635 two of the nobles sent John Winthrop, Jr., the son of Massachusetts governor John WINTHROP, to establish a colony in Connecticut and serve as governor. He founded the coastal town of Saybrook. Three years later Puritan leaders and merchants founded New Haven. They had two basic goals: to create a religiously controlled colony and to establish a base from which to carry on FUR TRADE with the Indians.

 See map in British Colonies (vol. 1).

Founding of Connecticut. At first, the Connecticut "river towns" of Windsor, Wethersfield, and Hartford were under the control of the General Court, the governing body of Massachusetts Bay colony. Not wanting to be part of Massachusetts, the Connecticut towns sent representatives to Hartford in 1639 and formed the colony of Connecticut, with John Winthrop, Jr., acting as governor. They adopted the FUNDAMENTAL ORDERS OF CONNECTICUT, a document modeled after the charter* of Massachusetts, which created a government for the new colony. Connecticut did not include Saybrook and New Haven, which had their own governments. In 1644 the founders of Saybrook sold their colony to Connecticut, but New Haven remained a separate colony for a number of years.

As more settlers moved into the Connecticut region, tensions arose with the local PEQUOT INDIANS. Conflict over the lands led to the outbreak of the PEQUOT WAR in 1636, which almost completely wiped out the tribe. The Pequot War, as well as the threat of Dutch expansion into the region from neighboring New Netherland, led the Connecticut and New Haven colonies to join with Massachusetts and the PLYMOUTH COLONY in 1644 in a loose alliance called the NEW ENGLAND CONFEDERATION. Lasting for 40 years, the confederation played a role in defending New England settlements from the NARRAGANSETT INDIANS during KING PHILIP'S WAR (1675–1676). The colonists' victory in this war marked the end of major armed resistance by Native Americans in New England. No longer in fear of Indian attack, colonists founded numerous communities on either side of the Connecticut River and along the coast.

* ***charter*** written grant from a ruler conferring certain rights and privileges

Settlers from the Massachusetts Bay colony founded towns along the rivers of Connecticut in the mid-1630s. After a few years, they declared Connecticut a separate colony and formed a government. In 1662 Connecticut finally received a charter from the English crown.

Charter Oak

Connecticut colonists treasured their 1662 charter, which granted broad powers of self-government. Thus, they were dismayed when Edmund Andros, governor of the Dominion of New England, called for the return of the document in 1687. While Connecticut governor Robert Treat protested, another Connecticut official took the charter and hid it in a large, hollow tree. The charter remained in this tree—known as the Charter Oak—until Andros was overthrown in 1688 and the charter government was reestablished. The Charter Oak held a place of special honor until it died in 1856—at the estimated age of 1,000 years.

* *annul* to cancel

* *subsistence farming* raising only enough food to live on

Changes in Government.   In 1662 John Winthrop, Jr., now governor of the colony, received a charter for Connecticut from the English crown. The charter recognized the right of the colony to exist, established its boundaries, and granted a considerable amount of self-government. The charter also made provisions for New Haven to join the Connecticut colony. New Haven resisted at first, but it finally agreed to become a part of Connecticut in 1665.

The charter called for the annual election of a governor, deputy governor, and 12 "assistants" to rule the colony. These officials also formed the council, the upper house of a colonial assembly. The lower house of the assembly was composed of two elected members from each town in the colony. The assembly had the power to make laws for the colony as long as these laws did not contradict the laws of England.

Connecticut enjoyed self-government until the 1680s, when England decided to annul* the charters of several colonies and unite them in the DOMINION OF NEW ENGLAND. Sir Edmund ANDROS, who was named governor of the dominion by King James II, announced the plan in Hartford in late 1687. Connecticut settlers accepted royal rule for a few years, but they hid the colony's charter to prevent its seizure. When a new king took the English throne in 1689, Connecticut settlers quickly voted to restore self-government under their old charter, a move that was approved by the crown. The charter—with a few changes in 1776—remained the basic law of Connecticut until 1818.

Growing Prosperity.   Connecticut grew and prospered throughout the 1700s. By 1766 it had a population of more than 130,000. The vast majority of the colonists were of British ancestry, but about 3,000 African Americans lived in the colony as well. Virtually all the colonists belonged to Protestant churches. Most were Puritans. There were no Roman Catholics and only a few Jewish settlers.

About 90 percent of the settlers engaged in farming. Over time, the economy of the colony shifted from subsistence farming* to raising surplus crops and livestock for trade. Most of the trade was with Boston, New York, and the West Indies. Connecticut merchants supplied rural shopkeepers with imported foods such as pepper and molasses; dry goods such as lace and gloves; manufactured items like pots, pans, needles, knives, and gunpowder; and a few books. Shopkeepers traded these goods to local farmers for meat, livestock, potatoes, and other farm produce, which were exchanged with the merchants for the goods they supplied.

During the 1700s, manufacturing began to develop in the larger towns of Connecticut. Among the colony's major industries were clock making, iron making, and shipbuilding. Shipbuilding became especially important in coastal towns such as New Haven and New London.

Religion in the Colony.   The Puritan church played a vital role in the political and cultural life of Connecticut. The close link between CHURCH AND STATE had been established in the colony's first settlements by their Puritan founders. The colonial government supported the Puritans and discouraged other faiths. Although the QUAKERS and some other religious groups challenged church authority in the 1600s, they were unable to achieve equal standing in the colony. In 1689, when England allowed Connecticut to reestablish its charter, the colony agreed to uphold the English ACT OF TOLERATION, a law that granted all Protestant groups the right to worship. In practice, however, the Puritan leaders of Connecticut continued to discourage other religions.

In the 1730s and 1740s, preachers traveled throughout the Connecticut countryside giving emotional sermons that challenged certain Puritan beliefs and stirred religious feeling among the colonists. This was part of a broad religious revival known as the GREAT AWAKENING. Thousands of Connecticut colonists followed the teachings of these preachers, which led to a bitter split with those who remained faithful to traditional Puritan beliefs. Prompted by Puritan leaders, Connecticut passed a law requiring the ministers to obtain permission from local clergy* before preaching. The law threatened fines and banishment, but many revivalist preachers simply ignored it and continued their activities.

Colonial policy toward other religions eventually changed. By the late 1700s, Connecticut allowed Baptists, Anglicans, and Quakers to form their own churches and hold religious services. Not until after the AMERICAN REVOLUTION, though, did the state formally end its connection to the Puritan church.

Intellectual Life. Dedication to religion spurred a movement for public EDUCATION in Connecticut. The colony's religious leaders wanted young people to learn to read so they could study the Bible, thereby gaining religious instruction and moral improvement.

A law passed in 1650 required two types of schooling in the colony. Towns with at least 50 families had to hire a teacher to instruct children in reading and writing. Towns with 100 families or more had to establish a grammar school to teach students and prepare them for college. Communities did not always meet their obligations, however. By the mid-1700s, at least 50 towns in the colony contained enough families to support a grammar school, but only 4 of them actually established schools. The desire for advanced religious training led to the founding of Yale College in 1701.

A growing population and widespread literacy helped spur the development of newspapers in Connecticut. The first newspaper in the colony was the *Connecticut Gazette* of New Haven, founded in 1755. Nine years later, the *Connecticut Courant* began publication in Hartford. Still in existence today, the *Courant* is the oldest newspaper in continuous publication in the United States.

Connecticut and the Revolution. In 1765 Connecticut joined with other colonies in protesting British actions during the STAMP ACT CRISIS. The Connecticut assembly condemned the Stamp Act, and units of the SONS OF LIBERTY—an organization devoted to defending colonial rights—began forming in opposition to it. In the elections of 1766, the Sons of Liberty managed to defeat the governor of Connecticut, who had backed the Stamp Act, as well as members of the colonial council who had supported him.

Groups of Connecticut patriots* remained active in the years just before the American Revolution. In the early 1770s they formed COMMITTEES OF

* *clergy* ministers, priests, and other church officials

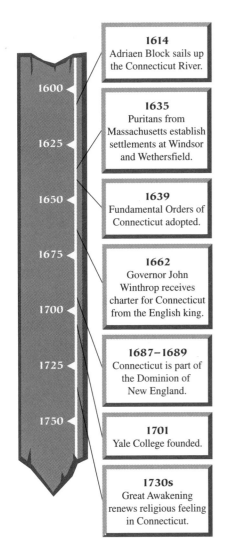

1614
Adriaen Block sails up the Connecticut River.

1600

1635
Puritans from Massachusetts establish settlements at Windsor and Wethersfield.

1625

1650

1639
Fundamental Orders of Connecticut adopted.

1675

1662
Governor John Winthrop receives charter for Connecticut from the English king.

1700

1687–1689
Connecticut is part of the Dominion of New England.

1725

1701
Yale College founded.

1750

1730s
Great Awakening renews religious feeling in Connecticut.

* *patriot* American colonist who supported independence from Britain

* *militia* army of citizens who may be called into action in a time of emergency

CORRESPONDENCE and issued angry protests against such British actions as the INTOLERABLE ACTS. After the Battles of LEXINGTON AND CONCORD, Connecticut militia* joined the struggle against the British. Some of the Connecticut forces helped capture FORT TICONDEROGA in New York; others fought at the Battle of BUNKER HILL outside Boston. Meanwhile, the colony's assembly instructed its delegates to the SECOND CONTINENTAL CONGRESS to vote for independence. Connecticut played an important role throughout the war. Although only a few battles took place in the state, it contributed food, supplies, weapons, and soldiers. (*See also* **British Colonies; Colonial Administration; Government, Provincial.**)

Conquistadors

See first map in Exploration, Age of (vol. 2).

See color plate 1, vol. 4.

The conquistadors—*conquistadores* in Spanish—were military leaders who carried out Spain's earliest conquests in the Americas. The term sometimes includes the men who followed these leaders and fought under their command.

In the early 1500s, Hernando CORTÉS, one of the most successful conquistadors, defeated the Aztec Indians to win control of central Mexico. His victory opened the way for other conquistadors to push farther north into North America. Among them were Hernando DE SOTO, who led an expedition north from Florida into the heart of the continent, Francisco Vásquez de CORONADO, who searched for legendary cities in the Southwest, and Juan de OÑATE, who launched Spanish settlement in New Mexico. Other conquistadors explored present-day Arizona and California, laying the groundwork for Spanish colonization there.

The conquistadors were both bold and ruthless. Inspired by the immense wealth Cortés found in Mexico, they pursued gold and silver greedily. They also tried to claim land for Spain and, in some cases, to open up new territory for Roman Catholic missionaries. Although the conquistadors provided many detailed and useful reports on the geography, native peoples, and wildlife of the Americas, they were not simply explorers. They waged violent, sometimes brutal, military campaigns against the Indians, from the PUEBLO of New Mexico to the Inca of Peru. Besides providing Spain with a territorial claim to a huge portion of the "New World," the conquistadors left behind a string of settlements that established the Spanish language and culture in lands from California to South America. (*See also* **Cabeza de Vaca, Alvar Núñez; Exploration, Age of; Missions and Missionaries.**)

Constitutions, Colonial

A constitution is a plan of government that establishes basic principles and provides a framework for organization and administration. It may be written, as in the United States, or largely unwritten, as in Great Britain. The English constitution, a collection of principles, customs, institutions, and laws, dates back to the Middle Ages. It includes the Magna Carta of 1215, in which King John agreed to certain limits on his power and certain rights for his people. English settlers in North America brought with them a belief in their rights as English citizens. During the 1600s, they wrote

documents based on their traditions that laid the foundation for law and government in their colonies. Though not constitutions in the modern sense, these documents—called charters, covenants, compacts, and agreements—served as the basis for the state constitutions adopted during and after the American Revolution.

The earliest guidelines for colonial government appeared in the MAYFLOWER COMPACT. Written in 1620 by the PILGRIMS who founded the PLYMOUTH COLONY, the compact was an agreement to work together to enact laws and choose leaders for the colony. Although the Mayflower Compact was not a constitution because it did not create a framework for government, it did establish the rule of law.

The FUNDAMENTAL ORDERS OF CONNECTICUT, the first written plan of government in the colonies, was adopted in 1639. It set up a system for electing a governor, judges, and representatives to make laws. Very democratic for its time, the Fundamental Orders later became the foundation for Connecticut's state constitution.

* **proprietor** person granted land and the right to establish a colony

The proprietors* of West Jersey (now part of New Jersey) drafted a document known as the Concessions and Agreements in 1677. Besides creating a representative assembly, it guaranteed rights such as freedom of religion and trial by jury. Pennsylvania granted similar rights in its Frame of Government, adopted in 1682. This plan also placed certain limits on the powers of government.

In 1669 the proprietors of the Carolinas drew up an agreement called the Fundamental Constitutions, which established a government run by the upper class that was based on a complex system of land ownership. The system proved to be unworkable because the landowners could not find colonists willing to work on their estates. With no accepted plan of government, the Carolinas remained unstable for decades.

Building on these early plans, the colonies developed systems of laws and representative government. During and after the Revolution, when the colonies had become states in a new nation, Americans wrote state constitutions to provide a framework of government and protect the rights and liberties of the people. (*See also* **Government, Provincial; Laws and Legal Systems; Political Thought.**)

Construction and Building Techniques

*E*uropean colonists built houses, barns, churches, forts, and government buildings in North America. They modified the construction methods and designs of their homelands to suit their new environments. The kind of structures they built was determined by the materials and skills available in the region as well as by the local climate. The settlers also used some techniques learned from Native Americans.

Building Materials. The colonists had to rely on local resources for construction. Because many areas settled by Europeans had dense forests, wood became a common building material. Structures often had wooden frames covered with wood or other materials. The earliest settlers used wooden pegs to connect the timbers, but during the 1600s handmade nails came into use, and by the late 1700s machine-made nails became available.

In the British colonies, settlers generally covered the building's frame with large wooden planks. Sometimes they applied plaster or whitewash to these planks, both on the inside and outside of the building. Settlers also used wood for moldings and other forms of decoration. For more elegant structures, British colonists began to work with brick rather than timber and to cover the roofs in slate and tile.

Builders in the Dutch settlements combined wood framing with brick walls and covered the outside of the building with wooden boards. They usually made roofs of wooden shingles, though thatch roofs sometimes appeared on farmhouses. In some rural areas of New Netherland, brick or stone was the primary material for houses. Stone houses built by Dutch settlers in the 1600s can still be seen west of the Hudson River.

In New France*, builders filled the spaces within wall frames with rubble or wooden posts. In the colony of Louisiana, settlers used bricks or a moss-and-clay mixture for the same purpose and then covered the walls with a layer of whitewashed plaster. Roofing materials included tree bark, thatch, and wooden shingles. Chimneys were made of brick or stone in the French colonies and also in the British and Dutch colonies.

Buildings in the Spanish Borderlands* developed along different lines from those in other colonial regions. One reason was that the Spanish colonies, except for Florida, had limited supplies of wood. Settlers in the southwest used adobe, a sun-dried brick made from clay, in construction. Most buildings had adobe walls covered with layers of plaster, and often only window and door frames were made of wood. Spanish colonists topped their buildings with roofs of thatch or ceramic tile. They used regular brick as flooring or to form decorative details, such as moldings and columns. Some Spanish mission churches with domed or vaulted ceilings were built of brick because it was stronger than adobe.

Building Techniques. In the early colonial period, European settlers sometimes copied Indian structures and methods of construction. For example, colonists often placed the frame of the building directly on the ground, as the Indians did, perhaps anchoring it with posts in the dirt. In the 1700s, foundations and cellars became more common in colonial buildings, especially in damp climates where a foundation helped protect the wooden frame from rotting. In Virginia, colonists adopted the Native American practice of using bark on the outside of their houses and woven reed mats inside.

Many of the building techniques used in the colonies reflected environmental conditions. In the cold climate of New France, for example, the colonists devised ways to insulate walls and floors and to shelter doorways from cold winds. In the hot climate of Louisiana, houses had large windows for ventilation along with covered balconies to shield the windows from the sun. Colonists in New England decided to cut lumber in standard sizes, which saved on labor—always in short supply.

Throughout colonial North America, most construction was done by trained crafts workers such as carpenters and masons. These builders prepared a rough plan on site with the client. Quite often, the plan was modified during actual construction. Builders generally used standard rules for laying out stairs and determining the height and thickness of walls. These rules,

* **New France** French colony centered in the St. Lawrence River valley, an area known as Canada; included the Great Lakes region and, until 1713, Acadia (present-day Nova Scotia)

* **Spanish Borderlands** northern part of New Spain, area now occupied by Florida, Texas, New Mexico, Arizona, and California

Spanish Adobe

Adobe bricks, a distinctive feature of Spanish colonial architecture, were easy to make in dry climates. Clay was set in wooden molds and laid in the sun to dry. When hardened, the clay had turned into adobe bricks. These were used to construct thick walls for buildings that kept heat in during the winter and out during the summer. Although quite durable, adobe disintegrates when exposed to water. For this reason, the colonists often covered the adobe with plaster and whitewash to protect it from rain.

which builders learned through APPRENTICESHIP training, might differ from region to region. New crafts workers continued to arrive from Europe, bringing with them knowledge of the latest styles and developments in construction. (*See also* **Architecture.**)

Continental Army

*T*he Continental Army was the professional army formed by the American colonists to fight for independence from Britain. Many soldiers who served in the Revolutionary War belonged to state militia* units rather than the Continental Army. But the Continental Army formed the core of the colonial fighting force and took part in important engagements from the siege of Boston in 1775 to the final battle at Yorktown in 1781.

Formation of the Army. The AMERICAN REVOLUTION began when colonial MINUTEMEN clashed with British soldiers at the Battles of LEXINGTON AND CONCORD in April 1775. Following these battles, Massachusetts and Connecticut began to organize an army by enlisting volunteers and appointing officers to lead them. At the same time, patriot* leaders in Massachusetts asked the SECOND CONTINENTAL CONGRESS to take charge of assembling troops. On June 14, the congress voted to raise ten companies of riflemen in Pennsylvania, Maryland, and Virginia. The next day, it appointed Virginian George WASHINGTON as commander in chief of the new Continental Army. Two days later—before Washington had a chance to take command—troops from New England met the British outside Boston at the Battle of BUNKER HILL.

Washington arrived in the Boston area on July 3 and took command of the New England soldiers. A few weeks later rifle companies from Pennsylvania, Maryland, and Virginia joined the troops. Washington faced the difficult task of simultaneously organizing an army and fighting a war. Working with leaders in the congress, he developed a plan for a Continental Army consisting of 26 regiments* of infantry, 1 of riflemen, and 1 of artillery. This would amount to a total of 20,372 men. According to the plan, soldiers would serve until the end of 1776.

By January 1, 1776, the new army still was not in place. Many men in the militia refused to join the Continental Army. Some considered the enlistment period too long. Others objected to serving under officers they had not selected. Many militia officers hesitated to enlist as well, unwilling to accept a lower rank in the new army. By spring 1776, Washington had fewer than half the desired number of soldiers.

Congress authorized the formation of additional regiments, including cavalry units. The plan was to build a fighting force of about 80,000. At no time during the war, however, did Washington have more than 15,000 troops under his command—and 10,000 was more typical. To supplement his army, Washington called on state-controlled regiments and local militia units. He had to rely on this mixture of different types of troops throughout the war.

All soldiers in the Continental Army were volunteers. Early enlistments lasted a year, but the men who signed up after 1776 agreed to serve for either

* *militia* army of citizens who may be called into action in a time of emergency

* *patriot* American colonist who supported independence from Britain

* *regiment* army unit; during the Revolution, each regiment consisted of 728 men

173

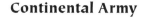

Continental Army

The Continental Army spent the winter of 1777–1778 encamped at Valley Forge, Pennsylvania. The soldiers suffered from shortages of food, clothing, and blankets, but they did benefit from skillful training by Baron Friedrich Wilhelm von Steuben.

* **quota** number or amount required

three years or the duration of the war. To raise troops, some states set quotas* for each town, asking local officials to supply money if they could not provide their quota of volunteers. A number of states encouraged men to enlist by offering gifts of land or money. The Continental Congress also promised a cash bonus to volunteers. Some states offered more, however, which led men to join state regiments rather than the Continental Army. All free men, both white and African American, were welcome in the Continental Army, and many regiments included veteran black troops. By the end of the war, the Rhode Island regiment was almost entirely black because the state agreed to buy the freedom of any slave who enlisted.

Equipment and Training. The Continental Army suffered from a shortage of supplies throughout the war. Most soldiers wore clothes of buckskin or homespun cloth rather than the official blue uniform because the colonies did not have enough blue wool. More importantly, the troops lacked shoes, blankets, and food. Although congress authorized a daily ration of a pound of bread, a pound of meat, a pint of milk, a few ounces of butter, and some beans and other foods, the soldiers never received this generous ration. A Connecticut man wrote of going four days without food and watching his fellow soldiers cook and eat their old shoes. This lack of food was not unusual.

* **flintlock musket** heavy, long-barreled gun with a firing mechanism that caused a spark that ignited gunpowder and propelled a bullet

* **bayonet** short blade attached to the barrel of a gun and used for stabbing

The basic weapon of the infantry was a flintlock musket* with a bayonet*. Though not very accurate, these guns could be reloaded easily. More reliable rifles took longer to load, so they were used primarily by long-range sharpshooters who could hide while reloading. Cavalry troops carried pistols and swords. Throughout the war, the army struggled with shortages of both weapons and gunpowder.

Soldiers in the Continental Army went through training to learn how to perform well in combat. In the early years of the war, commanders used a variety of methods of drilling and disciplining their men. Baron Friedrich Wilhelm von Steuben, a German officer who joined the Continental Army at Valley Forge in February 1778, made military training more consistent. He simplified the commands, drilled the soldiers every day, and wrote a manual for the army on training and discipline. With Steuben's help, the Continental Army became a well-trained and effective fighting force—one that was able to meet and defeat the British army on its own terms. (*See also* **Military Forces; Weapons.**)

Continental Association

** **boycott*** refusal to buy goods as a means of protest

** **repeal*** to undo a law

*I*n October 1774 the FIRST CONTINENTAL CONGRESS formed the Continental Association to prevent American colonists from trading with Great Britain. The congress hoped that this boycott* would force the British government to repeal* the INTOLERABLE ACTS—harsh measures designed to assert British authority in the colonies and punish resistance to it.

The colonists had used boycotts in the past to protest British policy. The earlier ones, however, involved restrictions on importing British goods. The Continental Association broadened the boycott to include a ban on selling goods to Britain or even using British goods. Moreover, the new plan came from the Continental Congress of the American colonies, not from a group of colonial merchants. Local committees enforced the boycott, using public opinion and community pressure to persuade merchants and consumers to participate.

The Continental Association received broad backing from the delegates to the Continental Congress. Some saw it as a way of achieving changes in British policy while avoiding war. They hoped that the loss of business would encourage British merchants to support the colonists' goals in Parliament. Although the Continental Association did not succeed in overturning the Intolerable Acts, it did help the colonists unite in their opposition to British policies. (*See also* **Stamp Act Crisis; Townshend Acts.**)

Continental Congress

See *First Continental Congress; Second Continental Congress.*

Copley, John Singleton

1738–1815
Painter

*J*ohn Singleton Copley is considered to be the most important portrait artist of colonial America. His paintings of prosperous American men and women capture the spirit of colonial life in the 1770s. His subjects included such well-known people as Samuel ADAMS, Paul REVERE, and John HANCOCK.

Born and raised in Boston, Copley began painting at an early age. His work was probably influenced by his stepfather, Peter Pelham, an engraver, and by an English artist, John Smibert. Copley painted his earliest known portrait when he was about 15 years old and started his professional career at age 20. He soon became known as a portrait painter, and his work was much in demand. Many of Boston's wealthy merchants and officials hired Copley to paint portraits of themselves and their families.

Copley attracted the attention of the British art world in 1766 after sending a portrait of his half-brother, entitled *The Boy with a Squirrel,* to London.

On seeing the painting, the famous British painter Sir Joshua Reynolds and the American painter Benjamin WEST, then living in London, urged Copley to come to Europe to study. Copley delayed the move for several years because of the success of his portrait business, but he eventually left America in 1774. After a tour of Italy, he settled in Great Britain, where he began painting historical pictures that combined portraits with historical events. One of the most successful was *Watson and the Shark,* based on a real event. The painting shows a young man being attacked by a shark as his friends try to rescue him. A few years after his arrival in London, Copley was elected a member of the distinguished Royal Academy of Arts.

Copley's last years were not happy ones. His later paintings were not as successful as his earlier works, and he was deeply in debt. His physical and mental health also declined. Copley died in 1815.

The paintings of John Singleton Copley are noted for being exceptionally true-to-life, with a richness of texture and color and a skillful use of light and shade. His portraits often show people in informal settings with objects from their everyday lives. Most critics believe that Copley's most significant works are the vivid, realistic portraits he painted in colonial America. (*See also* **Art: Painting and Sculpture, European.**)

Corn

See *Maize.*

Coronado, Francisco Vásquez de

1510–1554
Spanish explorer

* **viceroy** person appointed as a monarch's representative to govern a province or colony

* **friar** member of a religious brotherhood

See first map in Exploration, Age of (vol. 2).

*F*rancisco Vásquez de Coronado was the last of the CONQUISTADORS, the military commanders who sought treasure and territory for Spain in the Americas. Coronado had hoped to find and conquer a wealthy civilization, as Hernando CORTÉS had done in Mexico. Although he never found riches, Coronado did explore vast territories never before seen by Europeans, including present-day Arizona, Texas, and Oklahoma.

Born in Salamanca, Spain, Coronado came to Mexico in 1535 in the service of Antonio de Mendoza, viceroy* of the colony of NEW SPAIN. He became governor of the western province of Nueva Galicia a few years later. In 1540 Mendoza sent Coronado northward with 300 Spaniards and 800 Indians under his command. Coronado's mission was to find the treasures rumored to exist in the interior of what is now the American Southwest.

The chief source of these rumors was a friar* named Marcos de Niza, who had traveled in the region. He reported that he had seen the incredibly rich SEVEN CITIES OF CÍBOLA in the distance. Coronado found the cities, but they turned out to be ordinary pueblos of the ZUNI INDIANS. An Indian told Coronado of great wealth in a place called Gran Quivira somewhere to the north, and the frustrated conquistador headed for this new goal.

During their wanderings, Coronado and his lieutenants explored the valleys of the Rio Grande and the Pecos, Yaqui, and Colorado rivers. One lieutenant, Garcia López de Cárdenas, led the party that stumbled upon one of the natural wonders of the continent—the Grand Canyon. Coronado roamed as far as present-day Kansas before giving up the dream of Quivira.

Coronado and his men explored the Southwest in search of riches and sites for Spanish settlements. They failed to find treasure, but they did explore vast lands as yet uncharted by Europeans.

The conquistador went back to Mexico in 1542. Although his expedition had gathered a wealth of geographic knowledge, he had failed to find material riches, and his trip was considered a disaster. Coronado returned to his post as governor but was soon removed because of his cruel treatment of the Native Americans in his province. He ended his days as a petty official in Mexico City. (*See also* **Exploration, Age of.**)

Cortés, Hernando

1485–1547
Spanish conqueror of Mexico

See first map in Exploration, Age of (vol. 2).

*H*ernando Cortés was one of the most successful of the CONQUISTA-DORS, the Spanish conquerors who sought treasure and territory in the Americas. He seized control of the Aztec empire, bringing the vast lands of present-day Mexico under Spanish rule and paving the way for a long-lasting Spanish presence in North America.

Born in Medellín, Spain, Cortés briefly attended the University of Salamanca to study law. Then, in search of adventure and riches, the young man joined a voyage to the Americas. In 1511 he served under Diego Velásquez in the Spanish campaign to conquer Cuba. After taking the island, Velásquez became its governor and named Cortés the mayor of the new colony's capital, Santiago.

Spanish explorers who visited the eastern coast of Mexico in 1517 and 1518 returned with reports of Indians wearing gold. Velásquez, eager to share in the riches, planned a large expedition to the region and appointed Cortés its commander. But Velásquez began to have doubts about the ambitious young man and decided to send another Spaniard in his place. Hearing rumors of the governor's change of mind, Cortés quietly slipped away before the official orders arrived. He set sail with 11 ships, more than 500 soldiers, 16 horses, and several large guns.

Cortés landed at several places along the Mexican coast in 1519, making alliances with Indians who had been conquered by the powerful Aztec. At

See
color plate 1,
vol. 4.

one of these stops, native people presented Cortés with an Indian woman named Malintzin, or Malinche, who became his interpreter and mistress. Her diplomacy, language abilities, and knowledge of the region's cultures contributed greatly to Cortés's campaign to conquer the Aztec. At his final landing along the coast, Cortés founded Vera Cruz and proclaimed himself captain general of the new colony. He destroyed his ships, so his men could not retreat, and then marched west toward the heart of the Aztec empire.

Montezuma, the Aztec emperor, had heard of the Spaniards' arrival on the coast. He believed that the conquistador might be an Aztec god called Quetzalcoatl. When the Spaniards reached the capital of Tenochtitlán, they were greeted with great ceremony by the Aztec chiefs. In return, Cortés took Montezuma hostage and forced him to swear allegiance to the king of Spain.

Receiving word that Velásquez had sent troops to relieve him of his command, Cortés hurried to the coast. He captured the commander of the new expedition and headed back to Tenochtitlán. On arriving, Cortés found his men at war with the Aztec. He learned that the Spaniards had killed several Aztec for making human sacrifices, a common Indian religious practice at this time. Cortés asked Montezuma to appeal to his people to end the fighting. But when the emperor tried to calm the Aztec, they responded by stoning him to death. Cortés and his soldiers fought their way out of the city in a bloody battle that cost the lives of half his men.

In May 1521, the Spanish forces and their Indian allies surrounded Tenochtitlán, cutting off its supplies of food and water. Cortés repeatedly attacked the city, destroying it building by building. After three months the Aztec surrendered, their once mighty empire broken. On the ruins of Tenochtitlán, Cortés founded Mexico City as the capital of the colony of NEW SPAIN.

By 1526 Cortés had conquered all of what is now Mexico and Honduras. King Charles I of Spain confirmed his position as captain general of New Spain and granted him huge estates in the colony. Cortés proved to be a capable administrator, but his wealth and power made others jealous. His many enemies at court plotted to turn the king against him. Fearing that Cortés wanted to make New Spain into an independent country, Charles sent a viceroy* to Mexico City to take control of the colony.

* **viceroy** person appointed as a monarch's representative to govern a province or colony

A discouraged and bitter Cortés returned to Spain in 1540, never again to see the territory he had conquered and governed. He died at his estate near Seville, Spain. (*See also* **Exploration, Age of.**)

Cotton

* **cash crop** crop grown primarily for profit

European explorers in the Americas discovered that Indians grew cotton and wove it into cloth. English settlers in the JAMESTOWN COLONY began raising cotton in 1607, but they did so on a small scale for local use. Cotton did not become a major cash crop* in the South until the 1790s.

In colonial times, making cotton cloth was a long and backbreaking procedure. Short-staple cotton, the variety of cotton that could be grown inland in southern colonies, had sticky green seeds that were difficult to separate from the fiber, the part of the plant used for cloth. A worker had to pick the seeds out by hand and could only process a pound of short-staple cotton a day.

To turn the cotton into cloth, workers had to spin it and weave it. Two British inventions of the 1700s dramatically reduced the time needed for this process—the spinning jenny, which transformed cotton into thread, and the power loom, which wove the thread into cloth. Both machines were powered by water, not by hand. As the British textile industry boomed, the demand for raw cotton rose sharply. But farmers in the southern colonies could not increase their production significantly because of the time it took to process the cotton.

In 1793 Eli Whitney revolutionized the cotton industry with the invention of the cotton gin. The machine had a roller with teeth and a brush to separate the seeds from the fibers. Using this device, a worker could produce 50 pounds of cotton in a day—50 times more than by hand. In the 10 years after the invention of the gin, southern planters increased cotton production almost 800 percent. Eager for profit, they pushed westward and settled the lands that became Mississippi, Louisiana, and Arkansas. Cotton became so important to the economy of the South that people said that cotton was king.

The cotton gin had some unexpected consequences. Because cotton became so profitable, southern planters wanted to expand their production. To do so they needed more slaves to work in the fields, harvest the crops, and run the cotton gin. The economy of the southern states in the early 1800s was built on cotton and based on slave labor. (*See also* **Slavery.**)

Cotton, John

1584–1652
Clergyman and author

* *Anglican* of the Church of England
* *vicar* priest of a parish in the Church of England

* *nonconformist* not following traditional views or customs

John Cotton was a religious leader of the PURITANS. He played a leading role in church and government affairs in the early years of the Massachusetts Bay colony. Cotton wrote extensively on religious theory and practice and on government's responsibility for the religious affairs of its citizens.

Born in England to deeply religious parents, Cotton was educated at Cambridge University. Anglican* officials recognized his intelligence and preaching ability and named him vicar* of a large church in the English town of Boston. A supporter of the Puritan ideal of simplicity, Cotton began to eliminate the elaborate Anglican ceremonies from his services. Over the years he grew closer to the Puritans, demonstrated by a special farewell sermon he preached for John WINTHROP and other Puritans when they left England for Massachusetts in 1630.

For 20 years Anglican officials allowed Cotton to lead his church in his own way, even though he did not follow the traditions of the Church of England. In 1632, however, a church court finally summoned the nonconformist* vicar to appear before it. Fearing punishment for his Puritan views, Cotton fled to North America with his family.

In Massachusetts, Cotton became preacher of the First Church of Boston, a position that gave him great influence in government and church matters. He was involved in several of the controversies that divided the early Puritan community. A student of his, Anne HUTCHINSON, argued that faith alone, not good works, could lead to salvation. Although Cotton supported her view at first, he eventually joined church officials in banishing Hutchinson and her followers from the colony in 1638. Later, he wrote pamphlets that defended the Puritan leadership against the criticisms of Roger WILLIAMS, who argued that the government should not play a role in spiritual matters. Cotton believed that citizens needed a strong government to keep them in order.

Cotton devoted much of his later life to writing religious works. A catechism* he published in 1646, called *Milk for Babes,* was used by New England children for many years after his death.

* **catechism** book containing the basic teachings of a religion

Coureurs de Bois

Coureurs de bois—which means "woods runners" in French—were fur trappers and traders who left the settlements of NEW FRANCE in the mid-1600s to live in the wilderness. These men adopted the customs of Native Americans and often took Indian wives. They were driven by a love of adventure and by the profits they could make in the FUR TRADE. These independent woodsmen differed from voyageurs, or engagés, who were employees of the French and English fur companies.

The coureurs de bois were mostly young men who had arrived in New France with the intention of clearing the land to farm and raising families. But because clearing the land was backbreaking work and the colony had few women, many men headed into the wilderness, hoping to get rich in the fur trade. The woodsmen dressed to suit the wilderness in fringed jackets made of animal skin and loose, knee-length pants of wool or leather. They also wore knee-high stockings that could be removed when wading across streams.

The colonial government wanted to develop an economy based on agriculture, and so it restricted the number of licenses granted for fur trading. The coureurs de bois simply traded without the licenses. Within a few decades, so many men had left for the interior that the settlements of New France were seriously weakened by a loss of population.

The coureurs de bois made major contributions to the exploration and development of the lands north and west of the GREAT LAKES. They provided valuable firsthand knowledge of Indian culture and language and of the geography of the region.

Courts

See *Laws and Legal Systems.*

Courtship

Courtship is the process of selecting possible marriage partners. In colonial America, British, Dutch, French, and Spanish colonists and African Americans each followed their own patterns of courtship, shaped by their cultural backgrounds, their religious beliefs, and their views of marriage. Native American courtship customs differed from those of the Europeans.

Almost every group in North America shared one belief—that courtship involved both the family and the community. Because Europeans considered marriage to be the foundation of the community, the preparations for

In colonial times, courtship was practically a community affair. Males and females socialized under controlled conditions, but they sometimes found interesting ways to communicate personal messages. This device is called the "whispering rod."

* *status* social position

* *tolerant* allowing different views and behavior

marriage were—to some extent—the community's business. Marriage linked different families, produced children to be raised in the community, and determined how money and property would be passed on from one generation to the next. Individuals were expected to choose partners who met with the approval of their families and neighbors—people of their own religion, economic class, and racial group. The higher a family's social status*, the more important it was for the children to make a "proper" match and the less freedom they had to make their own choices.

Courtship in colonial times also came under the watchful eye of the church, which attempted to regulate sexual and social behavior. The church, for example, frowned on young people spending time with members of the opposite sex except under tightly controlled conditions supervised by adults. Nevertheless, a fair number of colonial youth managed to break the "rules" of their churches and societies.

Over time, parents, the church, and social expectations came to play a less important role in courtship. As people of different cultures and backgrounds settled in North America, colonial society became more flexible and tolerant*. As a result, young people gained more independence, and their courtships reflected personal choices rather than the expectations of others.

British Colonists.   In the British colonies, courtship behavior took a variety of forms. Among the PURITANS of New England, courtship was closely controlled by parents. A young man could not call on a girl without her father's permission. Although parents did not arrange the marriages of their children, they used all kinds of pressure to discourage them from marrying partners considered unsuitable. Most young couples needed land, goods, or money from parents to set up their own household. By withholding these things, parents could control the timing of a child's marriage.

The Puritans, along with young people in other colonies and in Europe, followed the practice of "bundling" in courtship. This custom allowed an unmarried courting couple to sleep in the same bed as long as they remained fully dressed or were separated by a board. Supporters claimed that bundling gave young folk a chance to see what it would be like to spend their lives together. Critics charged that bundling encouraged unacceptable sexual behavior.

In the Chesapeake Bay region and the South, young people enjoyed a considerable amount of freedom in courtship. They had less adult supervision than couples in New England for two reasons. Many adults in these regions had died of disease at an early age, leaving adolescent children without parents. In addition, many young people in the South had come to the colonies as laborers or servants without their families. Greater sexual freedom led to a higher rate of pregnancy outside of marriage in the southern colonies than in the northern colonies. By the 1700s, changes in population and economic conditions made courtship patterns in the region more similar to those in the North.

Dutch Colonists.   The Dutch colonists in New Netherland gave their children a fair amount of freedom in associating with individuals of the opposite sex and in choosing their marriage partners. Most parents, however, encouraged their children to choose a partner within their own social class and to come to them for advice and consent. When a courtship became serious, a young couple would probably experiment with bundling. Many couples also lived together without being married, which sometimes led to the birth of children outside of marriage.

After the mid-1640s, the leaders of New Netherland became concerned about public morals. To strengthen family ties, they outlawed the practice of living together without marriage. In several cases, officials declared marriages illegal because they had taken place without the consent of both sets of parents. However, officials also investigated some courtships to make sure that parents were not pushing their daughters into unwanted marriages.

New France French colony centered in the St. Lawrence River valley, known as Canada; included the Great Lakes region and, until 1713, Acadia (present-day Novia Scotia)

French Colonists.   Courtship was a serious matter in New France*, especially among the upper classes. Many French colonists viewed marriage not as an individual choice but as a way for families to advance socially and economically. Family members who disapproved of a match could block the

marriage. Young people sometimes responded to objections by obtaining a legal document that asked the parents to reconsider.

In New France, a man could not legally marry before age 30 without the consent of his parents. Couples denied permission to marry, however, could take matters into their own hands with a ceremony called *mariage à la gaumine.* While attending church, the couple stood up and announced their vows as if at a wedding. From then on they acted as husband and wife. This practice became popular in the early 1700s, but both the ROMAN CATHOLIC CHURCH and the French government disapproved of the custom. It disappeared in 1789.

* ***Spanish Borderlands*** northern part of New Spain, area now occupied by Florida, Texas, New Mexico, Arizona, and California

Spanish Colonists.   Courtship customs in the Spanish Borderlands* were shaped by two powerful influences—the church and the notion of "honor." The Spanish Catholic Church viewed marriage as a holy union that must be freely chosen by individuals. Under church law, parents could not force their children to marry against their will. At the same time, the church frowned on any type of sexual activity outside of marriage.

Spanish culture revolved around the concept of honor and the idea that the conduct of individuals affected both their own and their family's honor. A young woman's honor—her sexual purity—was thus, in a sense, the property of the family. Unmarried women were not supposed to go anywhere without fathers, brothers, or other guardians to protect them. A father not only could punish a daughter for sexual misbehavior, but he also considered it his right to control her courtship and marriage. Many parents put pressure on sons as well to obey their wishes on courtship and marriage.

Young people who wished to marry in spite of parental objections often turned to priests, who would occasionally marry them in secret. In some cases, however, priests helped parents push their children into marriages that advanced the family's economic and social interests.

African Americans.   The institution of slavery drastically altered the traditional social patterns of the Africans brought as slaves to the colonies. In the early days, there were far more male than female slaves, preventing many men from marrying and starting families. This uneven ratio also made the African practice of polygamy—in which one man had several wives—nearly impossible. Because slave families were often divided by slaveholders, elders no longer arranged marriages for young relatives as they had done in Africa.

Native Americans.   In general, the courtship customs of Native Americans were less rigid than those of European colonists. In many cultures, young Indians were free to choose their mates. In some, however, parents or tribal elders chose partners for the young, or at least influenced their choices. Indian men and women generally had considerable freedom in their relationships with the opposite sex. In addition, most Native American cultures did not regard sexuality as sinful or shameful. Europeans considered Native American courtship and marriage customs to be "primitive." Even so, thousands of European men entered into informal relationships or marriages with Native American women, especially during the early years of colonial settlement when white men far outnumbered white women. (*See also* **Family; Marriage.**)

Crafts

Pewter Goods

Pewter, made by combining tin with other metals, looks much like silver and can have a highly polished or a dull finish. Colonists used it as an inexpensive substitute for silver in plates, bowls, and candlesticks.

The British colonists did not produce pewter themselves. Tin, its main ingredient, had to be imported and the import tax was high. As a result, most pewter items made in the colonies were produced from existing pieces that had been melted down.

See color plate 6, vol. 2.

See color plate 1, vol. 2.

* **burgher** citizen of a town

Handicrafts—handmade goods—have been a part of life in North America since the first settlers arrived. Early colonial families had to make most of the items they needed for personal and household use for themselves. These first examples of American handicrafts were often quite crude. As the colonies developed, skilled workers took over the production of many everyday goods.

In the early days, handicrafts were simple, practical objects—cooking utensils, tools, CLOTHING, and FURNITURE. The colonists valued these items for their usefulness and cared little about decoration or artistry. As the colonies grew wealthier and more urban, people began to take a greater interest in the quality of the workmanship of these everyday objects.

The increasing demand for well-made goods provided business for crafts workers. Many opened small shops, sometimes employing one or more assistants. The goods that they produced ranged from silverware and furniture to clocks and guns.

Crafts workers, also known as ARTISANS, went through long periods of training to master their trade. They began as apprentices, working for a master crafts worker. As their skills increased, the apprentices became journeymen. Eventually, if they could save enough money, they would open a shop and go into business for themselves.

During the colonial period, most independent artisans and their apprentices were white males. However, slaves often served as assistants. Many women played a role in the production of crafts, by spinning and weaving material for clothing and household linens and doing needlework. They also made women's hats and dresses.

British Colonial Crafts. Crafts workers in the British colonies enjoyed two advantages: they could earn a good, steady income, and they held a respected position in society. They were proud and independent tradespeople who took a leading role in the community. Because political and economic events affected their business, crafts workers followed such developments closely and often took a stand defending their rights or protesting policies of the colonial government.

Artisans who worked in cities often specialized. Cabinetmakers might concentrate on making furniture, for example. However, artisans were usually willing to perform related work when necessary. During times of economic hardship, a woodworker might build houses or make barrels, furniture, or coffins. Crafts workers who lived in rural areas had a smaller market for their goods and were more likely to practice a variety of crafts. Many produced handicrafts only part-time. Farmers might turn out handicrafts during the winter when they had little farmwork to do. If a farm was not profitable, family members might make and sell handicrafts to contribute to the household income.

Dutch Colonial Crafts. In the Dutch city of New Amsterdam crafts workers were carefully regulated. Skilled artisans could register as burghers*, which gave them specific rights, such as operating a business in the city. Among the earliest Dutch artisans were carpenters, chair makers, locksmiths, masons, painters, potters, and BLACKSMITHS.

Crafts workers were often prominent people in public life. Patriot Paul Revere, shown here in a 1768 painting by John Singleton Copley, was a noted silversmith in Boston.

* **Spanish Borderlands** northern part of New Spain, area now occupied by Florida, Texas, New Mexico, Arizona, and California

Crafts workers were trained in an apprenticeship system. Boys, usually from age 14 and up, were apprenticed to a master to learn a craft. The city regulated the indentures, agreements between the apprentice and the master.

Crafts workers in New Amsterdam produced a wide range of goods. When the colony passed into British hands, artisans began to specialize according to nationality. The Dutch tended to work as goldsmiths, silversmiths, gunsmiths, and painters, while English crafts workers took over furniture making, watchmaking, and clock making.

French and Spanish Colonial Crafts. The French colonies were smaller and poorer than the British colonies and could support fewer artisans. Nevertheless, crafts workers provided many of the practical items needed by the colonists. The French colonies had highly skilled woodworkers and cabinetmakers who produced fine furniture and became known for their wood carving. Metalworking and silversmithing were also well-established crafts. Although colonists imported most of the high-quality cloth they used, artisans in female religious orders created fine examples of embroidery, knitting, and crocheting.

In the Spanish Borderlands*, the population was made up mainly of soldiers, missionaries, government officials, and some traders and settlers. Too few people lived in these Spanish settlements to provide a living for artisans. Most items were either imported or produced by Native Americans, whom missionaries taught to make European-style goods. Only in the settlements of New Mexico did crafts, notably textiles and woodworking, reach a high level of quality. (*See also* **Apprenticeship; Weaving.**)

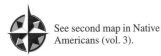

Cree Indians

* *pelt* skin and fur of an animal

See second map in Native Americans (vol. 3).

The Cree, one of the largest groups of Native Americans in North America, played an important role in the colonial FUR TRADE. They lived in the forests of what are now the Canadian provinces of Quebec and Ontario, but they eventually spread as far west as the Great Plains.

French and English fur traders first came into contact with the Cree in the 1600s. The Indians supplied the Europeans with beaver pelts* and, in exchange, received goods such as traps and weapons. The Cree used these items to trade and form alliances with other Indian tribes.

By the mid-1700s, groups of Cree had expanded into the plains of the present-day Canadian provinces of Alberta and Saskatchewan. Known as the Plains Cree, these people adopted many of the customs of other PLAINS INDIANS. They became BUFFALO hunters and began using horses, which they obtained from the Blackfoot Indians in exchange for guns. The Cree who had remained in their native forests, the Woodlands Cree, continued to take an active part in the fur trade.

In the 1800s, several epidemics of smallpox drastically reduced the Cree population. The near extinction of the buffalo and the decline of the fur trade in southern Canada created additional hardships. Many of the Cree were forced by the American and Canadian governments to move to reservations. Today, Cree Indians live throughout Canada and Montana.

Creek Indians

confederacy alliance or league of peoples or states

cede to yield or surrender

The Creek Indians were a loosely organized confederacy* of tribes who spoke dialects of the Muskogean language. Located throughout Alabama and Georgia, these tribes united to defend their territory against the European settlers. The British called them "Creek" Indians because they lived along rivers.

The Creek's first encounter with Europeans was a deadly one. The Spanish explorers of the 1500s introduced smallpox and other DISEASES that wiped out much of the Indian population. In the 1600s the Creek began trading with the European powers in North America—the French, the English, and the Spanish. After the English established the city of CHARLESTON, South Carolina, in 1680, the Creek carried on a lively trade with its settlers, exchanging deerskins and Indian slaves from other tribes for guns and other European goods.

In the early 1700s, a lack of deer and slaves drove some southeastern tribes, including the YAMASSEE INDIANS, into debt to the British. Traders in the Carolinas began seizing Yamassee women and children in payment for the tribe's debt. The Creek, fearing that they might also be enslaved, joined the Yamassee and other Indians in attacks on British frontier towns and trading posts. The colonists were only able to stop the conflict after convincing the Creek's old enemy, the CHEROKEE, to join them.

Despite this setback, the Creek remained a powerful military force. The European powers were engaged in a fierce competition for control of North America, and they wanted to form alliances with strong Indian tribes. The Creek remained neutral and maintained their independence for many years by playing the European powers against each other.

In 1733 the Creek allowed the British to establish the colony of Georgia in their territory. Soon, however, white settlers moved beyond the agreed-upon boundaries, leading to tensions between the colonists and the Indians. Nevertheless, the Creek refused to take sides during the FRENCH AND INDIAN WAR between Great Britain and France.

The British victory in the war altered the world of the Creek Indians. With France no longer a threat in the region, the British did not need the Indians' support. Furthermore, the Creek had become dependent on European goods, and the British now controlled the market completely. The Indians' reliance on European goods had also caused them to go deeply into debt to traders. British colonists demanded that the tribe cede* several million acres of land as payment.

The AMERICAN REVOLUTION divided the Creek, with some villages wanting to remain neutral and others favoring the British. In 1778 the Creek entered the war on the side of the British. After winning the war, the newly formed United States forced the Creek to give up additional territory.

Creoles

In the colonial period, the term *Creole* was generally used to refer to people of European ancestry who lived in the Americas. The meaning of Creole changed over the years, and the word was applied to different groups in different regions.

The word comes from the Spanish *criollo,* which means "native." It was first used in New Spain in the 1600s to distinguish colonists born in the

Americas, Creoles, from those born in Europe, *peninsulares.* Later, the term was applied only to colonists of French, Spanish, or Portuguese ancestry.

Creole had a slightly different sense in the French colonies. In 1755 the British forced thousands of French-speaking ACADIANS to leave their homeland in what is now Canada. Many ended up settling in LOUISIANA, a French colony that was taken over by the Spanish in 1763. The long-established members of the colony's French community looked down on the Acadian immigrants. To set themselves apart, they called themselves and their dialect Creole, while the newcomers became known as Cajuns. Over time, though, the meaning of the term expanded. By the early 1800s, numerous African Americans in Louisiana who had some French or Spanish ancestry began referring to themselves as Creoles. The meaning of the term continued to change. Today it is used to refer to a broad group of people in Louisiana, who still speak a French dialect. (*See also* **Languages; Race Relations.**)

Crime and Punishment

*L*aws, courts, and criminal justice systems in the North American colonies reflected—but did not entirely match—the legal traditions of the European countries that established them. Colonists had to adjust the practices of their homeland to suit the special circumstances of life in the "New World."

Four facts shaped crime and punishment in all the colonies. First, the justice systems depended on the cooperation of everyone in the community. There were no formal police forces, and the undeveloped countryside offered suspects ample opportunities for escape. Colonial officials needed the help of settlers in identifying crimes and catching the people accused of committing them.

Second, during the early years of settlement, the judicial system was fairly crude, and most law keepers had little training. Judges were often respected members of the community who knew something of the law but had not been schooled in it. They combined their judicial duties with other occupations. In the 1700s, however, the situation began to change, and most of the British colonies had trained lawyers and judges.

Third, punishment had two goals—to make the criminals pay for their actions and to hold criminals up as an example that would discourage others from similar behavior. Finally, the legal definition of crime was closely linked to the religious notion of sin. In early New England, for example, the most common crimes were drunkenness, sexual misbehavior, and failure to attend church. The most serious offenses were heresy* and witchcraft. By the 1700s, crimes against property had become the most frequent type of misconduct. Many punishments aimed to shame criminals rather than to hurt them physically or financially.

* ***heresy*** belief that is contrary to church teachings

British Colonies

Although criminal justice in British North America was based on British law, colonial practices differed in a number of respects. These differences developed as a result of the particular circumstances of life in the colonies as well as colonists' dissatisfaction with the British system. In setting up their governments, the colonists put their own ideas about crime and punishment into

Crime and Punishment

Humiliation was an effective form of punishment in the colonies. Those accused of breaking the community's rules had to stand in a pillory in the center of town for all to see, with their head and hands locked between two pieces of wood.

* **misdemeanor** minor crime
* **vagrancy** homelessness
* **charter** written grant from a ruler conferring certain rights and privileges
* **statute** law made by a legislative body

* **capital crime** crime punishable by death

law. These laws changed over time, reflecting developments in British legal practice and in colonial society.

The Court System. The British colonies had lower and higher courts, which had responsibility for handling different kinds of criminal offenses. Justices of the peace ran the lower courts. Meeting in towns or county seats throughout each colony, they tried misdemeanors*—the crimes most frequently committed in the colonies—such as fighting, rioting, vagrancy*, or failure to attend church. Each colony had one higher court, which handled felonies, including murder, rape, arson, and treason. The way the higher courts operated varied. The Superior Court of Massachusetts moved throughout the colony, while the General Court of Virginia met only in the colony's capital, and all accused persons had to go there for trial.

Criminal Codes. The tradition of British law reached North America in three ways. The home government could require—through colonial charters* or acts of Parliament—that the colonies have certain laws. Colonists brought law books with them. Finally, a number of colonists arrived with a knowledge of British laws and court practices.

Captain John SMITH, who led the JAMESTOWN COLONY in its early years, created Virginia's first laws. In 1619 the colony established its own legislative assembly, the VIRGINIA HOUSE OF BURGESSES, which began to pass criminal laws. The statutes* differed somewhat from those in the home country. For instance, in Virginia commoners could carry firearms and anyone could kill game in the public forests. Both practices were illegal in England.

The PURITANS of New England wanted several changes to English law, including clearer law codes and harsh penalties for immoral or sinful acts. These goals were embodied in the first MASSACHUSETTS code of laws. Written by Nathaniel Ward, who had legal training, the code was adopted in 1641 and revised in 1648. Although based partly on English law, it included some provisions adopted from the Bible. CONNECTICUT's laws were similar—not surprisingly, as settlers from Massachusetts founded Connecticut. The laws of New Haven, originally a separate colony, showed a strong biblical influence. The law code of RHODE ISLAND, however, was less severe than that of Massachusetts.

The legal systems of the middle colonies took a slightly different course. In NEW YORK, the English kept the Dutch court system when they took over the colony in 1664, but they eventually made changes to conform to legal practices in England. The QUAKERS of New Jersey and Pennsylvania developed less severe law codes than those of the Puritans. Under the constitution that Quaker William PENN wrote for Pennsylvania in 1682, murder was the only capital crime*. Other colonies required the death penalty for a number of crimes.

Colonial law treated Indians and African Americans under separate rules. In Massachusetts, Native Americans who attacked white settlers would be tried and severely punished. Although colonists who attacked Indians could also be charged with crimes, they rarely were. In Rhode Island and the middle colonies, Indians received fairer treatment. In the southern colonies, "black codes" established special laws for African Americans. Slaves were tried in courts without juries and had no lawyers to represent them. Punishments were severe and often included prolonged whippings. A Virginia law excused owners who killed their slaves in the course of punishing them.

Between the late 1600s and the American Revolution, colonial law changed in several ways. As in Britain, the colonies passed more and more laws protecting property against crimes such as theft and burglary. At the same time, laws against immoral behavior—failure to attend church, drunkenness, or sexual relations outside marriage—became less important. The number of judges with legal knowledge and experience increased. In addition, the courts began to recognize the rights of the accused. By the early 1700s, Massachusetts, Connecticut, New Jersey, and Pennsylvania gave defendants in criminal trials the right to a lawyer; by the 1760s, more than half the colonies had such statutes. The colonies granted this right to defendants years before Britain did.

Crimes and Trials. Violent crimes such as assault, wounding, or homicide usually arose from quarrels. Southern colonies had higher rates of these crimes, although the homicide rate in the colonies was generally low in the 1600s and even lower in the 1700s. Both homicide and theft occurred more frequently in cities than in the countryside. Stealing was four times more common in the city of New York than in the rural areas of the colony. Colonists carefully watched members of certain groups—slaves, Indians, servant women, and colonists not from Great Britain—for criminal activity. Despite the suspicion, these "outsiders" were convicted of fewer crimes than would be expected from their share of the population. If found guilty, however, they generally received harsher punishments than white males received for similar crimes.

When an individual was accused of a crime, the case came before the grand jury—a group of free white men who heard the evidence and decided whether to charge the person with the crime. Anyone formally charged with a crime had the right to a jury trial. People often gave up this right, however, because an individual who asked for a jury trial had to pay for it. At the trial, the jury determined whether the accused was innocent or guilty. Wealthy people generally sought jury trials, while poor people allowed their cases to be decided by the judge. Defendants frequently used the tactic of plea bargaining—accepting guilt for a lesser crime rather than standing trial.

Punishment. In colonial times, punishment was swift—and generally public—when someone was found guilty of a crime. People convicted of misdemeanors paid fines, were whipped, or suffered public humiliation. Some who were convicted had to give the court money as a bond along with a promise never to commit the crime again. The criminal's neighbors or relatives might also have to post a bond as an assurance that the crime would not be repeated. This encouraged them to keep a close eye on the criminal.

Hanging was the punishment for serious offenses. Murder was a capital crime in all colonies. New England punished witchcraft and heresy by death, and robbery was a capital crime in some colonies. Few convicted criminals went to prison—jails were for people awaiting trial, rarely for punishment. Only debtors were routinely jailed. Punishment practices changed somewhat

Stocks

Stocks, or the pillory, were a form of punishment used in the colonies to persuade criminals to reform through humiliation. Criminals were placed in a wooden frame with their head and hands—and sometimes legs—sticking through holes in a wooden frame. Unable to move and in plain sight of everyone in the community, the criminals were expected to feel shame. Townspeople could add to their discomfort by hurling insults—or rotten fruit and vegetables.

in the late 1700s as a result of a reform movement that swept Great Britain and influenced the colonies. Reformers began to urge prison terms as punishment, rather than public shaming or whipping.

Dutch Colony

The law in NEW NETHERLAND was based on the Dutch system of law. The officials of the DUTCH WEST INDIA COMPANY, which ran the colony, used a legal textbook from their homeland as a guide. When unusual situations arose, they created new laws. The director-general of New Netherland led a council of officials that heard criminal cases. As the colony's population increased, the company established lower courts in the towns. The judge in each court heard the evidence and reached a verdict. Unlike the British colonies, New Netherland had no tradition of trial by jury.

Most cases involved men rather than women. A large proportion of the criminals were soldiers of the West India Company or sailors who roamed the bustling port of New Amsterdam. Few of those convicted of crimes were Africans or Indians.

The commonest crimes were theft, slander, assault, sexual misconduct, and drunkenness. Convicted criminals rarely went to prison. Punishments for men included whipping, branding, and the pillory, which held the criminal for public viewing and humiliation. Women were fined, ordered to restore stolen goods, or banished. Soldiers might be forced to "ride the wooden horse," sitting for hours on a saddle mounted on a wooden rail, with weights attached to their legs. People convicted of murder were sentenced to death, but many of them, including slaves, received last-minute pardons and banishment.

The company passed strong laws against selling liquor to Native Americans. Violations resulted in a stiff fine. But the laws and penalties seem to have had little effect on these liquor sales. Officials also had little success in curbing drunkenness among the people or in preventing rowdy behavior on Sundays.

French Colonies

French law followed ancient Roman law, which used what is called the inquisitorial system. Unlike the German and English tradition in which each side argued its case, the French legal system gave responsibility for discovering the truth of a charge to the judge hearing the case. On one hand, judges had to follow a strict set of procedures in examining cases. On the other hand, they had a great deal of freedom in choosing punishments. As a result, judges often weighed a defendant's social position, as well as the circumstances of the case, before arriving at the punishment.

Crime in New France.   Colonial criminal records are spotty and may obscure the truth about crime in NEW FRANCE. For instance, 60 percent of all reported crimes occurred in towns, although only 20 percent of the people lived in towns. But the government was better able to exercise its authority—and make arrests—in urban areas. The town of Montreal had far more crime than

Remember: *Consult the index at the end of Volume 4 to find more information on many topics.*

Quebec, which was larger. Undisciplined fur traders visited Montreal on a regular basis, boosting the crime rate. In addition, Montreal lacked the network of family, church, and social connections that helped ensure order in Quebec.

Most of those convicted of crimes were men. A good number were bachelors or soldiers—groups considered especially rowdy and troublesome. French colonial officials rarely tried Native Americans in their courts because they did not want to risk offending their Indian allies.

The most common crime was assault, accounting for about one-third of all recorded cases. In a colony that valued social position, harsh words could easily lead to fights. About 10 percent of all court cases grew out of insults. Only 5 percent of cases involved homicide—a rate similar to that of Virginia, Britain, and France. As in British North America, crimes against property increased during the colonial period. The French colonists, however, punished certain forms of theft less harshly than the British colonists. For example, an individual who stole while drunk or because of need was unlikely to receive a severe penalty.

Criminal Law. In the English system, each side presented its evidence to a judge or jury. The defendant heard the accusers and could answer them directly. Under French law, all investigative and trial proceedings were held in secret with only the judge present. The goal was to ensure justice by limiting the influence of persuasive lawyers.

In the French system, judges had to follow a series of steps in handling criminal cases. First came the accusation, which could be brought by a private citizen or the public prosecutor. To prevent people from lying, accusers could be charged with libel* if a defendant was found innocent of the charge. An investigation called the inquiry followed. If the evidence was sufficient, the judge issued a warrant for the accused person's arrest.

* *libel* making a false statement that damages a person's reputation

Next came the interrogation, during which the judge questioned the accused. A court clerk read the defendant's statement aloud and he or she had a chance to revise it before signing. The judge then called back the others who had testified, and they were asked to confirm their statements. At this point the defendant was brought to confront the accusers and could try to discredit the testimony of any witnesses.

At the end of this stage—called the confrontation—the prosecutor asked for a judgment. If the case involved the death penalty, the prisoner might be tortured to bring a confession or information about others involved in the crime. Torture was supposed to be applied according to strict rules, and afterwards, the accused had a right to deny any confession made during the torture. However, torture was very rarely used in New France.

Three judges considered the case. If they doubted the guilt of the defendant, that person would be released. If they found the defendant guilty, the original judge would pronounce sentence. The convicted person could appeal a harsh sentence to councils in France. In the history of New France, seven colonists successfully appealed their sentences.

Judges had great freedom in setting sentences but generally limited harsh penalties to serious crimes. They punished simple assault or disturbing the peace with fines; burglary or robbery with banishment, branding, or serving on the king's ships; and murder with death. As in the other colonies, imprisonment was rarely used as punishment because the colony lacked jails.

Most criminals were punished where they were tried—except those condemned to death. These unfortunate individuals were taken to Quebec, where the executioner lived. Most people despised the executioner and sometimes refused to carry him by boat or wagon to the place where the condemned prisoner was held. Character had a lot to do with the poor reputation of the executioner in New France. Ten of the 14 people who held the job were condemned murderers who became executioners to save their own lives.

Spanish Borderlands

The justice system of the Spanish colonies, like that of the French colonies, had roots in ancient Roman law. Judges had sole responsibility for handling criminal cases and had much freedom in determining punishments. Because the Spanish colonial government was far away in Mexico, officials of the Spanish Borderlands—the region that is now the southwestern United States as well as Florida—could adjust the law to suit their own circumstances and values. Little is known about colonial law in California because all records on the subject were destroyed in the San Francisco earthquake of 1906.

Court System. The officials who had the power to make and carry out laws in the Spanish colonies generally tried criminal cases as well. These included provincial governors, appointed by the Spanish crown, and town officials called *alcaldes.* The governors tended to be drawn from the military, while the *alcaldes* usually came from the local population. Both types of officials had responsibility for maintaining law and order, but little formal legal training to do so.

The criminal process in the Spanish colonies resembled that in the French colonies, except that Spanish law allowed defendants to be represented by lawyers. There were few trained lawyers in the Borderlands, but sometimes respected or learned local citizens helped the accused present their cases. In the late 1700s and early 1800s, provincial governors sometimes named military officers to serve as attorneys.

Crime. Official records show a high proportion of violent crimes in the Borderlands. About 17 percent of all crimes in New Mexico between 1700 and 1780 were homicides, and another 28 percent were assaults. Although Spanish law did not draw distinctions between different categories of murder, judges considered the circumstances of a case and punished planned murders more harshly than those committed in the heat of the moment.

Sexual crimes also appear frequently in official records. Common offenses included breaking marriage promises, sexual relations outside of marriage, and homosexuality. Reports of rape were relatively rare. In cases of sexual misbehavior, judges were more likely to try to reform a person's behavior than to inflict a harsh punishment. Judges did the same with accusations of witchcraft.

Punishment. In determining how to punish criminals, judges drew upon several sources of information: Spanish laws, the writings of legal scholars, custom, and *equidad*—the community's sense of fairness. Because judges

Remember: *Consult the index at the end of Volume 4 to find more information on many topics.*

were greatly concerned with promoting harmony in society, they tended to give more weight to local custom and the community's feelings than to law codes and legal texts.

Punishment was supposed to serve as an example to the community, so sentences were often proclaimed and carried out in public. Judges might choose punishments that shamed or humiliated the criminal. One cattle thief, for instance, was sentenced to walk the streets of San Antonio with the intestines of the animal wrapped around his neck. A New Mexico man who beat his father-in-law was forced not only to pay the medical costs but also to offer an apology in public. Other common punishments included fines and forced labor on public works. Authorities sometimes banished criminals, particularly repeat offenders.

Physical punishment was relatively rare. Although lower-class criminals were more likely to be whipped than wealthy criminals, only those who had committed violent crimes received such punishments. A death sentence was quite unusual and only became official after a trained legal adviser reviewed the case. (*See also* **Laws and Legal Systems; Salem Witchcraft Trials.**)

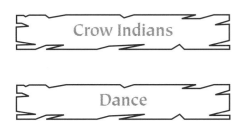

Crow Indians

See *Plains Indians.*

Dance

See *Music and Dance.*

Daughters of Liberty

*T*he Daughters of Liberty, loosely organized groups of women in the American colonies, were formed to protest British taxes and support the boycott* of British goods. Although the movement lasted only a few years, newspapers celebrated the women's contribution to the patriot* cause. The Daughters of Liberty were not connected with the more prominent Sons of Liberty.

In the late 1760s, colonists and the British government clashed several times over taxes passed by Parliament. The duties on imported goods imposed by one of the Townshend Acts particularly angered the colonists. In protest, many colonists refused to buy British goods.

A piece that appeared in 1767 in the *Massachusetts Gazette*—and was reprinted throughout the colonies—appealed to women to join in the protest. Addressing the "Daughters of Liberty," the writer asked colonial women to reduce the demand for imported cloth by devoting themselves to spinning thread and weaving wool. "Wear none but your own country linen," the writer urged. "Let your pride be the most to show cloaths [clothes] of your make and spinning."

Hundreds of women rose to the challenge. In groups ranging from 15 to 100, they gathered together with their spinning wheels—often at the home of the local minister—to spin wool and cotton yarn. These spinning bees took place in Massachusetts, Rhode Island, Georgia, North Carolina, and New

* **boycott** refusal to buy goods as a means of protest
* **patriot** American colonist who supported independence from Britain

York City. The women usually donated what they produced to the host of the meeting.

Death and Burial

eath was an ever-present threat in the North American colonies. Most people died at home, surrounded by relatives and friends, and were buried in churchyards or graveyards. In dealing with death and burial, European settlers and the Africans who came as slaves followed the customs of their homelands. Their diverse views and practices became part of the heritage of the American colonies.

Death shaped colonial families. Many people died very young. In New England, one of the healthiest regions of colonial America, more than 25 percent of the population perished before age 20. Almost everyone had lost brothers and sisters during childhood. Children also lost parents, especially in the Chesapeake Bay area and the Carolinas, where the death rate from disease was much higher than in other parts of the British colonies. Men and women commonly married more than once, rebuilding families after the deaths of their wives or husbands. Orphans were so numerous that the colonists created special courts to protect them.

British Colonists. Attitudes toward death varied widely among the British colonists, as did their burial customs. The New England PURITANS were deeply concerned with death. They believed the dying should express regret over their sinfulness and pray for salvation. Puritans expected children to be present at deathbeds and to view the corpses of family members. These experiences taught the young to fear death and to worry about their own salvation.

Deathbed scenes were important to the QUAKERS as well, but for different reasons. The Quakers believed that a dying person was closer to God and could give advice about leading a proper Christian life. Both Puritans and Quakers held simple funerals, and mourners were expected to control their grief. Showing too much grief meant that a person had not accepted God's will.

Planters in the Chesapeake Bay area and in the South viewed death in a practical, matter-of-fact way. Knowing that they could fall sick and die at any time, they planned for the care of their families and estates after their deaths. Southern colonists were often buried on family property rather than on church grounds. The funerals of wealthy or important people could turn into extravagant public occasions with huge processions.

Scotch-Irish settlers on the frontier followed many of the mourning customs of their homeland. When someone died, the family removed dishes from cupboards, covered mirrors, and stopped clocks until after the funeral. Neighbors put a plate of soil and salt on the corpse's stomach— the soil represented flesh, and the salt represented spirit. Members of the community were expected to pay their respects to the family and to touch the corpse.

African Americans. Blacks in North America—even those who became Christians—continued to hold many traditional African ideas about death. For example, they believed that if death rituals* were not properly performed, the dead person's spirit could haunt the living. Funerals were

Remember: *Words in small capital letters have separate entries, and the index at the end of Volume 4 will guide you to more information on many topics.*

* *ritual* ceremony that follows a set pattern

emotional ceremonies, with crying, shouting, and praying. African Americans often covered the graves of their loved ones with mounds of earth and marked them with seashells or items that had belonged to the dead.

Dutch Colonists.   The Dutch colonists continued to practice the funeral customs of their homeland even after New Netherland was taken over by the English and became New York. For the Dutch, care of the sick and dying was a community affair. The church sent "consolers" to visit and read the Bible to those who were seriously ill. After a death, friends and neighbors prepared the body for burial. They placed it in a sturdy wooden casket covered with a dark cloth and displayed it in the largest room in the house. Then they watched over the body all night. A "funeral inviter," dressed in black, called on the dead person's friends and relatives, who could not attend the funeral without an invitation. The family of the deceased provided food, drink, and tobacco for the mourners and gave them gifts such as scarves, rings, or spoons in memory of the one who had died.

Spanish Colonists.   Spanish settlers brought Roman Catholic beliefs and traditions to the Southwest. Whenever possible, a priest came to the bedside of a dying person to give the last rites, a Catholic ritual for the dying. Some ceremonies blended Native American traditions with Catholic ones. For example, on November 2, the Day of the Dead, colonists decorated the graves of their loved ones and celebrated death with music, dancing, and picnics. Through this festival, people acknowledged death as a natural part of life.

Settlers in the Southwest used salt and vinegar to preserve the bodies of the dead until burial. If these substances were scarce, the deceased was buried quickly. A wake, or gathering of mourners, followed the burial. Women prayed that the dead person's sins would be forgiven. Mourners wailed aloud and said special prayers to help the individual who died enter heaven.

French Colonists.   Like the Spanish colonies, the French colonies of New France and Louisiana were largely Roman Catholic. Priests prayed for the dying and presided over burials. Funerals were community events, with relatives, friends, and neighbors of the deceased taking part. A priest sprinkled the body with holy water, after which mourners carried it to the church for Mass. In Louisiana funeral processions gradually became parades with music, food, and drink. Like the Spanish colonists, the French remembered and honored their dead on November 2, which they called All Souls' Day. (*See also* **Diseases and Disorders; Old Age.**)

Declaration of Independence

The Declaration of Independence announced to the world the intention of the 13 British colonies of North America to separate from Great Britain and establish a new nation. Since its creation in 1776, this document has come to represent more than the struggle of a few colonists against the unjust policies of the British government. The ideas contained in the Declaration have inspired generations of people around the world in their own fight for freedom.

Declaration of Independence

The Liberty Bell

A treasured symbol of the United States, the Liberty Bell originally hung in the State House in Philadelphia, where the Continental Congress met. It was rung on July 8, 1776, when the Declaration of Independence was first read to the public. According to legend, the bell cracked that day and was never used again. Actually, the bell was rung at celebrations for many years until silenced by a large crack in 1846. The bell—made in 1751—was inscribed with a Bible verse that seemed to hint at its future role: "Proclaim liberty throughout all the land." It was not actually called the "Liberty Bell" until the 1830s, when the name was used by people in the antislavery movement. Still in Philadelphia, the Liberty Bell is a notable landmark.

tyranny unjust use of power

Prelude to the Declaration.   Many delegates to the SECOND CONTINENTAL CONGRESS in May of 1775 believed that the colonies should separate from Britain, but the assemblies of several colonies had specifically instructed their delegates *not* to vote for independence. John ADAMS, a delegate of Massachusetts and a strong supporter of independence, delayed pushing for a decision on the issue. He believed that a vote for independence had to be unanimous.

By the first months of 1776, shocking news from Britain had changed the views of many colonists. PARLIAMENT, with the approval of the king, had banned all trade to the colonies, and the British government was hiring foreign soldiers to fight the colonists. These developments convinced several colonial assemblies to drop their earlier restrictions and allow delegates to vote in favor of independence.

The congress took a major step toward independence on May 15, when it directed the colonies to create new governments to replace those appointed by the British government. On that same day, the Virginia assembly instructed its delegates in the congress to introduce a resolution calling for independence from Britain. This was done on June 7 by Richard Henry LEE. The resolution stated that "these United Colonies are, and of right ought to be, free and independent States . . . and that all political connection between them and the State of Great Britain is, and ought to be, totally dissolved."

A heated debate followed the introduction of the resolution, and a determined minority of the delegates refused to approve it. Consequently, the congress agreed on June 10 to postpone a vote on the issue for three weeks. In the meantime, it selected a committee to draft a document that would set forth the reasons for independence. Thomas JEFFERSON headed the committee, which also included John Adams, Benjamin FRANKLIN, Robert Livingston of New York, and Roger Sherman of Connecticut.

Content of the Declaration.   After a brief debate, the committee selected Jefferson to write the Declaration of Independence, and he produced a draft that argued persuasively for separation from Britain. Jefferson opened by stating that the colonies were not rebelling against Britain but were "dissolving" the ties that bound Britain and the colonies together. Drawing on the ideas of the ENLIGHTENMENT, he declared that the colonies were entitled to be "separate and equal" because of the "Laws of Nature."

In the second paragraph of the Declaration, its most memorable, Jefferson outlined the rights that all people enjoy, including "Life, Liberty, and the Pursuit of Happiness." He explained that to protect such rights, people form governments, which in turn receive their powers from the "consent of the governed." When a government fails to protect those rights, Jefferson wrote, the people have not only the right but also the "duty" to overthrow that government. Jefferson's proclamation of the right to take action against a cruel and unjust government lies at the heart of the Declaration of Independence. The idea has inspired people throughout the world to challenge tyranny*.

Another famous phrase in Jefferson's second paragraph has caused much debate in later generations. His statement that "all men are created equal" seemed to be contradicted by the practice of SLAVERY in the colonies. Most delegates to the Continental Congress disliked slavery, and many hoped for its end. Indeed, the words and ideals of the Declaration helped stimulate the

In this historical painting by John Trumbull, the drafting committee is shown submitting the Declaration of Independence to Congress. The members of the committee, from left to right, are John Adams, Roger Sherman, Robert Livingston, Thomas Jefferson, and Benjamin Franklin.

movements to end slavery in the 1800s and the civil rights movement in the mid-1900s.

After his philosophical opening paragraphs, Jefferson devoted most of the remainder of the Declaration to summarizing the "long train of Abuses" that King GEORGE III had committed against the colonists. He charged the king with trying to establish "an absolute Tyranny" over the colonies and implied that the colonists were only responding to the king's oppression*. This argument reflected a shift in colonial attitude. For years, the colonists had blamed the unfair actions of the British government on Parliament. They claimed that Parliament had no right to make laws for them because the body did not include representatives from the colonies to defend their interests. In effect, the Americans had already declared their independence of Parliament. To separate from Britain, they had to break their ties to the king.

After listing the grievances against the king, Jefferson formally declared the colonies to be "Free and Independent States" with the same powers and rights of independent nations. He then called on delegates in the congress to support the Declaration by pledging to each other "our Lives, our Fortunes, and our sacred Honor."

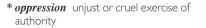

* *oppression* unjust or cruel exercise of authority

See color plate 7, vol. 3.

Approving the Declaration. Jefferson presented his draft—revised slightly by other members of the committee—to the congress on June 28, 1776. On July 1, delegates debated Richard Henry Lee's resolution for independence. They postponed voting on the issue for a day, however, when it became clear that four colonies—New York, Pennsylvania, South Carolina, and Delaware—were still opposed or undecided. On July 2, 12 colonies approved the resolution and the Declaration of Independence. New York abstained* but a week later gave its support to the resolution and the Declaration.

After voting for independence, the congress turned to polishing the document that would explain the colonies' decision. The delegates made only minor alterations in Jefferson's opening paragraphs of the Declaration. They made greater changes in the list of grievances against the king. In one

* *abstain* to keep from doing something

instance, they removed a reference to slavery because of pressure from southern states. The congress also dropped a number of charges against the king that were considered personal attacks not suitable for a political document.

The Continental Congress completed its revision of the Declaration of Independence and approved it on July 4. The finished document was sent to a printer, who placed that date on the top of the printed version. Thus July 4, 1776—rather than July 2, when independence was actually declared—came to be celebrated as the nation's birthday. The delegates to the Continental Congress signed the Declaration at a special ceremony on August 2. Delegates not present on that date signed later. (*See also* **American Revolution; Independence Movements: British Colonies; Revolutionary Thought.**)

Declaratory Act of 1766

* *repeal* to undo a law
* *boycott* refusal to buy goods as a means of protest

The Declaratory Act of 1766, a proclamation of the British PARLIAMENT, was part of an arrangement to improve relations with the American colonies. The act, which asserted Parliament's authority over the American colonies, eventually led to increased tension between Britain and the colonies.

In 1765 American colonists had reacted angrily to the STAMP ACT, which Parliament had passed as a way of collecting taxes. The colonists argued that the British government did not have the right to tax them because they had no delegates in Parliament to represent their interests. Parliament agreed to repeal* the Stamp Act after the colonists organized a series of riots and a boycott* of British goods. Many people in Britain feared that repealing the Stamp Act would make the British government look weak. As a result, Parliament passed the Declaratory Act at the same time.

The Declaratory Act stated that Parliament had the "full power and authority to make laws" for the colonies "in all cases whatsoever." In addition, the act declared that any laws passed by colonial assemblies that questioned the authority of Parliament were "utterly null and void," that is, they had no legal force.

Most Americans, busy celebrating the repeal of the hated Stamp Tax, paid little attention to the Declaratory Act. They believed it was merely Parliament's way of saving face after backing down on the taxation issue. It was not until Parliament suspended the New York Assembly in 1767 that Americans began to realize that Parliament intended to exercise the power contained in the Declaratory Act. The Declaratory Act, although originally part of a peacemaking arrangement, became a further source of conflict between Great Britain and the American colonies.

Deism

* *divinity* quality of being divine; a god

Deism was a system of religious beliefs popular among many leading thinkers of the 1700s and 1800s. Deists accepted the existence of a supreme being but not the divinity* of Christ. They believed that God created an ordered world that runs according to certain natural laws, but that God does not intervene in human events or perform miracles. This view of God's role led deists to focus on human reason. They believed that people had an obligation to use the reason given to them by God to create a moral society.

First developed in the 1600s in Europe, deism took root in colonial America in the late 1700s and claimed supporters in most of the Protestant religions. It gained the backing of prominent political and intellectual figures, including Benjamin FRANKLIN, Thomas JEFFERSON, Thomas PAINE, and Ethan ALLEN. Most of them viewed Christianity as a guide for developing moral principles, not as the one true religion. They placed a high value on virtue, ethics, and learning as the means of discovering truth and guiding human behavior. Their moderate* views and religious tolerance influenced society and politics during and immediately following the American Revolution. (*See also* **Enlightenment; Freedom of Religion.**)

* moderate not severe, avoiding extremes

De Lancey Family

Prominent New York colonists

The De Lancey family was one of the most powerful families in colonial New York. Its founder, Etienne (Stephen) De Lancey, immigrated to New York from France in 1686. He became a wealthy merchant and married into a powerful New York family, the Van Cortlandts. The De Lancey family increased its wealth, social position, and political power through marriage and friendships with important people.

Stephen's son, James De Lancey (1703–1760), was chief justice and lieutenant governor of New York and one of the most powerful political leaders in the colony. He was extremely successful in looking after the "De Lancey interest," that is, the political and financial well-being of the De Lancey family and its supporters. His brother, Oliver De Lancey (1718–1785), was also active in New York politics.

James's son, also named James (1732–1800), continued to expand the family's power. However, the De Lancey interest, which was built on connections to the British political system, conflicted with the colonies' movement toward independence in the 1770s. The family's opposition to the American Revolution proved to be its downfall. In 1775, James De Lancey moved with his family to Britain. During the Revolutionary War, Oliver served as a general in the British army. The De Lancey holdings were taken over by the new American government.

Delaware

See map in British Colonies (vol. 1).

The second smallest of Britain's North American colonies, Delaware was located on the west bank of the Delaware River near the Atlantic Ocean. Though officially part of PENNSYLVANIA after the 1680s, Delaware enjoyed a significant degree of self-government. It became a separate colony at the beginning of the American Revolution.

Early Settlement.   The explorer Henry HUDSON sighted the Delaware River in 1609, while leading an expedition for the Dutch. He called it the South River. An Englishman later renamed the river for Lord De La Warr, the first governor of the JAMESTOWN COLONY.

In the 1630s, the Netherlands, Sweden, and Britain all became interested in founding settlements in the Delaware region, primarily to establish trade along the river. The Dutch and English, in particular, competed for control of the area. Early European settlers met two Native American groups—the Nanticoke and Lenni Lenape, later called the DELAWARE INDIANS. The Indians enjoyed relatively good relations with the Europeans. Eventually, however, white settlement forced both groups of Native Americans to leave the region.

In 1631 a group of Dutch investors founded a settlement called Swanendael at a site near present-day Lewes, Delaware. The investors chose the location because of the large number of whales in Delaware Bay. Whale oil was quite valuable at the time, and the Dutch hoped to make a profit from hunting the animals. Within a year, however, disagreements with the Indians led to the deaths of all 32 colonists.

A Swedish trading company established another settlement in 1638. The company hired Peter Minuit, a former employee of the DUTCH WEST INDIA COMPANY, to organize a colony along the Delaware. Minuit purchased land from local Indians and started a trading post he named Fort Christina (after Sweden's queen) at the site of present-day Wilmington.

Swedish attempts to expand control led to conflict with the Dutch, who still claimed the area and had a prosperous FUR TRADE along the Delaware River. In 1651 the Dutch built Fort Casimir on the river just below Fort Christina. The Swedes captured the fort in 1654, but the following year Peter STUYVESANT, the leader of NEW NETHERLAND, conquered all of New Sweden. Swedish officials returned to Europe, but the Swedish and Finnish settlers in the colony remained and accepted Dutch rule.

Though the colony of New Sweden did not last long, it left an imprint. Swedish settlers had introduced a style of building log houses that was later widely used on the frontier.

William Penn attempted to combine Delaware with his colony of Pennsylvania. Delaware settlers resisted the union, and in 1701 Penn allowed them to have a separate government. This etching shows the countryside between the town of Wilmington and the Delaware River in 1789.

English Rule.   In 1664 an English fleet commanded by the Duke of York captured New Netherland, while a smaller fleet seized the Delaware River settlements. The Duke of York ruled the Delaware region as part of the colony of NEW YORK. He encouraged English settlement in the area and introduced English law. The Dutch had organized Delaware into three districts, and the duke continued this arrangement.

In 1682 the Duke of York transferred control of Delaware to William PENN. Penn wanted the area because the Delaware River connected his colony of Pennsylvania to the Atlantic Ocean. Under Penn, the region became known as the "Lower Counties." He tried to unite these counties with Pennsylvania, but settlers in Delaware—a mixture of Swedes, Finns, Dutch, and English—resisted because they feared domination by Pennsylvania's QUAKERS. In 1701 Penn granted the Lower Counties a charter* that guaranteed a separate government, but he retained overall authority as proprietor* of both Pennsylvania and the Lower Counties.

Meanwhile, Penn had to deal with conflicting claims to the land. The CALVERT FAMILY argued that the Delaware region was included in their 1632 charter for the colony of MARYLAND. The Calverts had not challenged the Duke of York's claim to the land because he was the king's brother. However, the family was willing to take on William Penn. The conflict between the Calverts and Penns continued until 1750, when the Penn family won the right to Delaware in court. English surveyors Charles Mason and Jeremiah Dixon finally established the boundaries between Pennsylvania, Delaware, and Maryland in the 1760s. Part of their survey, the Mason-Dixon Line, later became the unofficial dividing line between free states in the North and slave states in the South.

Delaware in the 1700s.   Although three European nations had established settlements in Delaware in the 1600s, most of the people who lived there in the late 1700s were of British background. African Americans formed a small part of the population—about 6 percent. Many were slaves who worked on tobacco plantations in the southern part of the colony. Delaware remained a slaveholding area until after the Civil War.

Delaware had considerable religious diversity. The Lower Counties' charter guaranteed people the "freedom of their consciences" as long as they were Christian. Even Roman Catholics—who suffered discrimination in some colonies—were welcomed in Delaware. Beginning in 1730, Catholic missionaries from Maryland visited the colony to preach, and land was purchased for the colony's first Catholic church in 1772.

Like New York and other middle colonies, Delaware was slow to support the movement for American independence. Wealthy planters in southern Delaware remained loyal to Britain, while people in northern Delaware generally favored separation. Nevertheless, Delaware's delegates to the SECOND CONTINENTAL CONGRESS voted for independence. When the AMERICAN REVOLUTION began, Delaware quickly established its sovereignty* by declaring itself a state. On December 7, 1787, Delaware became the first state to ratify the newly written United States Constitution, thus earning the nickname the "First State." (*See also* **British Colonies; Colonial Administration; Economic Systems; Swedish Settlements.**)

* **charter** written grant from a ruler conferring certain rights and privileges
* **proprietor** person granted land and the right to establish a colony

Rodney's Ride

When the Second Continental Congress in Philadelphia scheduled a vote on independence from Britain for July 2, 1776, the Delaware delegation found itself divided. One delegate favored independence, another opposed it. The third delegate, Caesar Rodney, remained at home in Delaware tending his sick wife. The night before the vote, a messenger rode 90 miles to summon Rodney back to Philadelphia. Rodney traveled through the night, arriving in time for the vote on July 2. Rodney's vote brought Delaware to the side of independence, and his midnight ride became one of the most famous events in Delaware history.

* **sovereignty** supreme power or authority

Delaware Indians

See second map in Native Americans (vol. 3).

* **confederacy** alliance or league of peoples or states
* **clan** related families

* **pelt** skin and fur of an animal

When Europeans first arrived in North America, the Delaware Indians occupied the area around the Delaware and lower Hudson rivers in present-day New Jersey, New York, Pennsylvania, and Delaware. The name Delaware came from early colonists. The Indians called themselves the Lenape or Lenni Lenape, which means "people who are the standard" or "original people."

The Delaware Indians lived by hunting and farming. Men did the hunting, usually alone, while women raised crops such as corn, beans, and squash. The Delaware also had a far-reaching trading network with other Indian groups that extended as far west as the Ohio and Mississippi River valleys. They spoke a language of the Algonquian language family.

The Delaware moved about seasonally within their traditional homelands. During the summer, they settled in large farming villages near rivers or in coastal areas. When fall arrived, they moved to hunting camps in the hills farther inland. In their villages, the Indians built wigwams and longhouses, both covered with bark, grass mats, or animal skins. The wigwams were small dome-shaped dwellings; the longhouses were long rectangular buildings used for living quarters and for tribal meetings.

The Delaware had three major divisions—the Munsee (Wolf), Unami (Turtle), and Unalachtigo (Turkey)—that were joined in a loose confederacy*. Tribal organization was based on kinship within a particular clan*, and membership in a clan came from the women of the tribe.

European explorers and fishermen visited the coastal regions of Delaware territory in the 1500s, but regular contact with Europeans began when Henry HUDSON sailed to the region in 1609. Soon after, the Delaware began trading with the Dutch settlers of NEW NETHERLAND. They became involved in the Dutch FUR TRADE, exchanging beaver pelts* for beads, tools, and other items.

While the Dutch controlled New Netherland, the Delaware maintained a firm hold on their homelands. After the English took over the colony in 1664, the Indians came under increasing pressure to surrender land to colonists. The Delaware gradually left their traditional homelands and retreated farther and farther west, first to Pennsylvania and then to Ohio.

During the FRENCH AND INDIAN WAR, many Delaware sided with the French against the British. When the AMERICAN REVOLUTION broke out, the Delaware divided into three main groups according to their role in the war. One group near present-day Pittsburgh supported the Americans. Another group in northwestern Ohio backed the British. A third group in Ohio remained neutral. Following the Revolution, many of the Delaware who had supported the British moved into Canada. Most of the other Delaware continued migrating farther westward to escape the consequences of spreading white settlement. The tribe eventually settled in Indian Territory (present-day Oklahoma), where many Delaware continue to live today. (*See also* **Agriculture: Native American; Languages: Native American.**)

Democracy

See *Assemblies; Political Thought; Voting Rights.*

de Soto, Hernando

ca. 1496–1542
Spanish conqueror and explorer

See first map in Exploration, Age of (vol. 2).

ernando de Soto was one of the CONQUISTADORS, the Spanish conquerors who sought treasure and land in the Americas. During his search for wealth, de Soto explored the southeastern part of North America. He and his men became the first Europeans to cross the APPALACHIAN MOUNTAINS and the MISSISSIPPI RIVER.

De Soto was born in Barcarrota, Spain. While still in his teens, he went to Central America in the service of Pedrarias Dávila, governor of the Spanish colony of Panama. There, de Soto gained a reputation for bravery in several campaigns against local Indians. In 1531 he joined an expedition against the Inca empire in South America. The Spaniards seized the Inca capital city of Cuzco and executed the Inca ruler, Atahuallpa. For his part in the conquest, de Soto received a share of the Inca treasure and returned to Spain a rich man.

In 1537 King Charles V of Spain named de Soto governor of the Spanish colony of Cuba. More importantly, the king granted him the right to "conquer, pacify, and populate" La Florida, the Spanish name for the territory north of Cuba. There de Soto hoped to find and conquer a wealthy civilization like that of the Inca or the Aztec of Mexico. In 1539, he sailed north from Cuba with nine ships carrying over 600 men, a few women, and over 200 horses. The expedition landed on the west coast of modern Florida in the Gulf of Mexico. After setting up camp, de Soto began his search for gold.

Hernando de Soto, shown here in a 1615 engraving, explored thousands of miles of American wilderness in his search for gold and other riches. Although he never found gold, he and his men did collect useful information about Indian cultures and American wildlife.

De Soto and his men roamed far beyond Florida, marching north through present-day Georgia and the Carolinas and west across the Appalachian Mountains. In May 1541 the expedition stumbled upon a mighty river—the Mississippi. After crossing it on rafts, they explored parts of what are now Arkansas and Louisiana. Throughout their journey, the Spaniards terrorized native villages and seized Indians to use as slaves and guides. As a result, de Soto and his men spent much of their expedition fighting off attacks from hostile Native Americans. The invaders also unknowingly introduced small-pox and other European DISEASES to the area, wiping out a large percentage of the Indian population.

Three years of battering by harsh weather and Indian attacks greatly weakened de Soto's army. The exhausted commander decided to return to the camp in Florida. The Spaniards headed east, wading through miles of swampland. As they reached the banks of the Mississippi River, de Soto fell ill with a fever and died on May 21, 1542. To hide their leader's death from the local Indians, the soldiers wrapped his body in chains and sank it in the river. Under the command of Luis de Moscoso, the men abandoned the plan to return to Florida and continued their quest for gold. After six more months of marching, the Spaniards built boats and sailed down the Mississippi to the Gulf of Mexico and west along the coast. By the time they reached some Spanish settlements, only half of the original army remained.

Despite great efforts, de Soto never found gold or the fabulously rich civilization he searched for. His expedition did, however, explore over 4,000 miles of wilderness and in the process gathered a wealth of information about Indian cultures and wildlife in the southeastern part of North America. (*See also* **Exploration, Age of.**)

Diaries

*M*any colonists in North America kept diaries and journals of their experiences. These documents provide valuable information about the personal interests and concerns of the colonists. The style and focus of the journals varied considerably.

One of the most notable journals from the colonial period is that of John WINTHROP, the first governor of the Massachusetts Bay colony. In his diary, Winthrop focused on the activities of this PURITAN community rather than on his personal life. Other New England Puritans dwelled on spiritual matters in their diaries. Many of them discussed their efforts to live up to the strict standards of their religion. Michael Wigglesworth wrote with sorrow that his "goodness (if any there be) is like the morning dew that is dried up." Samuel Sewall used his diary to deal with inner conflicts. A judge at the SALEM WITCH TRIALS, Sewall had come to regret his role in the trials. He recorded his attempts to make up for past mistakes, including a public apology for his part in the events at Salem. Other well-known Puritan journals include the diary of Cotton MATHER and the *Personal Narrative* of Jonathan EDWARDS.

William BYRD, the son of a wealthy Anglican* planter in Virginia, had quite different interests. Educated in England, Byrd socialized with some of the most prominent people in the colonies, and he wrote about the social

* *Anglican* member of the Church of England

events he attended, London theater, and financial matters. His journals reveal his keen interest in business as well as the small role religion played in his life.

The diaries of Dutch colonists were usually simple, chronological accounts of everyday life—often attempts to explain life in the colonies to others or to write something that might be published. The journal of Harmen van den Bogaert of Fort Orange, for example, tells the story of the expedition he led among the IROQUOIS. He described in vivid detail Indian life and the hardships and dangers he encountered during the trip. (*See also* **Literature.**)

Dickinson, John

1732–1808
American political writer

* *repeal* to undo a law

* *boycott* refusal to buy goods as a means of protest

* *reconciliation* reaching agreement after a dispute

*J*ohn Dickinson was a prominent leader during the Revolutionary period. Though a strong supporter of colonial rights, he opposed violent resistance to British policies and hoped to avoid separation from Britain. His many writings on the issues of the day earned him the name the "Penman of the Revolution."

Born in Maryland, Dickinson spent much of his boyhood in Delaware. He studied law in Philadelphia and London and became a prominent lawyer. Dickinson held various public offices in both Pennsylvania and Delaware. While a member of the Pennsylvania assembly, he frequently clashed with fellow assembly member Benjamin FRANKLIN over financial and political issues.

In response to the SUGAR ACT of 1764 and the STAMP ACT CRISIS of 1765, Dickinson wrote a pamphlet in which he argued that the best course for colonists would be to persuade British merchants to support the repeal* of these acts in Parliament. As a member of the Stamp Act Congress, he drafted a petition to King GEORGE III asking for repeal of the act that required colonists to pay a stamp tax on all papers they used. After Parliament passed the TOWNSHEND ACTS in 1767, Dickinson wrote a series of essays called *Letters from a Farmer in Pennsylvania.* These challenged Britain's right to tax the colonies and argued for peaceful opposition to the acts through a boycott* on British imports.

Dickinson's repeated calls for nonviolent resistance to British policies made him a leader of the colonists who favored reconciliation* with Britain. His position made him unpopular with those who called for American independence. As a delegate to the FIRST CONTINENTAL CONGRESS, Dickinson wrote a petition to the king urging a peaceful settlement of colonial grievances. Although he supported the move to take up arms against Britain after the Battles of LEXINGTON AND CONCORD, Dickinson voted against the DECLARATION OF INDEPENDENCE. He still hoped that the colonies and Britain would resolve their differences. When it became clear, however, that the British were not ready to negotiate, he joined the colonial forces.

In 1787 Dickinson served as a delegate from Delaware to the convention that drew up the United States Constitution, and he wrote a series of letters in support of the new government. Following the convention, Dickinson retired from public office but continued to write about public issues. (*See also* **Press in Colonial America.**)

Diseases and Disorders

Sickness was a part of life in the North American colonies. Native Americans, colonists from Europe, and slaves from Africa and the West Indies all suffered from a variety of diseases and disorders. However, certain health problems occurred more often, or had more severe effects, on particular groups of the population. Climate, age, income, and diet all influenced the chances of becoming ill.

In general, wealthy colonists suffered less from illness than the poor because they could eat well, dress warmly, and live in decent housing. The rich could also afford to flee their homes during epidemics of disease. Epidemics struck hardest in the cities, where people were crowded closely together and diseases could easily spread from one person to another. Rural areas were safer from epidemic outbreaks because of their isolation.

The very old and the very young were particularly at risk. Elderly people were more likely than younger adults to die of illnesses such as pneumonia or influenza. Disease and infection also killed large numbers of infants and young children. Between 11 and 14 percent of all children in the colonies died in the first year of life.

Causes of Disease. In the 1600s and 1700s, people held various theories about the cause of disease. Many colonists thought that the human body contained four vital fluids, called "humors," and that an imbalance in these liquids resulted in sickness. The PURITANS of Massachusetts believed that God sent illnesses to punish sinners, while Native Americans and people of African descent blamed evil spirits for disease.

In reality, many health problems came from poor sanitation. People dumped garbage and human waste into the streets or into rivers and streams, polluting their drinking water. Colonists rarely bathed, and most of them owned only a few changes of clothing. Lice and mites infested dirty clothes and beds, spreading diseases. Military camps were notoriously unsanitary. Epidemics of ailments such as dysentery, an intestinal disease carried by infected food and water, often swept through army barracks. People did recognize that

These drawings from Benjamin Bell's *A System of Surgery,* published in 1791, show some of the tools and techniques used to perform surgery in the 1700s. Surgery was a grisly business because little was known about how to prevent infection.

illness often spread from person to person. Sometimes the sick were confined in special buildings called pesthouses to keep them from infecting others.

Diet also played an important role in health. Native American tribes who hunted and farmed ate well-balanced diets that included meats, grains, and plenty of fruits and vegetables. European colonists and their black slaves generally did not eat as well. They consumed few fruits and vegetables, particularly in the northern British and French colonies, where the growing season was short. Scurvy, a disease caused by a shortage of the vitamin C found in fruits and vegetables, was common in northern regions. In the South the disease primarily affected slaves, who lived mostly on corn and meat. While scurvy and other kinds of malnutrition were rarely fatal, poor diets weakened people, making it easier for deadly diseases to take hold.

Common Illnesses.   Medical records from the colonial period are patchy and incomplete. People often did not know what illness had caused someone to sicken or die, and in many cases the names they gave to medical conditions do not match terms used today. Many old accounts speak of deaths from "fever," yet "fever" could refer to half a dozen or more different diseases known today.

Contagious diseases thrived in the crowded and unsanitary conditions of the ships that brought immigrants to the colonies. Losses were high—in 1738, for example, 1,600 people died on 15 ships bound for Philadelphia. Newly arrived passengers often started outbreaks of disease in port cities.

Slaves from Africa and the West Indies brought malaria and yellow fever, tropical diseases carried by mosquitoes, to North America. Africans had been exposed to these diseases for centuries and had built up some immunity, or resistance, to them. As a result, fewer blacks than Europeans died from these illnesses, which were especially severe around Chesapeake Bay and in the southern colonies. Colonists new to the South endured what they called the "seasoning"—repeated bouts of sickness, often including malaria and dysentery. Those who survived were less likely to suffer future attacks. Although now a mild illness of childhood, measles was also a serious threat to people of all ages in colonial times. Severe outbreaks erupted regularly, leaving hundreds dead.

Smallpox was perhaps the most dreaded disease of colonial times. Raging through the colonies in a series of epidemics, smallpox killed between 15 and 25 percent of the colonists who caught it and often left those who survived with terrible scars. The death toll was much higher among Native Americans, who had never been exposed to smallpox before the arrival of the Europeans and had no immunity to it. Severe outbreaks of smallpox first occurred among the Indians in the 1630s. Within a century, smallpox and other European diseases such as measles and influenza had devastated the Native Americans, killing perhaps as much as 90 percent of the population.

Diseases of the lungs, such as pneumonia and tuberculosis, also ravaged the colonies. Pneumonia struck hardest in the cold North. Tuberculosis was widespread, accounting for as many as one out of every four deaths. It was

Poisoned Milk

Colonists in some parts of North America, particularly Pennsylvania, suffered attacks of an illness they called "the trembles," "the slows," or "the milk sickness." The illness struck people who ate meat or drank milk from cows that had eaten a poisonous plant called white snakeroot. As the cows digested the root, the poison entered their milk or flesh. The milk sickness was not always fatal, but survivors could remain weak and shaky for months— or for the rest of their lives.

especially deadly to Africans, who had not been exposed to the disease before being brought to America.

Other Health Problems.

Colonial doctors knew little about treating infections. Soldiers wounded in battle often survived their injuries only to perish as a result of infections in their wounds. Surgery performed in unsanitary conditions frequently caused infections. Patients who lived through the shock of surgery were at risk of becoming sick or dying from infection afterward.

Alcoholism was a health problem in colonial North America, although at the time people did not recognize it as a disease. Alcohol was especially dangerous for Native Americans, who had little or no experience with liquor before the arrival of Europeans. Numerous accounts from colonial times mention the destructive effects of alcohol on Indian communities.

Tooth decay was common, as were eye disorders. Spectacles could correct some vision problems, but little information survives about the manufacture and distribution of eyeglasses in the 1700s. Older colonists frequently complained of "arthritis," a category that included many joint diseases caused or made worse by constant physical labor.

Despite these diseases and disorders, colonists in North America were generally healthier and suffered fewer epidemics than people living in Europe at this time. By 1700 the average American colonist lived slightly longer than the average western European. (*See also* **Death and Burial; Health and Safety; Medical Practice.**)

Divorce

See *Marriage.*

Dominion of New England

* **charter** written grant from a ruler conferring certain rights and privileges

The Dominion of New England was a short-lived province in North America made up of English colonies. In 1686 the English king James II decided that the original charters* of the New England colonies should be canceled and the colonies combined into one large province, the Dominion of New England. In 1688, New York and New Jersey were added to the dominion.

The Dominion of New England was created to make it easier for the English crown to govern and defend its colonies. In addition, the crown hoped to gain greater control over the colonies, which had been enjoying a considerable degree of independence under their separate charters.

The king appointed a governor and a council to head the dominion government. The governor, Sir Edmund ANDROS, had military experience and took a strict approach to running the province. He expected his orders to be followed without question. Not only had the colonists lost their representative assemblies, they were also faced with Andros's absolute rule. They promptly opposed the new administration.

The experiment with provincial government ended in 1689 after James II was overthrown and replaced by the Protestant rulers William and Mary. The colonists immediately seized Andros and sent him back to England, and they jailed his few supporters. The colonial governments in the region were soon reorganized.

Drake, Sir Francis

ca. 1543–1596
English explorer and sea captain

* **privateer** privately owned ship authorized by the government to attack and capture enemy vessels; also the ship's master

Sir Francis Drake was the most famous English sea captain of his time and the second European to sail around the world. His raids on Spanish ships and settlements in the Americas brought his country great riches. To the English, Drake was a hero. To the Spanish, he was a feared and hated pirate.

Born to a poor farming family, Drake went to sea in his early teens. In the 1560s, he joined the expeditions organized by his cousin John Hawkins, which carried African slaves to the WEST INDIES. The Spanish regarded the West Indies as their territory and attacked Hawkins's fleet, destroying all but two of the ships. Drake vowed revenge on the Spanish. When he returned to the Caribbean in 1570, he had a commission from Queen ELIZABETH I to act as a privateer*. Launching a series of raids on Spanish lands and on Spanish treasure ships bound for Europe, Drake gained great wealth and fame.

In 1577 Drake received approval from the queen for a voyage to the Pacific coast of the Americas. He set sail from Plymouth in December with a crew of 166 and five ships. After passing through the Strait of Magellan at the southern tip of South America in August 1578, he sailed north along the Pacific coast, raiding Spanish settlements and capturing Spanish treasure ships. He continued north, perhaps as far as present-day Washington, hoping to discover a NORTHWEST PASSAGE—a water route between the Pacific and Atlantic oceans. Failing to find such a waterway, Drake turned south and stopped near what is now San Francisco to repair his only remaining ship, the *Golden Hind.* Drake claimed the surrounding land for England, naming it New Albion. As proof of his visit, he left behind a brass plate, dated June 17, 1579.

Drake feared that the Spanish would be waiting for him if he returned to England the way he had come, around the tip of South America. So he sailed across the Pacific Ocean instead, becoming the second European after Spanish explorer Ferdinand Magellan to make this long voyage. Drake finally arrived in England in 1580 in a ship loaded with Spanish treasure and valuable spices from the East Indies. Queen Elizabeth rewarded him with a knighthood.

Between 1585 and 1587, Drake led additional raids against the Spanish, including an attack on the town of Vigo in Spain. While in the Americas, he destroyed the Spanish settlement of ST. AUGUSTINE in Florida and rescued English settlers from the ill-fated colony on ROANOKE ISLAND in present-day North Carolina. During this time Spain had been building a large fleet, known as the Spanish Armada, in preparation for an attack on England. As an admiral of the English navy, Drake played a key role in defeating the Spanish Armada in 1588.

Drake began a final expedition against the Spanish in 1595. The next year, while off the coast of Panama in Central America, he died and was buried at sea. (*See also* **Exploration, Age of; Privateers.**)

Drama

*T*he theater had been a subject of constant dispute in Europe, and it continued to be controversial long after its introduction in North America. While many colonists considered watching and performing in plays to be a pleasant pastime, others—particularly certain religious groups—regarded acting and the theater as immoral.

The public's attitude toward theater depended largely on the religious and cultural background of the colonists. The Dutch settlers of NEW NETHERLAND had little interest in dramatic activity, and plays were not performed in the colony until it came under English rule in 1664. The theater flourished in some British colonies, but New England officials banned it completely. In the French and Spanish colonies, plays became a tool for teaching the principles of Christianity to Native Americans.

British Colonies. The first actors in British North America were leading members of society who put on plays for their own entertainment. Amateur theatricals, popular in England, probably took place throughout the colonies in the 1600s. Some performances were private; some welcomed the public.

From the beginning, however, members of many religious groups condemned the theater as an unwholesome or dangerous influence. In 1665 authorities in Virginia put three men on trial for presenting an English play called *Ye Bare and Ye Cubb* (The Bear and the Cub), the first recorded performance in the British colonies. After having the play reenacted in the courtroom, the judge found the men innocent of any wrongdoing. In 1690 authorities in Boston objected to a performance staged by students at Harvard College.

Opposition to the theater continued to grow, especially in communities with large groups of PURITANS, Methodists, QUAKERS, and Presbyterians. In 1750 Boston banned all theater, and many other cities followed its lead. Although plays were not prohibited in Virginia and Maryland, the colonial governments strictly regulated performers' activities. In 1752 a touring theatrical company that arrived in Williamsburg, Virginia, had to seek permission from the governor before scheduling performances. When the actors moved on to New York after a successful year in Williamsburg, they carried a certificate of good behavior to reassure New Yorkers that they were not rowdy or immoral.

Despite the restrictions, theater managed to survive and grow in the colonies during the 1700s. Professional actors traveled throughout the middle and southern colonies, performing in barns, inns, or fields on the outskirts of town to avoid the notice of local authorities. A merchant in Williamsburg, Virginia, built the first legal theater in the colonies in 1717. It did not last long because the small town was unable to support a theater. The first permanent theater that hired professional actors was the Southwark, built in Philadelphia in 1766. During the 1700s, the British colonies supported several traveling companies. The managers and most of the actors came from Britain, but many of the musicians and scenery painters, as well as a few actors, were colonists.

For the most part, these companies presented works by British playwrights. The plays of William Shakespeare remained popular through the 1700s, as did British comedies. *The Prince of Parthia* (1763), one of the few American plays staged by professional companies, was a long, highly emotional tragedy. The play apparently failed to please the audience, as it was never performed again. Major Robert Rogers, a veteran of the FRENCH AND

Remember: Consult the index at the end of Volume 4 to find more information on many topics.

Mrs. Lewis Hallam was one of the leading actresses of the colonial era. In the mid-1750s, she and her husband toured the colonies with a British theater company. In this painting by Charles Willson Peale, Mrs. Hallam appears as Cymbeline in an Annapolis theater.

* **Anglican** member of the Church of England
* **Jesuit** Roman Catholic religious order

* **clergy** ministers, priests, and other church officials

* **Spanish Borderlands** northern part of New Spain, area now occupied by Florida, Texas, New Mexico, Arizona, and California

INDIAN WAR, wrote *Ponteach; or, The Savages of America* (1766), a sympathetic portrayal of the Native American leader PONTIAC.

Although people from all classes went to see plays, the typical colonial theatergoer was well-educated, Anglican*, and lived in a city. In the years before the Revolutionary War, George WASHINGTON attended the theater frequently, sometimes seeing several plays a week. Thomas JEFFERSON was also a great supporter of drama.

The beginning of the American Revolution abruptly halted the development of theater in the colonies. In 1775 the SECOND CONTINENTAL CONGRESS banned all forms of public entertainment, including theater, in the hope that people would devote their money and energy to the coming war with Britain. During the war the congress passed several strong measures against the theater. This ban, however, did not apply to "pamphlet plays"—dramas that were meant to be read, not performed. A popular example was John Leacock's *The Fall of British Tyranny; or, American Liberty Triumphant, The First Campaign* (1776), one of many historical dramas to feature George Washington as the hero. After the Revolution, theater gradually revived in the United States.

French Colonies. Theatrical productions in NEW FRANCE included both plays from France and local works. Although the colony's population was small, it supported a surprising amount of theatrical activity throughout most of the 1700s.

The first play written and performed in New France was staged in 1606. Like most French plays of the time, *La Théâtre de Neptune en la Nouvelle-France* was meant for a highly educated audience and included many references to ancient Greek and Roman history. Following the tradition of French Jesuits*, the play consisted largely of long speeches.

In Quebec audiences frequently enjoyed works by leading French playwrights. Colonial authors did write some new plays, usually for special occasions. In 1640 the governor asked a group of amateur actors to include material in a production they were preparing that would teach Native Americans about Christianity. The performers added a scene in which two demons—speaking a Native American language—chased an unbeliever and cast him into a flaming hell. The impressive spectacle was the first of several plays to include Indian languages.

In the 1690s the governor of New France agreed to allow a production of *Tartuffe,* the comedy by French playwright Molière about the religious hypocrisy of the clergy*. Alarmed by the antireligious nature of the work, the bishop of the Catholic Church bribed the governor to halt production of the play. The bishop used the controversy over the work as an excuse to ban all theatrical activity in the colony, even Christian plays in religious schools. As a result, public theater almost disappeared from New France. Only four plays are known to have been staged in New France between the bishop's ruling in 1699 and 1763, when Britain gained control of the colony. Other performances may well have taken place in private homes.

Spanish Borderlands. Drama in the Spanish Borderlands* was often used to serve the goals of the Spanish empire and the ROMAN CATHOLIC CHURCH. In Spain, festivals frequently included plays about religious and patriotic subjects, and Spanish colonists brought this tradition with them to North America.

The first theatrical performance in the Borderlands occurred on April 30, 1598. Led by Juan de OÑATE, a group of colonists had spent several difficult months traveling over mountains and across deserts before reaching the territory that became New Mexico. When the weary Spaniards arrived on the banks of the Rio Grande, they rested and prepared a religious celebration in gratitude for their survival. As part of the festivities, they performed a play written by a member of the expedition, a work about local Indians asking to be baptized as Christians.

Six months later Oñate's followers presented another play during a festival in honor of the settlement's first church. The play, *Los Moros y Cristianos* (The Moors* and the Christians), concerned the centuries-long battle between the Spanish Christians and the Moors who had invaded Spain. The play glorified the virtues of Christian warriors and the strength of the Spanish empire. It reinforced the idea that Spain had the right to conquer non-Christians and to convert them to Christianity—as it was doing to the Native Americans. Versions of *Los Moros y Cristianos* remained popular throughout the Borderlands.

Two other historical dramas written during the Spanish colonial period were widely performed. Based on important battles between the Spanish settlers and the COMANCHE INDIANS in the 1770s, *Los Comanches* ends with the Spanish driving off or converting the Indians. Colonial communities presented this play every year in celebration of the Spanish victory. The other popular historical drama was *Los Matachines,* a combination of music, dance, and drama performed by Christianized Native Americans. It represented Spain's conquest of the Aztec of Mexico and the Aztec acceptance of Christianity.

The Spanish colonists staged religious plays as well. The biblical tales of Adam and Eve and Cain and Abel were popular. One widely performed religious drama, *Los pastores,* tells the story of a group of shepherds who received a visit from an angel announcing the birth of Jesus. The shepherds set out to see the infant, but along the way the Devil tried to trick them into forgetting their mission. Hundreds of versions of this play survive today.

Whether historical or religious in subject, the drama of the Spanish colonies was often intended to teach Native Americans in the audience about the might of Spain and the glory of Christianity. Performed over and over again at festivals and on holidays, these dramas became a part of the cultural life of the Borderlands and were staged long after the colonial era ended. (*See also* **Hallam, Mrs. Lewis; Literature.**)

* ***Moors*** North African Muslims

Opening Night

In the British colonies, the audience determined a play's fate. If the first performance was a success, the company performed the play again. If opening night went badly, however, the play could close then and there. Audience members—who commonly ate, drank, and chatted or played cards with their friends during performances—were not shy about showing their opinions. They cheered and applauded speeches they liked and hissed and booed at poor writing or acting. In extreme cases they pelted the stage with orange peels, bellowing "Off! Off!" at the unfortunate performers.

Dress

See *Clothing.*

Dueling

See *Social Customs.*

Dutch East India Company

* **charter** written grant from a government conferring certain rights and privileges

* **monopoly** exclusive right to engage in a certain kind of business

*T*he Dutch East India Company was one of most powerful trading companies of the 1600s and 1700s. Established in 1602 by a charter* from the government of the Netherlands, the company had exclusive trading privileges in Asia. When the company sent an expedition to North America to find a sea route to Asia—the fabled NORTHWEST PASSAGE—it laid the grounds for Dutch claims to territory in the Americas.

During the 1500s, Portugal controlled the spice trade between Europe and the East Indies, groups of islands in southeast Asia. In 1594 some Dutch merchants organized an expedition to the East Indies in hopes of breaking the Portuguese spice monopoly*. The success of their voyage encouraged other Dutch companies to join the spice trade. By 1601 no fewer than 14 fleets with 65 ships were sailing back and forth between the Netherlands and the East Indies laden with rich cargoes of spices. The quantity of imports was so great that it threatened to flood the market in Amsterdam. Finally, to restore order, the Dutch government declared that the trading companies must merge. This led to the formation of the Dutch East India Company.

The directors of the East India Company received broad powers over an area that extended from the Cape of Good Hope at the southern tip of Africa eastward to the Straits of Magellan at the southern tip of South America. Within this area the company exercised all the rights of a nation. It could make treaties with foreign leaders, build fortresses and military and naval bases, punish criminals, set economic policies, and wage war.

One of company's early goals was to locate a safer sea route to Asia. The Dutch had been at war with Spain and Portugal for decades, and Dutch trading ships often encountered enemy vessels during the long and dangerous voyage around Africa. The high costs of protecting and insuring trading expeditions cut deeply into company profits. In 1607 the company hired Henry HUDSON, an English sea captain, to locate a safe passage to the East Indies through North America. Hudson failed to find such a passage, but his explorations opened a portion of North America to Dutch trade. In the years that followed, the DUTCH WEST INDIA COMPANY established the colony of NEW NETHERLAND in the region that Hudson had explored.

The East India Company eventually gained control of the sea route around Africa from the Portuguese and Spanish. It also drove the Portuguese from the East Indies and took over the spice trade. By the 1700s, however, the company had begun to lose money, partly due to increasing competition from the British and French, and partly because of corruption within the company. The Dutch East India Company ceased operations in 1799, and its possessions in the East Indies were taken over by the Dutch government. (*See also* **European Empires; Exploration, Age of; Trade and Commerce.**)

Dutch Reformed Church

See *Protestant Churches.*

See *New Netherland.*

* *charter* written grant from a government conferring certain rights and privileges

*D*uring the 1600s, European merchants competed for the riches of Asia, Africa, and the Americas. Hoping to expand trade and set up colonies in West Africa and the Americas, a group of Dutch merchants formed the Dutch West India Company in 1621. The new trading company received a charter* from the government of the Netherlands and began settling Dutch families in North America.

Modeled after the DUTCH EAST INDIA COMPANY, which operated in Asia, the Dutch West India Company had exclusive trading privileges in certain areas of the world. It was the only Dutch company permitted to trade on the west coast of Africa, in the WEST INDIES, in Australia, and on the east or west coasts of the Americas. Administered by 19 directors, the West India Company also enjoyed broad political powers. It could build forts and establish colonies in the regions under its control and could make alliances with the inhabitants.

The West India Company had five divisions, or chambers, based in different cities. Each chamber had authority to maintain its own fleet of trading ships and to establish its own colonies. In 1624 and 1625, the chamber of Amsterdam sent 30 families to start the colony of NEW NETHERLAND on the eastern coast of North America. Among its early settlements were Fort Orange on the Hudson River (now Albany, New York) and NEW AMSTERDAM on Manhattan Island (now New York City).

The West India Company demanded strict obedience from the settlers to its rules and policies. It acted as both ruler and employer. To administer the colony's affairs, it appointed a director and a council. From the beginning, though, most of the settlers were more interested in their families and small plots of land than in taking part in the FUR TRADE, which the company hoped would bring great profits.

The West India Company needed to make a profit for its investors, and it also needed to strengthen its claim to New Netherland by encouraging settlement. The company tried to attract colonists in various ways, including offers of free land. Settlement expanded, but the company had increasing difficulty making a profit from its colonial activities. Financial problems finally forced the company to give up its monopoly* over the fur trade in the late 1630s. However, the colony remained under the authority of the Dutch West India Company until the English took control of New Netherland in 1664.

The Dutch West India Company continued to have financial difficulties. After reorganizing under a new charter in 1674, the company engaged primarily in the SLAVE TRADE and administered small colonies in the Caribbean and on the coast of South America. When the company's charter expired in 1791, the Dutch government took over all its colonies and its debts. The Dutch West India Company ceased operations three years later when the Netherlands was conquered by the French. (*See also* **Colonial Administration; Trade and Commerce.**)

* *monopoly* exclusive right to engage in a certain kind of business

Dyer, Mary

ca. 1610–1660
Quaker missionary

* **repeal** to undo a law
* **doctrine** set of principles or beliefs accepted by a religious or political group
* **excommunicate** to expel from the church

Mary Dyer was hanged for defying laws against QUAKERS in the PURITAN colony of Massachusetts Bay. Her stubborn defense of the Quaker religion led to her death, but it also resulted in the repeal* of the colony's extreme anti-Quaker laws.

Born Mary Barrett, the young woman married William Dyer in London in 1633. A year or so later, the couple went to MASSACHUSETTS. There Mary Dyer became friendly with Anne HUTCHINSON, who was banished from the colony because her religious beliefs conflicted with Puritan doctrine*. According to one story, Mary Dyer was the only person to walk out of the church with Hutchinson when she was excommunicated* in 1638. The Dyers, also banished from Massachusetts, accompanied the Hutchinsons to Rhode Island. There William Dyer helped found the town of Portsmouth and became a leading local figure.

Returning to England in 1650, Mary Dyer joined the Society of Friends, or Quakers. Many Protestant churches considered the Quakers to be a dangerous influence because of their belief that an individual could know God's will directly through an "inner light" and did not need church officials and doctrines. On her way back to Rhode Island in 1657, Dyer passed through Boston in spite of the law prohibiting Quakers. Puritan officials arrested Dyer but released her after an appeal from her husband.

* **martyr** someone who suffers or dies for the sake of a cause or principle

In the following years, Dyer was driven out of New Haven for preaching Quakerism. She was jailed and released twice in Boston, the second time just escaping hanging only because of her son's pleas for her life. In the spring of 1660, when Dyer returned once more to Boston, authorities arrested her and condemned her to death. Hoping to bring about the end of the "wicked law" against Quakers, Mary Dyer chose to be a martyr* for her beliefs. She was hanged on June 1, 1660. The next year, under pressure from the English government, the Massachusetts colony repealed its law requiring death for Quakers.

East India Company

See *British East India Company; Dutch East India Company.*

Economic Systems

* **gathering** collecting wild plants, nuts, and berries for food

A study of the economic systems of the North American colonies reveals surprising complexity. Although agriculture was the main livelihood of most colonists and industrial activity was limited, the economies of the British, Dutch, French, and Spanish colonies reached far beyond their borders. They were in fact part of a global economic system based on trade between continents.

The economies of North America's Native American groups were also quite complex and interconnected. They included different forms of agriculture, hunting, fishing, and gathering* that varied according to the land and climate of a region as well as the culture and traditions of the Indians. The chief food crops originated in what is now Latin America and came north through connections among Indian groups. Native Americans throughout the continent engaged in a lively trade that covered great distances.

cash crop crop grown primarily for profit

As Europeans colonized North America, both they and the Indians adapted to new circumstances. The early colonial economies were shaped as much by Native American as by European traditions. From the Indians, colonists learned about such important food crops as corn and beans and also about TOBACCO, which became a major cash crop*. Many early European settlements rose on the sites of Indian farming villages, and colonists planted crops on fields cleared years before by the Indians. Even colonial roads followed routes Indians had used for generations.

Likewise, Native American economies were greatly influenced by contact with the colonists. Whether they took part in the FUR TRADE with Europeans or lived and worked on Spanish MISSIONS, Indians adopted new ways of life that changed their traditional economies. They came to rely on European manufactured goods in intertribal trade, and they reorganized their economies around these goods. The desire for trade with Europeans led to increased competition among Indian groups, which changed traditional economic patterns and political alliances. Even Native Americans who lived beyond the reach of European settlement felt the impact of changes brought by colonization because of the close connections among all Indian groups.

European Economies

The driving force behind the economies of the North American colonies was the idea of MERCANTILISM. This economic theory encouraged European governments to develop and control their economies in ways that would enrich their nations and increase their power. Among the leading principles of mercantilism were the importance of expanding trade and acquiring colonies. Colonies would provide precious metals and raw materials and serve as markets for European goods, particularly manufactured items. Increasing the supply of gold became a primary goal for European powers because they measured their wealth in gold.

At first, most British colonists focused on growing enough food to feed themselves and their families. In time, they began to raise crops such as tobacco, rice, and indigo for export. This engraving by James Peake shows a Pennsylvania farm settlement in the late 1750s.

The nations of Europe thus tried to shape the colonial economies to advance the interests of the home country. To ensure a steady supply of revenue, they passed laws encouraging their colonies to produce goods in high demand throughout Europe, such as tobacco and furs. To promote the growth of a wealthy merchant class, they passed laws limiting colonial trade to ships owned by European merchants. To encourage the development of industries at home, they made it difficult for colonists to establish new industries.

Although European nations attempted to shape colonial economies, they usually could not prevent the colonies from pursuing their own economic interests. Many colonists were scarcely involved in the trade-oriented economy favored by mercantilism. Instead they focused only on raising enough food to feed themselves and their families. At the same time, a wealthy class arose in the colonies that benefited from trade with Europe as well as from the growing colonial trade. These prosperous individuals eventually pursued their own interests—interests that often clashed with those of the home country.

British Colonies. The economy of the British colonies expanded tremendously during the colonial period. This growth was spurred by two great bursts of economic activity. The first burst, which occurred at a different time in each colony, began soon after the first settlers arrived. Lasting about a generation, this growth was fueled by the process of creating farms, communities, and markets.

The second burst of economic expansion began in the 1740s and lasted until the American Revolution. It was launched by an increase in foreign trade that developed from changes on both sides of the Atlantic Ocean. Population growth in Europe resulted in a greater demand for American agricultural products. Meanwhile, in the colonies, population growth and lower prices for British manufactured goods led to increased demand for imported products.

Over time, the colonial economy began to produce more goods with less LABOR. This increase in productivity came from the use of more efficient technology and improvements in workers' skills. The main factor in the higher productivity, though, was that colonists were shifting away from subsistence farming* toward the production of surplus products for sale. This change affected both agriculture and the development of industry.

The southern colonies focused on raising such crops as tobacco, rice, and indigo* for export. In the middle colonies, farmers grew grain for shipment to European markets. In New England, where poor soil limited agricultural productivity, colonists exported large quantities of fish. Throughout the colonies, trees were felled and turned into lumber for export. Colonists also used trees to make masts for ships and to provide pitch and tar for waterproofing ships' hulls.

Only a few major industries developed in the colonies. The most important was shipbuilding. Shipyards sprang up all along the Atlantic coast, particularly in New England. By the mid-1700s, about one-third of all British merchant ships were built in the colonies. An iron industry also developed in the colonies, and iron exports to Britain doubled between the 1730s and 1770s.

* *subsistence farming* raising only enough food to live on

* *indigo* plant used to make a blue dye

> **Remember:** *Words in small capital letters have separate entries, and the index at the end of Volume 4 will guide you to more information on many topics.*

As the colonial economy expanded, Britain introduced new policies to influence the direction it would take. Between 1649 and 1764, Parliament passed a series of laws known as the NAVIGATION ACTS. These laws encouraged the production of certain crops—including tobacco, rice, and indigo—and required that they be sold only in Britain or its colonies. The acts also restricted trade by specifying that goods moving between Britain and the colonies must travel on British ships with mostly British crews. Furthermore, Parliament banned the export of certain manufactured goods made in the colonies and placed other limitations on colonial manufacturing.

Despite these policies, the British colonies continued to enjoy the benefits of economic growth. By the standards of the time, the colonists of the 1700s were well fed, and they spent a smaller share of income on food than did people living in Europe. Many colonists were well clothed, too, and could easily obtain items that made life more comfortable and enjoyable, such as bedding, tableware, sugar, tea, and spices.

Economic expansion did not benefit all colonists equally. In the early colonial period, the distance between the rich and the poor was very small. As the colonies developed, this gap began to widen. Some individuals—most notably merchants and the owners of large PLANTATIONS—began to accumulate great wealth. At the same time, population growth in communities along the coast created greater demand for housing and jobs, which led to higher rents, lower wages, and increased poverty. Still, colonial society remained fairly equal, especially on the frontier, which had abundant land and opportunities.

One group that contributed much to the colonial economy but gained little from it was African Americans. Most of them lived in SLAVERY. Slave labor played a crucial role in the economy, especially in the southern colonies, and helped raise the living standards of the white population. In terms of food, clothing, and housing, black slaves in the British colonies seem to have fared better than slaves in other regions, and their living conditions generally improved during the colonial period. Nevertheless, they suffered terrible oppression*, and any gains they made were offset by the hardship of their daily lives.

*** oppression** unjust or cruel exercise of authority

Dutch Colony.   Founded as a trading colony, NEW NETHERLAND lasted only from 1621 to 1664. It had difficulty attracting settlers, and the population never exceeded 9,000. During the early years, the Dutch tried to establish an agricultural economy.

By the 1650s, New Netherland had developed a thriving transatlantic trade, as well as coastal commerce with the English colonies and regional trade with the WEST INDIES. Furs were the most important product, but the Dutch also traded lumber, grain, salt, and luxury items such as spices and furniture. With the passage of England's Navigation Acts, which placed numerous limits on the trading activities of its colonies, smugglers carrying restricted goods used New Netherland as a haven. In its later years, the Dutch colony became heavily involved in the SLAVE TRADE.

French Colonies.   During its early years, the economy of Canada—a region along the St. Lawrence Valley—was dominated by the fur trade and subsistence agriculture. The area's poor soil and harsh climate made farming difficult and kept the settlement from flourishing. The economy expanded between 1700 and 1740, largely a result of increased supplies of resources and modest gains in agricultural production. During that time, Canada began to export grain to French colonies in the West Indies. After that period, the economy remained fairly stable until the British takeover in 1763.

The economic systems of NEWFOUNDLAND and Acadia differed somewhat from that of Canada. Newfoundland, which had only a few thousand permanent settlers, had a seasonal economy dominated completely by fishing. Each spring, the local population swelled with the arrival of fishing fleets from France, and it fell again in the fall when the ships left. Acadia had an economy based on fishing and farming. Agricultural production was somewhat greater than in Canada, and surplus products were traded with neighboring French regions as well as with Britain's New England colonies. After the British took control of Acadia—which they called NOVA SCOTIA—the region formed an even stronger trading connection with northern New England, with an emphasis on forest products and fishing.

In LOUISIANA, a small colony in which Native Americans outnumbered French settlers, the main economic activity was trade in deerskins. But British traders in the Carolinas dominated the profitable fur trade because they offered Indians more desirable goods in exchange for pelts*. French settlers did establish some plantations, which used slave labor to raise tobacco, indigo, and timber for export, as well as food crops for local markets. After Spain gained control of Louisiana in the 1760s, the plantation economy expanded, and the value of agricultural exports increased dramatically. This growth created a prosperous class of planters and merchants in the area around NEW ORLEANS. Much of Louisiana, however, remained undeveloped economically.

Spanish Colonies. Most of the regions within the Spanish Borderlands* never developed strong and varied economies. Growth was limited by the Borderlands' small and widely scattered populations and by the nature of its settlements. To colonize their northern regions, the Spanish established a series of military posts, or PRESIDIOS, and missions. These outposts* concentrated on producing food for their own needs and trading with Indians for supplies rather than developing products for export. In the late 1700s, some regions began to create economies comparable to those of the British and French colonies.

Spanish FLORIDA never developed a self-sufficient economy. The lack of any profitable economic activities in the colony made it almost completely dependent on NEW SPAIN and the West Indies for funds and supplies. The economy of TEXAS was based on subsistence agriculture, but trade in cattle began to develop in the mid-1700s.

The colonists of CALIFORNIA, the last region of the Borderlands to be settled, lived by RANCHING and subsistence farming. The region's isolation prevented the development of trade with other colonial areas, although local settlers did establish some contacts with Russian fur traders along the northern California coast.

See color plate 4, vol. 1.

* *pelt* skin and fur of an animal

* *Spanish Borderlands* northern part of New Spain, area now occupied by Florida, Texas, New Mexico, Arizona, and California

* *outpost* frontier settlement or military base

Economic Systems

Before Europeans arrived in North America, Native Americans had already established a wide network of trade in items ranging from corn and pottery to copper and furs. Indians in Florida used canoes and rafts to transport their goods, as shown in this drawing by French colonist Jacques le Moyne.

NEW MEXICO was the most prosperous Borderlands province. By the late 1700s, it had developed a stable economy based on agriculture and a fairly profitable ranching industry. The colony also developed a significant regional trade in such items as pottery, cotton goods, ironware, and horses. Neighboring ARIZONA also had an economy based on farming and ranching, but it had too few people to develop and prosper.

Native Americans

The arrival of the Europeans in North America caused significant changes in Native American economic systems. The impact can best be understood by comparing Indian economies before and after European contact.

Economic Systems Before Contact.   For hundreds of years, agriculture was the chief economic activity of Native Americans in much of North America. Small-scale farming began about 4,000 years ago with some regional crops. Then, about 1500 B.C. in the Southwest and A.D. 200 in northeastern regions, a number of food plants—most notably corn, beans, and squash—were introduced from what is now Mexico. Easier to grow and more productive than the earlier plants, these crops spread gradually through the two regions.

To grow these crops, Native Americans adapted farming techniques to suit the soil and climate where they lived. Indians living in the Southeast cut and burned trees to clear land for farm plots. In eastern forests and on the Great Plains, they planted crops along rivers to take advantage of water that seeped into the soil. In the arid Southwest, farmers built elaborate irrigation systems to bring water to their fields.

Throughout North America, Indians also obtained food by HUNTING, fishing, and gathering. They hunted deer, rabbits, ducks, geese, moose, and

elk in many areas and BUFFALO on the Great Plains. Indians who lived near rivers and lakes fished, while those at the seacoasts could find seals, fish, and other sea life. Some groups along the northern Atlantic and Pacific coasts even hunted whales. Native Americans sought and harvested a great variety of wild plants, nuts, and berries. Gathering was especially important to the CALIFORNIA INDIANS, who relied on acorns as one of their principal foods. Indians living in the far north and west of the Rocky Mountains got their food almost entirely from hunting, fishing, and gathering rather than from farming.

Native Americans tended to divide labor for agriculture, hunting, and gathering along gender lines. While all adults might have roles in farming, hunting and fishing typically were considered tasks for men and gathering a job for women.

Indians generally obtained food locally, but they developed extensive trading networks to acquire resources and goods not available within their own societies. Local trade included such items as corn, dried meat, baskets, pottery, and furs. Long-distance trade included eagle feathers, copper from the Great Lakes area, mica—a mineral valued for its spiritual power—from the Appalachians, and seashells from California and the Gulf of Mexico. Commerce in these products dated back to ancient times, and trade routes crisscrossed the continent.

The early Native Americans lacked domesticated* animals that could carry heavy loads. Therefore, trade goods tended to be light and valuable enough to make the commerce worthwhile. Products were usually traded from village to village in a series of exchanges that took them, after many months, far from their place of origin. Indians often carried trade goods on their backs. However, those living along coasts or rivers transported products in various types and sizes of CANOES, rafts, and other boats. Water routes sometimes covered thousands of miles.

Some places became well known for their annual trade fairs. At the appointed time, Indian tribes would arrive from near and far for several days of trading, feasting, and dancing. In some areas, the language of certain groups that specialized in trading became the common language of trade. This was the case with the Chinook Indians in the Pacific Northwest, the CREE INDIANS in the far north, the POTAWATOMI INDIANS around the Great Lakes, and the Mandan Indians along the Missouri River. In the central Great Plains, several different groups used a language of hand signals to communicate.

domesticated raised by humans as farm animals or pets

Sending a Sign

The sign language used by Indians of the Great Plains to carry on trade appeared in Texas as early as the 1540s. It eventually spread as far north as Canada. Hand signs for words and ideas generally represented objects or actions. *Bad* was a motion that suggested throwing away something. For *oat,* a signer moved the hand toward the mouth; using both hands indicated a large meal. Signs could also be combined. *Freeze* was indicated by putting together the signs for cold, water, and hard. While used mostly for communication between different tribes, sign language also helped Indians communicate with Europeans.

Economic Systems After Contact.   Initial contacts with Europeans had a enormous, often devastating, effect on Indian societies. European DISEASES killed countless Native Americans, causing major social and economic disruption. In many areas, Indians were enslaved by Europeans and forced to work on farms, which ruined Indian economies that relied on shared labor. Although most colonies stopped enslaving Indians by the 1720s, Spanish colonists in California forced Native Americans to live and work on missions throughout the 1700s. These Indians eventually abandoned their traditional ways of life and became dependent on the colonists for survival.

Despite these hardships, many Indians societies benefited from contact with Europeans—at least in the short run. The French relied on Native

Americans for the fur trade, and hired them as trappers, scouts, and boatmen. Groups such as the POWHATAN INDIANS and the IROQUOIS CONFEDERACY profited by acting as go-betweens in the trade between British colonists and other Indians. In time, however, expanding colonial settlement led to conflicts and resulted in the colonists taking over more and more Indian land. Those tribes that survived were forced to move and adapt their economies to new environments.

The agricultural practices of Native Americans changed little until the arrival of European metal tools, which the Indians quickly adopted for farming. Many tribes also began to raise European domesticated animals, such as pigs, cattle, and sheep. Hunting saw significant changes after the introduction of guns, which allowed Indians to kill from a greater distance than with bows and arrows. Another introduction, that of the HORSE by the Spanish, transformed the life of Native Americans on the Great Plains. Now able to follow herds of migrating buffalo, the PLAINS INDIANS developed a nomadic lifestyle and economic activities that revolved around the horse and buffalo. Some tribes specialized in breeding and raising horses and prospered by supplying them to other groups.

As trade between colonists and Indians increased, the Native Americans became more and more dependent on European goods. Their women wanted iron and brass kettles instead of traditional clay pots, and their men preferred metal knives and axes to their own stone and wood tools. The Indians reorganized their lives around the availability of such European products, and obtaining these goods became a focus of their economies during the colonial period.

Many Indian tribes adapted well to contacts with Europeans, changing their own economies and providing food, furs, and other goods to Europeans. By the end of the colonial period, however, a large number of tribes had been forced onto reservations, where they tried to establish economies based on European patterns. (*See also* **Acadians; Agriculture; Trade and Commerce.**)